CONQUISTADOR
VOICES

CONQUISTADOR VOICES

The Spanish Conquest of the Americas
As Recounted Largely by the Participants

Volume I

Christopher Columbus
Hernán Cortés

Kevin H. Siepel

Spruce Tree Press
Angola, New York

Spruce Tree Press   Website: www.spruce-tree-press.com
PO Box 211   E-mail: info@spruce-tree-press.com
Angola, NY 14006

Published 2015

ISBN   978-0-9786466-2-2 (paperback, Vol I)

Library of Congress Control Number: 2015908752

Publisher's Cataloging-in-Publication

Siepel, Kevin H.
    Conquistador voices : the Spanish conquest of the
Americas as recounted largely by the participants /
Kevin H. Siepel.
    volumes cm
    Includes bibliographical references and index.
    LCCN 2015908752
    CONTENTS: Volume I. Christopher Columbus ; Hernán
Cortés -- Volume II. Francisco Pizarro and his brothers ;
Álvar Núñez Cabeza de Vaca ; Hernando de Soto.
    ISBN 978-0-9786466-2-2 (paperback : vol. I)
    ISBN 978-0-9786466-3-9 (paperback : vol. II)

    1. America--Discovery and exploration--Spanish.
2. Conquerors--America--History. 3. Conquerors--Spain--
History.   I. Title. II. Title: Spanish conquest of
the Americas as recounted largely by the participants.

F1411.S577 2015   980'.013
                         QBI15-600125

Cover art courtesy of the artist, Jim Carson, www.JimCarsonStudio.com
Cover design by Karrie Ross, www.KarrieRoss.com
Maps by the author

Dedicated with gratitude to my wife

María Carmen García Pascual

without whose influence
I wouldn't have attempted this book
and without whose patience
I couldn't have finished it

And to my brother Tim

a faithful and helpful reader of drafts

Also by Kevin H. Siepel

Rebel: The Life and Times of John Singleton Mosby

Joseph Bennett of Evans and the Growing of New York's Niagara Frontier

ABOUT THE TRANSLATIONS

English translations of primary-source documents used in this volume are from the following:

Columbus
All translations by the author.

Cortés
All translations by the author except for the "Aztec account," which was taken from *The Broken Spears* by Miguel León-Portilla, copyright © 1962, 1990 by Miguel León-Portilla. Expanded and updated edition © 1992 by Miguel León-Portilla. Reprinted by permission of Beacon Press, Boston.

THE SETTING OF THESE EVENTS

When immersing oneself in the riveting events that occurred in the New World in the fifteenth and sixteenth centuries, it is easy to lose sight of what was happening at this same time in Europe.

During the era of the discovery and invasion of the American continents and the subjugation of their peoples by Europeans — during the interval of, say, 1490 to 1550, which is roughly the scope of these two volumes — the following historic events occurred in Europe: Leonardo da Vinci completed both his Last Supper and the Mona Lisa, among many other works; Michelangelo produced his large body of masterworks, including the famed Pietà in St. Peter's, David, The Last Judgment, and the Sistine Chapel ceiling; Machiavelli wrote *The Prince;* Martin Luther and Henry VIII both broke with the Church of Rome; Ignatius of Loyola founded the Society of Jesus; the Council of Trent, which would dictate Roman Catholic practice well into the twentieth century, was convened; and Thomas More, the Lord Chancellor of England, was tried for treason and executed.

CONTENTS

INTRODUCTION 1

CHRISTOPHER COLUMBUS 5

HERNÁN CORTÉS 127

FOR FURTHER READING 321

INDEX 323

INTRODUCTION

This book has been written for the general reader. It is intended to bring to life an important and fascinating historical period – the period known as the Spanish Conquest of the Americas. It is not an in-depth treatment of sixteenth-century Spain or its colonies, nor is it an exhaustive history of the so-called Conquest itself. Indeed many more pages would be required even to address adequately the tangled skein of events of Pizarran Peru.

What this two-volume work does is to sketch out the arc of the Conquest in terms of five narratives – narratives related to five high-profile men who participated in it, men who had set out across the sea from Europe at different times to make what they could of an opportunity. Its virtue is that they or their fellow participants are here allowed to speak extensively for themselves, with minimal help or commentary from a citizen of the twenty-first century. If it were a film about modern events it would be a documentary, a collection of film clips featuring the words and actions of protagonists and eyewitnesses, the clips being interconnected by the bare amount of narration necessary to create an engaging five-part series.

The selections appearing in these two volumes help us to see – to the extent possible – these invaders, explorers, and conquerors as they were, not necessarily as our school books might represent them to be. On the basis of their own words, then, how might we describe these men who ventured across the sea as initiators of, or participants in, this raw drama?

They were in the first place courageous and tough. They knew how to face death, and how to endure enormous suffering and pain. They were in fact quite remarkable in this respect. They were for the most part self-righteously religious, their arrogance in religious matters – as in most other matters – difficult for many of us to grasp. Most were profoundly rapacious, driven by a lust for gold that the Indians found impossible to comprehend. Gold was in fact the principal reason for their flooding into this dangerous New World. Many, though not all, could be surpassingly, horrifyingly cruel. If they knew how to endure suffering, they knew also how to inflict it, and — like many colonizers — did so without compunction and frequently in monstrous fashion. Most were deeply exploitative of the Indians, not least of Indian women, who were commonly treated as chattel. The leaders, finally, and a large number of their subordinates were quite intelligent, some outstandingly so.

Since the version of history that we inherit is normally the one written by the conqueror, the preponderance of what follows is from European sources. The lone exception to this is the Nahuatl account of Cortés's conquest of Mexico (Volume I), interspersed among European descriptions of the same events. Even this account, however, may not be free of Spanish influence.

Christopher Columbus, who began it all and whose story opens Volume I, was perhaps the most complex of the five men presented here, and certainly the least suited for leadership. Nevertheless his enormous self-esteem, his single-minded belief in an idea, his certainty of having been chosen by God to advance that idea, and his rapidly blossoming skill as a navigator made him ideally suited to the task at hand. His unavoidable foreignness, however, his lack of interest in administrative affairs, his deteriorating health, and his growing penchant for self-pity were his Achilles heel, and his death went all but unnoticed in the rush to colonize and ravish the lands that he had discovered.

Hernán Cortés was the deepest and possibly the most intelligent of the five. He was also one of the luckiest. Breaking away from Cuba with an expedition to the mainland just in time to avoid being arrested by the governor, he soon blundered upon two people whose language skills unlocked the mysterious Mexican empire, enabling him to contemplate actually bringing it down. After brazenly opening communications directly with the emperor in Europe, leapfrogging his superiors, he rallied thousands of Indians and many reluctant Spaniards to his cause by a combination of diplomacy, thinly veiled threat, and stunning violence. He showed enormous resilience in the face of devastating loss and defeat. Yet, like Columbus, he gradually lost hold over the land that he had conquered, and he met an old man's death in virtual oblivion.

Francisco Pizarro, whose story opens Volume II, was as uneducated and rude as his rudest follower. He was nonetheless as confident as Columbus, and as devious, ruthless, brazen, and lucky as Cortés. Abetted by his brothers, with a small Spanish force, and—at least at first—with no assistance from Indian allies, by valor and cunning alone, this illiterate man caused the fall of a kingdom, and was ultimately responsible for fueling Spain's meteoric rise to prominence in Europe with the silver produced by Peruvian mines. His legacy, however, is marred by great barbarity—much of it Spaniard upon Spaniard—and he himself suffered a violent death at the hands of his own people.

Álvar Núñez Cabeza de Vaca, like the others a man of these violent times, provides a breath of fresh air to the modern reader. No stranger to the excesses of the Conquest, he nonetheless learned of necessity what it meant to be an Indian, to be The Other. In the process, he turned himself into a monument to the Spanish capacity for simple endurance. He later became a monument to the Spanish capacity for vengeance, as he fell afoul of the colonists in his assignment as governor of South America's Plata River region. To us it may seem ironic that this man, who had perforce acquired such empathy with the poverty-stricken denizens of the Americas, ended his career accused of their maltreatment.

Hernando de Soto is perhaps the most tragic of the five men presented here, a consummate leader of vast ambition, with solid powers of administration—capable, like most of the others, of great brutality—yet a man destined for ultimate failure. Returning home weighted down with wealth following a successful few years in Peru, he sought further wealth and aggrandizement as governor of the wilds of Florida, which, in the Spanish mind, extended from the southeast coast of today's United States into northern Mexico. In three years of starving and suffering, losing men regularly to powerful Indian resistance, he found nothing in Florida of the wealth he was seeking. His last months spent in seeming loss of purpose, he died ingloriously of fever on the banks of the turbulent Mississippi, his body unceremoniously dumped into its dark waters.

Because they portray riveting events, albeit somewhat outside the mainstream, the accounts of Gonzalo Pizarro's journey into the jungles of South America in search of cinnamon, and of Francisco de Orellana's odyssey across that mighty continent have also been included.

What you will find featured in these two volumes—to the extent consonant with good storytelling—is the voices of the participants. Some of these accounts were set down on paper during or immediately after the chronicler's participation in the stirring events reported. Some were written many years later, perhaps dictated to a non-participant. The connecting narrative, with the assistance of many excellent resources, has been supplied by me. In a quest for a more modern-sounding translation of the primary-source material, I have translated a substantial portion of this material myself.

The narrative is in some places lengthy, in other places minimal. I have tried to provide only what has appeared essential for furnishing context, and for connecting what I feel to be the most revelatory "sound bites" of long ago. To add explanatory detail without disruption of narrative flow, footnotes have been supplied. Value judgments have been left to the reader.

You will, I hope, find this an engaging story.

CHRISTOPHER COLUMBUS

The Spanish Invasion of the Indies

CHAPTERS

1. Setting the Stage.............................. 9

2. First Voyage, 1492-93...............................19

3. Second Voyage, 1493-96.........................43

4. Third Voyage, 1498-1500........................65

5. Fourth Voyage, 1502-04.........................81

MAPS FOLLOWING PAGES 17, 41, 63, 79, 125

1

SETTING THE STAGE

Cristoforo Colombo, or Christopher Columbus as we know him, was born in 1451 into a family of Genoese weavers. Impatient of his surroundings and of his likely lot in life, he had gone to sea in his early teens. He had traveled widely, down the African coast and, it is thought, even to Iceland. Opinions differ as to his role in these maritime pursuits, but it appears that he was more of a seagoing trader than a sailor.

Around 1477, at the age of twenty-five or twenty-six, he found himself in Lisbon, ostensibly in a role related to Genoese trade. Whatever the exact nature of his business, it soon led him to the Portuguese island colony of Madeira, where he met and married the daughter of the founder and former governor of Porto Santo, Filipa Moniz Perestrelo. In 1480 Filipa would give birth to their son, a boy named Diego.

By now, Columbus's exposure to foreign climes and new sources of information, and especially his experience in this kingdom that had "written the book" on sailing and exploration,[1] had awakened in him a dream of possibilities that few had considered. Mariners of the day were not accustomed to sailing far out of sight of land. Few had ever tried sailing due west from Europe to find what might lie over the watery horizon. He knew, of course, that the world was a globe (albeit with the heavens whirling about the earth).[2] He reasoned, therefore, that if one sailed west, one might arrive at the same place that his hosts, the Portuguese, were hoping to reach by sailing south and east around Africa—namely the exotic Indies, source of spices. Spices from the East, highly prized in Europe for giving flavor to bland European food, were currently hauled overland through central Asia, with duties being levied at every step of the way—the heaviest by the Ottoman Turks—before they were shipped down the Mediterranean to Venice, which profited greatly from its role as gateway to Europe. The price on arrival in Flanders, say, or Castile, was therefore exorbitant. If one could reach the Indies from the other side, one might rewrite the rules

---

[1] The Portuguese at this time were the greatest mariners of Europe.

[2] He would later come to believe the earth was more pear-shaped.

of the game, he reasoned, and possibly one might find oneself atop a highly profitable commercial enterprise. And what if other lands were discovered to lie between Europe and the East? No one knew what treasures they might hold for a daring entrepreneur. Columbus — astute, but deeply religious, even mystical, by nature — grew convinced that God had selected him to carry out this bold plan.

Portugal, with its imaginative ship designers, long experience in taking accurate measurement of latitude, and a monarchy highly supportive of seagoing exploration — essential factors for any large-scale expedition — was clearly the country where Columbus's idea might find a hearing. The Portuguese had for years been systematically moving down the African coast, setting up trading stations for ivory and slaves, steadily advancing on the tip of Africa and on whatever might lie beyond. In 1483 or 1484 Columbus approached the king, João II, for support of his idea of sailing to the Indies by going west instead of east. The young monarch seriously considered the proposal — indeed it was debated strenuously among his advisors — but the final decision was for rejection. Columbus seemed to be grossly underestimating the distance to Asia, he was told, he expected too much in the way of rewards and titles, and he appeared to have an unfounded confidence in his own abilities. Added to this was the fact that Portugal had already committed significant resources to reaching the East by sailing around Africa, not straight out into the unknown Atlantic. Given that this course was bringing significant gain to the government, with its lucrative trade in slaves and other commodities, it made little sense to alter that course.

Deeply disappointed, Columbus in 1485 turned his feet toward Spain. Perhaps he could get a hearing there.

It was not only his own feet that Columbus directed toward Spain that year, but those of his five-year-old son Diego as well. While the long-accepted story is that Columbus left Portugal on the death of Filipa, some scholars question whether she in fact passed away, or whether young Columbus, more strongly possessed by a dream than by any notion of settled married life, simply left her. Regardless, he and little Diego arrived in the port of Palos, Castile, early in 1485. Near-penniless now, and a foreigner in yet another land, he placed his son under the care of the monks at the nearby monastery of La Rábida, and proceeded to spend a year cultivating the acquaintance of those who could help him secure an audience with the queen. Finally, in early 1486, he made his way to the royal court, now at Córdoba (there being as yet no fixed capital). At this time he spoke the dialect of Genoa, and presumably Portuguese. He doubtless spoke little Castilian, Catalán, or any other Iberian language. Some question whether he had any knowledge—beyond what he had been able to pick up from mariners with whom he had sailed—about navigation or the working of a ship. What is known is that, although he had vastly underestimated the westward distance to the Indies, as well as the likelihood of large continents lying in his path, he had boundless confidence in his ability to do what he had set out to do.

In Roman times the Iberian peninsula, then called Hispania, was known as a harsh and poor land lying at the empire's western edge. By the fifteenth century, Hispania, still harsh and poor, had grown into an aggregation of kingdoms—Portugal in the peninsula's furthest western reaches, and, moving eastward, Castile, Navarre, and the Crown of Aragon, which included the subkingdoms of Zaragoza, Barcelona, Valencia, and several polities beyond the peninsula, as far away as Greece. Rivalries existed among kingdoms, and, within each kingdom, severe social imbalances.

The overriding problem for the rulers of Iberia, however, had been neither inter-kingdom rivalries nor social imbalances. It had rather been the nearly eight-centuries-long occupation of the land by the followers of the Prophet Mohammed, whose militant hordes had swept across Iberia in 711. But Iberian rulers had eventually begun to push back against the Islamic presence, rooting it out slowly and painfully from north to south, defeating Islamic armies, eliminating Arab power, and gradually reclaiming the land for Christian rule. By the mid-thirteenth century this *Reconquista*, or Reconquest, was virtually complete: territory held by the invaders had been reduced to the emirate of Granada, in the far south. Granada, an opulent and civilized kingdom, coexisted with surrounding Christian kingdoms over the next two centuries, but uneasily. It remained a boil to be eventually lanced.

In the fifteenth century, Iberian society, as in most of Europe, was divided into three classes: nobles, clergy, and peasants. The gulf between nobles and clergy on the one hand, and the peasantry on the other, was great. The Castilian nobles, in particular, well armed and moneyed—having served as the very engine of the Reconquest—took all the liberties they liked with the peasantry and as many as they could with the Crown. They seized lands, committed abominable outrages against the defenseless lower classes, and ratcheted up their opposition to the monarchy to whatever extent the monarch's pale strength might permit. From the 1420s to the 1470s Castile, in particular—the largest of the peninsular kingdoms, but exceedingly poor—endured unending violence. The peasant class suffered greatly at the hands of the nobles, who by 1470 had taken over much of the land for themselves.

Throughout most of this period, Castile was ruled by Juan II, the father of a young Isabella. Upon his death in 1454, when Isabella was three years old, the scepter was passed to Isabella's half-brother, Enrique, who ruled as Enrique IV until his death in 1474. Neither man had been an effective monarch. Neither could stand up to the nobles, nor to the continuously felt pressure of rival kingdoms, notably Portugal.

Enrique's heir was his daughter Juana, Isabella's niece.[1] Despite the king's stated desire that Juana succeed him on the throne, many nobles were as much against her as a potential queen as they had been against Enrique as king, thereby putting the succession into question. On Enrique's death in 1474 the 23-year-old Isabella, doubtless emboldened by her marriage five years earlier to Ferdinand, the young heir of the crown of Aragon,[2] stepped forward to declare herself the rightful heir of the crown of Castile. In 1475, however, she and her young husband were forced to defend her claim by raising a military force to meet an invading Portuguese army intent upon defending the claim of the 13-year-old Juana. The reason for Portugal's interest: with a Portuguese victory, the 43-year-old Portuguese king, Afonso V, would marry the young princess and, by so doing, add Castile to his kingdom. By March 1476, however, the army of the young monarchs had fought a pitched battle with the Portuguese that was politically if not militarily conclusive, enabling Isabella to cement her position as ruler of Castile. Although Ferdinand had led Castilian armies in the field,[3] he would not come to power in his own kingdom, Aragon, till

---

[1] It was, however, widely suspected that Juana had been fathered not by Enrique, but by his wife's lover Beltrán de la Cueva.
[2] At the time of her marriage, Isabella was eighteen and Ferdinand seventeen. She had selected Ferdinand herself and married him in defiance of Enrique—who had wished to arrange a marriage for her into the ruling family of England, France, or Portugal.
[3] Isabella herself was frequently in the field with her army.

the death of his father in 1479.

The association of the kingdoms of Aragon and Castile under Ferdinand and Isabella was the first step toward the establishment of the modern Spanish nation.[1]

With the threat from without put down for the moment, Isabella turned her attention to affairs at home. She began to build a standing army and to use it for restoration of order. To bring the nobles to heel, she set the vigilante "brotherhoods" loose in the countryside — in the words of historian Henry Kamen, "organizing rather than eliminating violence." She offered an olive branch and new privileges to the recalcitrant nobility, but, for those slow to grasp the opportunity, commanded swift confiscation or destruction of property. She set the foundations for a sound economy throughout the kingdom. She and her young husband seemed ubiquitous, popping up unexpectedly in all corners of Castile, frequently dispensing justice personally. Careful to mete out mercy, however, as well as justice, they proved to be wise monarchs, increasingly beloved of their subjects.

Once the nobility had been tamed and a semblance of civil order established — a process that took only three years — this deeply Catholic monarch turned her attention to the Church, which had become thoroughly corrupt. Her efforts to reform the clergy and religious orders met with little success, but she found greater scope for activity in another area: investigating the depth of faith among Jews who, frequently for reasons of convenience, had converted to Christianity — the so-called *conversos*. To "inquire" into the character of their faith Isabella introduced the Spanish Inquisition, a powerful, invasive, and menacing arm of the state that would reach into every corner of Castile and its companion kingdom Aragon, and that would eventually be transformed for export to Castile's future colonies overseas.[2] Unconverted Jews were not targeted, but from about 1480

---

[1] The kingdoms nonetheless remained independent of one another, and not united. Aragon was run along somewhat democratic lines, with a parliamentary government that antedated England's by a century. Castile's tradition was more autocratic. For simplicity, the two kingdoms will sometimes be referred to as Spain.

[2] The Spanish Inquisition was a peculiarly Spanish attempt to ensure Christian doctrinal purity among Crown subjects. It operated independently of Inquisitions established both previously and subsequently by the Holy See.

to 1530—beyond the life-span of the queen—countless conversos would be imprisoned and tortured, and, by some estimates, as many as two thousand would be executed for persistence in Jewish practices. In Ferdinand's kingdom, this state-sponsored terror was violently resisted, at least at first. In 1485, in Zaragoza's La Seo cathedral, the Inquisitor of Aragon was murdered at his prayers.

With all power in Castile having been consolidated in the Crown, and measures to purify the Church under way, it was time for the next step: rooting out the remaining Islamic stronghold in Granada. The queen, although possessing a certain regard for both Jews and Moors, wished to preside over the reclamation of the last of Castile's usurped lands. She would see personally to the surrender of the Granada emirate, even to accompanying her armies in the field.

But in the mid-1480s, as she was occupied with making this final push, she had been momentarily distracted by an unrelated issue. A tall Genoese of about her own age, a persistent enthusiast, a man with an apparently inflated self-image and seemingly a bit of a dreamer, had come to seek royal backing for an odd voyage of exploration, a voyage not along the African coast, which was the purview of the Portuguese anyway, but a voyage straight out into the Atlantic in search of a kind of reverse route to the Indies. He had first come to her attention in 1486. His name was Cristoforo Colombo, but he'd had the apparent wit to hispanicize his name to Cristóbal Colón. Although she had to admit that his idea had a certain appeal, she'd been advised by her most expert counselors to pay no attention to him. At any rate, the business of this Genoese would have to wait until events in Granada had run their course.

Following his disappointing first hearing with the queen—who was not totally uninterested in the scheme, but for whom there were much more pressing issues—Columbus spent most of the next six years in Spain, traveling the land, presumably working at something, seeking out anyone who might advance his case at court.[1]

During his years in Spain, Columbus took a mistress in Córdoba—one Beatriz Enríquez de Arana—and in August 1488 he became the father of a second son, whom he named Ferdinand.

---

[1] In 1488 he briefly journeyed to Lisbon at the invitation of the Portuguese monarch, but the meeting led nowhere and he returned to Castile.

In Spain he labored at several disadvantages: his likely inability to express himself clearly, the outlandishness of his idea to many of the day's experts, and — with regard to the queen — the overriding presence in the royal mind of the need to excise the Moorish emirate from Granada. It was 1491 now, and the armies of Castile and Aragon, having spent the previous decade conquering, one by one, the emirate's network of outlying population centers, by year's end had surrounded the emir's stronghold on the heights of the Alhambra. Then on January 2, 1492, word was passed down to the monarchs — who were tenting with the army nearby at the new settlement of Santa Fé — that the Alhambra and city would be surrendered. Great jubilation ensued, generous terms were offered, and nearly eight centuries of Moorish rule in Iberia came to an end.

With the Reconquest now an accomplished fact, Columbus — who was at Santa Fé at the time — ensured that his own scheme would be next on the queen's agenda. Almost immediately after the surrender of Granada, he arranged an audience with the queen and her advisors in her very tent at Santa Fé. He ran through his standard arguments, virtually unchanged since his earlier meeting with her. Her advisors then mounted their standard technical objections, likely noting as well that the Indies already seemed within the grasp of the Portuguese, who had reached the southern cape of Africa more than three years before. It was but a matter of time before they reached the Indies. Their objections again carried the day. Columbus departed, low in spirit, resolved finally to bring his scheme to the French king. (He had in the meantime dispatched his brother Bartholomew — who shared his vision — to England to beg the support of Henry VII.)

During his nearly seven years in Castile, however, Columbus had taken care to cultivate influential men. One of these was an Aragonese converso named Luis de Santángel, of Zaragoza. Santángel, among the wealthiest men in Spain, was currently one of the queen's money men — in charge of funds for the royal household. He had slowly come around to seeing what Columbus saw, and seems to have believed that this earnest foreigner might well deliver on his promise. Importantly, Santángel had the ear of the queen. Another who came to believe in him was Fray Juan Pérez, superior of the monastery at La Rábida, where Columbus's son Diego had once been cared for. Fray Juan was also an intimate of the queen.

Both Santángel and Fray Juan now interceded with the queen, pointing out that — despite the technical arguments against such a voyage—the sum required to fund it was almost paltry in comparison to the return, should it prove successful. Isabella considered, and then changed her mind. She sent word that Columbus should return to Santa Fé, that she was ready to accept his plan in its entirety. Her decision was doubtless made easier by Santángel's assurance that he himself would put up a large part of the necessary funds.

A bailiff was sent to drag Columbus back, and affairs began to move in his direction.

A major sticking point for the queen had been Columbus's insistence on titles and monetary rewards should he be successful in his quest, the focus of which was still somewhat hazily defined. Yet she yielded on every point—perhaps believing that not much would come of it anyway—codifying complete terms in the Capitulations of April 17 and 30, 1492, she and the king endorsing the document point by point.

Incredibly to some, the foreigner Columbus was to be granted titles of Viceroy, Governor-general, and Admiral of the Ocean Sea in all islands and mainlands that might be discovered. Since clearly he could not hope to claim such titles in China or Japan—lands known from the nearly two-hundred-year-old account of Marco Polo—the possibility must have been in his mind of finding other lands as well. His heirs were guaranteed all rights and privileges stemming from his offices. He was to keep a tenth part of all merchandise taken from lands to be discovered, the remainder to go to the Crown. In return for paying an eighth part of equipment expenses, he was guaranteed an eighth part of whatever might be gained by use of that equipment.

As part of the Capitulations Columbus was also given a letter of introduction from the Catholic sovereigns to any potentate who might be encountered in the East. An item that proved of more immediate use, however, was a letter from the monarchs to the administration of the seacoast town of Palos, requiring the town—in atonement for some unnamed past offense against the Crown—to supply Columbus with two caravels.[1] A further item was a letter proclaiming that, on payment of a fair price, any merchant was required to supply Columbus with whatever he needed for his voyage. A related item cautioned that no taxes were to be charged on such purchases. Finally, an item of possibly dubious value to the explorer: for any accused

---

[1] Relatively small, highly maneuverable three-masted vessels, normally lateen-rigged.

criminal who agreed to ship with Columbus, all judicial proceedings were to be suspended. This grace period would expire two months after the man's return from his voyage.

In May Columbus headed for Palos to begin assembling and fitting out his little fleet. It should be remembered that he was a foreigner in a land not noted for its acceptance of outsiders. He had to purchase supplies and assemble a crew for what promised to be a hazardous undertaking, and it is easy to imagine a steady rumble of criticism and even ridicule as he went about enlisting reluctant sailors and outfitting his ships.

Among his first actions was the chartering of a third vessel, a three-masted carrack, or *nao*, with square-rigged main and foremast and lateen-rigged mizzen, called *Santa María*. It was owned partially by Juan de la Cosa, who would serve as its master. The two vessels supplied by the town of Palos were the three-masted, square-rigged caravel *Pinta* and the three-masted, lateen-rigged caravel *Niña*, each captained by one of the brothers Pinzón of that town. *Pinta* and *Niña* were each seventy to seventy-five feet long, *Santa María* somewhat longer. The newly minted Admiral of the Ocean Sea, whose skills as a navigator were possibly as untried as his skills as an administrator, would sail on *Santa María* with about forty men. Roughly two dozen men would embark on each of the caravels.

During these days of paperwork and preparation, the proudly Catholic sovereigns were busy "cleaning up" their realm still further, going a step beyond their concern for the purity of converso beliefs. On March 31 all unconverted Jews in Castile and Aragon were given four months to convert to Christianity or remove themselves from the kingdoms.[1] The Jewish exodus actually began in August, the very month of Columbus's departure.

No one in Castile or Aragon could have dreamed that the outcome of the small venture now preparing at Palos would one day far eclipse in importance the surrender of Granada or the expulsion from the land of forty thousand Jews.

---

[1] In 1502 Muslims throughout Castile would be offered a similar choice — baptism or exile. Most, with strong family ties in Castile, reluctantly chose baptism. Aragon's Muslims would not be faced with this ultimatum until 1526.

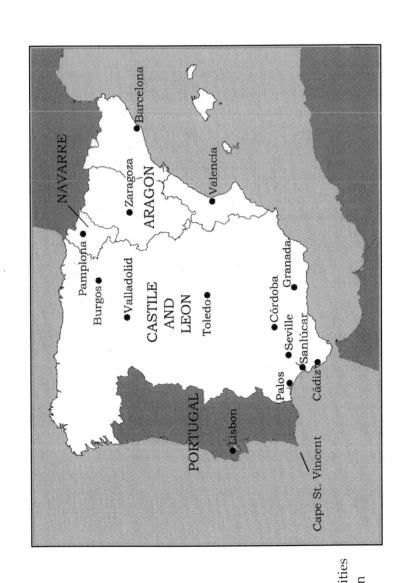

Sixteenth-century political
divisions on the Iberian
peninsula. Ports and major cities
or land features mentioned in
the text are shown.

2

FIRST VOYAGE, 1492-93

The little fleet, fitted out now as well as possible, cleared the bar at Saltés on August 3, with the Admiral's two young children, aged about twelve and four, waving from the quay. (They had been deposited in a school at Córdoba, likely to be cared for by Columbus's mistress, Beatriz.) In part to shorten the vessels' journey over unknown seas, in part to take the opportunity to re-rig *Niña* square,[1] a course was shaped south-southwest for Las Palmas, Canary Islands. Unfortunately, mechanical trouble arose almost immediately, with the rudder of *Pinta* on August 6 jumping its gudgeons. It was repaired at sea, but then broke again. More complete fixing would be required at Las Palmas. Following the necessary repairs and the re-rigging of *Niña*, and after taking on further supplies, the fleet departed from Las Palmas, only to spend two days becalmed out of La Gomera. On September 8, however, the wind picked up and a course was set straight out into the Atlantic.[2]

The three vessels carved the waters westward for nearly five weeks, Columbus keeping a double set of logs — one to show the three crews, understating distance traveled from home to keep their spirits up, and one for himself. But no crew member was unaware that they were hundreds of miles from known land, with a breeze that blew consistently westward, offering little hope of return. Columbus was kept busy calming the skittish crews, encouraging them, putting the best spin, the most portentous meaning, on every bird, floating plant, or other flotsam seen.

On the evening of Thursday October 11, the fast-sailing *Pinta* was, as usual, in the lead. Shortly before midnight a signal was made from her deck. A light had been seen.

---

[1] A necessary procedure to take advantage of following winds. Since a square-rigger was incapable of holding a course into the wind, however, many a crew member would complain loudly about the likelihood of never seeing Spain again.

[2] Possibly all three ships were rigged as carracks at this point, with the fore- and mainmasts square-rigged and the mizzen lateen-rigged.

From Bartolomé de Las Casas's abstract of the log of Columbus:[1]

> A sailor named Rodrigo, from Triana, was the first to see land. The Admiral, however, standing on the sterncastle at ten o'clock, had also seen a light, although it was so faint that he couldn't say whether it might indicate land. He called Pero Gutiérrez, steward of the king's table, telling him that he thought he'd seen a light, and asked him to look. He looked and saw it. The Admiral then called Rodrigo Sánchez, from Segovia, whom the king and queen had sent with the fleet as an overseer. He could see no light because he was in a bad position to see it. But after the Admiral spoke, the light could be seen once or twice, like a small candle being lifted up. Although few thought it meant land, the Admiral was certain they were near land. . . . Two hours after midnight land could be made out about two leagues away.[2] They took in all sail but a stormsail . . . and lay to, waiting for day.

What had been sighted by these dispirited but now vigilant mariners turned out to be not the mainland Columbus was seeking, but only a small island. When day broke, the flagship and two caravels coasted around the island's southern tip and then, carefully skirting a reef, moved northward along its leeward, or western shore. They anchored, and, on spying people on the beach, the Admiral ordered several parties — one of which he joined himself — to launch boats and row ashore.

It is widely accepted that this landing was made just north of Gardiner Reef on today's San Salvador (formerly Watlings) island in the Bahamas. Las Casas continues:

---

[1] Las Casas, once an entrepreneur, later a Dominican priest and relentless critic of Spanish actions in the New World, evidently had access to the Admiral's logs. His abstract of Columbus's log for this journey, as well as a letter written by Columbus himself near that journey's end, and three brief, obviously first-person, narratives in his son Ferdinand's biography of him are the only "first-hand" sources we have for these events.

[2] The Spanish league at this time may have been anywhere from about 2.6 nautical miles to about 4.25 nautical miles in length. In the literature of the Conquest, it is not easy to determine which measure is being used. Columbus himself seems to have used a league measuring just over one nautical mile. No attempt will be made here to interpret unverifiable distances.

It was Friday. They had reached a small island of the Lucayos, called by the Indians Guanahaní. Naked people started coming out, and the Admiral, along with Martín Alonso Pinzón [captain of *Pinta*] and Vicente Yáñez, his brother—captain of *Niña*—all headed for shore, the Admiral in the flagship's armed barge. The Admiral took with him the royal standard, and the captains the two banners with the green cross, which the Admiral carried on all his vessels. . . . On shore they saw very green trees, a lot of water, and various kinds of fruit. The Admiral summoned the two captains and the others who had come ashore, as well as Rodrigo de Escobedo, recording secretary of the fleet, and Rodrigo Sánchez, of Segovia, and ordered them to bear faithful witness that he was taking possession before all assembled—which he did—of this island for the king and queen, their sovereigns, making all required declarations, all of which may be found in the written record. Then many of the island's people came up to them.

The foregoing is the closest we have to a first-person account of that singular moment, the moment that set in motion a chain of virtually uncontrollable events that would affect whole peoples and continents for centuries, and that continue to affect them today. It was a seed-moment that would bear fruit of enormous and unforeseen magnitude. This account—set down by Las Casas—brief though it is, is not without clues about the tableau to be enacted again and again in this hemisphere over the next several decades: newcomers having the effrontery to lay claim for their own people to a strange but already inhabited land; their insistence upon a legalistic recording of the takeover, with formulaic declarations unintelligible to those whose lands were being seized; and the open-mouthed curiosity of the natives, who had never seen the like of these bearded and metal-encased white strangers with their giant seagoing conveyances, and who have no concept of what is about to happen.

For Columbus this island inhabited by Arawakan people was a distraction, since he had not come in search of islands, but of a mainland. He was fully expecting to land soon in the domain of the Grand Khan of China, the man to whom he would present his letter of introduction from the Catholic sovereigns. He had in his fleet speakers of biblical languages, and was confident that one of these languages would suffice for communication with the successor of Marco Polo's Oriental potentate.

Columbus's account of the first voyage was written to be read not by us, but by the king and queen, no doubt with the purpose of convincing the sovereigns to fund a second voyage. While much of the version that we have was actually written by Las Casas from a low-quality copy of Columbus's original log, large portions have been transmitted in the first person, as if from Columbus himself. Again, unsatisfactory as the document may be as a primary source, it nonetheless provides us with our best access to the Admiral's voice and thought with regard to this event that would have such an enormous impact on human history.

[FRIDAY OCTOBER 12, 1492][1] Because they were very friendly to us, and because I could see they were a people who could likely be converted to our holy faith by love more than force, I gave some of them a few red caps and glass rosary beads, which they hung about their necks, and other cheap trinkets in which they took a great deal of pleasure and which made them marvelously friendly to us. When we had put off again, they came swimming up to our boats, bringing us parrots, balls of cotton thread, light spears, and many other things, which they traded with us for other things that we gave them, like little glass beads and hawk's bells.[2] They took what we had and gave of their own very willingly. But they seem to be a very poverty-stricken people. All go about as naked as the day they were born, . . .

The only people I saw were young men, not one of them over thirty. They're very well built, with fine bodies and handsome faces. They have coarse hair, almost like a horse's tail, and wear it short. Their hair comes to just above their eyebrows, except for a few strands in back, which they wear long and never cut. They are the color of Canary Islanders— neither black nor white. Some paint themselves black, some white, some red, and others some other color. Some paint their faces, others the whole body, and others just their eyes or nose. They carry no arms and don't seem to know about them

---

[1] The journal actually proceeds directly from October 11 to October 13, recounting events of October 12 within.

[2] Small bells attached to the legs of hunting falcons in falconry.

because I showed them swords and they took them by the edge and cut themselves out of ignorance. They have no iron. Their light spears are just canes without iron. Some of them have a fish tooth at the tip, and others have something else. They are fairly tall people, good looking and well built. I saw some with evidence of wounds on their bodies. When I made signs asking about this, they indicated that people came there from nearby islands to capture them and they defended themselves. I believed and still believe that these people who came to take them captive are from the mainland.

The Europeans' attitude and their dawning intention toward these people appears clearly in the Admiral's next words.

They should prove to be good servants and intelligent, because I noticed that they can very quickly repeat everything I say to them. I feel it will be easy to make them Christians — it seems to me they in fact have no religion. If it please Our Lord, I'll bring a half-dozen of them back to Your Highnesses so that they can learn to speak.

They of course knew how to speak already, but not in a language intelligible to "civilized men," the only sort of language that mattered.

SATURDAY OCTOBER 13, 1492 They came out to the ship in boats like long-boats, each made of a single tree-trunk and carved out wonderfully in their manner.[1] Some of these craft are large, holding up to forty or forty-five men, while others are smaller, even down to holding only one man. They propel the boats beautifully with something like a baker's shovel. If they capsize, everyone jumps into the water, rights the vessel, and empties it with gourds that they carry with them. In these craft they brought us balls of spun cotton, parrots, spears, and other items that would be tedious to mention. They traded everything for whatever we offered them.

The Admiral now dropped a second significant clue to the Spaniards' interests.

I saw some men wearing a small piece of gold hanging from a piercing in their nose, and tried hard to learn if they had gold. I was able to understand by their signs that somewhere to the south there was a great king who had gold in large

---

[1] Canoes in the Indies and on the mainland were made of hollowed-out logs of various sizes.

quantities, including enormous golden vessels. I tried to get them to guide me there, but soon saw they had no intention of doing so.

Columbus's complete inability to speak or comprehend the language of this island's people proved to be no impediment to his understanding, as he easily fantasized what was being communicated to him, showing not the slightest doubt about the meaning of the islanders' words and gestures.

> SUNDAY OCTOBER 14, 1492 At dawn I ordered the flagship's gig and the caravels' boats made ready,[1] then coasted the island to the northeast. I wanted to see another part of the island — the eastern part — learn what was there, and see some villages. I found two or three settlements, their people coming down to the beach, calling out to us, and giving thanks to God. Some brought water to us, others things to eat. Still others, when they saw we had no intention of landing, swam out to us. It seemed that they were asking if we had come from the sky. An old man got into my gig. Others, both men and women called loudly: "Come and see the men who've come from the sky. Bring them food and drink." Many men and women came, each one bringing something, giving thanks to God, throwing themselves on the ground and raising their hands to heaven. They begged us to land.

He began almost at once to contemplate the construction of a defended settlement and showed the first signs of making what would become a common Spanish misjudgment, namely, that the docility of these people meant that they could be easily turned into both Christians and slaves. Within two days of arrival, he in fact captured his first human specimens for transport to Castile.

> This morning, in order to give an account to Your Highnesses as well as to learn the best place to build a fort, I went to have a look at all this. I found a piece of ground with six houses on it that's formed like an island, although it really isn't one. This piece of land could be turned into a real island in two days, although the project seems unnecessary because these people are very unschooled in arms. Your Highnesses will see this for yourselves from seven of them whom I've had

---

[1] The term "boat" refers to the rowed boats of various sizes or classification carried on board or towed behind the flagship and caravels.

seized in order to bring them back to learn our language and return. Depending on the will of Your Highnesses, the entire population could be brought back to Castile or kept captive on this island, because with fifty men the entire island could be subjugated and its people made to do whatever one wished.

Within the first two days of European arrival, the destruction of a native people had begun.

The three vessels now left the island, which had been christened by the Admiral San Salvador, and proceeded southwest to today's Rum Cay, called Santa María de la Concepción by Columbus. Ever alert to the possibility of gold, the Admiral longed to believe that he was being directed to its source by his new captives. To learn more about the presence of gold, he put an armed landing party ashore.

MONDAY OCTOBER 15, 1492 It was almost sunset when I anchored off this island's [western] cape in order to learn if there were gold there. The captives that I had taken on San Salvador had in fact told me that they wore large golden bracelets on their legs and arms here, although I took it all as a story to help them get away. Nonetheless I planned to pass no island without taking possession of it, although having taken possession of one, we might be considered to have taken possession of all. I remained there at anchor until today, Tuesday, when at dawn I headed for shore with the armed boats and landed. The people we saw there were as naked as those on San Salvador, and in much the same condition. They permitted us to look around the island, and gave us whatever we asked for. . . . On our arrival back at the flagship a large dugout was lying alongside *Niña*, and one of the prisoners from San Salvador who was aboard leaped over the side and went off in it. Another soon followed him and swam after the dugout, which was so fast and had such a head start that none of our boats could have caught it.

Likely stung by the audacity of mere savages daring to flee Spanish sailors, Columbus sent a few men ashore after the fugitives.

A few of my sailors went after them on shore, but they fled like hens. We took their dugout aboard *Niña*. At that moment another dugout appeared, a small one with one man in it. He had come from the other cape to barter a ball of cotton. Since he refused to climb aboard the caravel, a few sailors jumped overboard and seized him. I was standing on the flagship's sterncastle at the time and saw everything. I sent over for him and gave him a red cap and a string of small green glass beads that I hung upon his arm, and two hawk's bells that I affixed to his ears. I then told him to return to his dugout, which was with one of our boats, and to go ashore. . . .

It was to show him that we were good people that I set him free and gave him presents, so that when Your Highnesses send men here again, they won't find unfriendly people. What I gave him wasn't worth four *maravedís*.[1]

At midday the fleet proceeded westward to the northeastern tip of today's Long Island (Caribbean), visible in the distance. Columbus named the island Fernandina in honor of King Ferdinand. Moving northwest toward the island's tip, he discovered a large and deep harbor, but with an entrance too narrow to be negotiated safely by the ships. Next day he assembled a landing party, armed and bearing empty water casks, to go ashore in boats and procure fresh water at a nearby village. The astonished villagers, after recovering their composure, led the landing party to a water source some distance away, while Columbus remained for two hours strolling amid the trees along the shore, reveling in the idyllic beauty of the place. The men returned bearing filled water casks.

WEDNESDAY OCTOBER 17, 1492 The men who had gone for water told me they had gotten inside some of the houses, that they found them well swept and clean, and that the beds and furnishings they saw were like cotton nets.[2] The houses themselves are like large Moorish tents, with good chimneys. But I never saw more than twelve or fifteen houses in a village. The men learned here that married women wore cotton underpants, but that young girls wore nothing, at least below the age of eighteen.

Attempting to cope with almost daily rain and low visibility, Columbus now sailed along the island coast nearly to its southern tip. When the weather cleared, he headed generally east and south, where he encountered another island—today's Crooked Island, which he named Isabela in honor of the queen of Castile. At midday on October 19 the vessels anchored at some distance off Isabela's northern cape.

---

[1] The equivalent of pennies.
[2] The Europeans' first sight of *hamacas*, or hammocks.

FRIDAY OCTOBER 19, 1492 All these islands are so green and beautiful that I don't know where to go first. My eyes never tire of looking upon this gorgeous greenery, so different from what we have at home. I believe there are many plants and trees here that would be very useful in Spain as dyes and medicinal spices, but it pains me not to be able to identify them. Arriving off this cape I noted the most divinely sweet odor of flowers or trees coming off the land, the very sweetest odor on earth.

Columbus professed to have little time for geographical investigations, since he was in a hurry to find spices and gold. He proceeded a short distance southward along the Isabela shore, but was hesitant to anchor near shore because of widespread shallows. He stood off all night under sail, and in the morning began to edge carefully shoreward. By ten o'clock on the morning of October 21, the flagship and two caravels were safely anchored in the shadow of Cabo del Isleo, the island's northern promontory. He was told by his captive Indians (he used this term now) of a great island nearby called Colba, which he became certain was Marco Polo's Cipangu, or Japan. (It was in fact modern-day Cuba.) He was told of another large island whose name he heard as Bohío.[1] This island, when he eventually found it, he would christen Española—in English, Hispaniola.

SUNDAY OCTOBER 21, 1492 At ten in the morning I arrived off this cape, Cabo del Isleo, and dropped anchor, the caravels doing likewise. After eating we went ashore, where all we found was a single house, empty. They had evidently left out of fear of us, because all their things were there.

I ordered my men to touch nothing—I wanted simply to walk around the island with them and see it. If the islands that we had seen up to that time are beautiful and green and fertile, this one is even more so, filled as it is with great green forests. There are large lagoons here, surrounded by magnificent trees, everything so green. It's like April in Andalucía. The singing of the birds is so sweet that a man might never want to leave here. The flights of parrots even darken the sun. The diversity of large and small birds and their differences from ours is quite amazing. There are a thousand varieties of trees, each with its

---

[1] It was later discovered that *bohío* or *buhío* was the Arawakan word for hut, or dwelling.

own kind of fruit. Their odor is divine, and I regret deeply that I can't identify them, because I'm certain they have great value. I'm taking samples of everything back with me.

While walking near one of these lagoons I spotted a reptile,[1] which we killed. We'll bring its skin to Your Highnesses. When this animal saw us it raced into the water and we followed it, since the water wasn't very deep. We were able to kill it with spears. It's nearly five feet long, and I believe these lagoons harbor many more like it. Here I recognized aloe, and tomorrow I plan to have half a ton brought aboard the flagship, because I understand it has great value. While looking for a good source of fresh water we came across a village, half a league from where I'm anchored.

As soon as these people heard us coming they all fled to the forest, hiding their clothing and other possessions. I allowed nothing of theirs to be touched, down to the value of a pin. After a while a few of the village's men returned, and one of them came up to us. I gave him some hawk's bells and glass beads, leaving him quite contented. And in order to strengthen our friendship by seeking their assistance, I asked if he could get us some water. I then returned to the flagship. In a little while the people came down to the beach with gourds full of water, seemingly very happy to give it to us. I ordered that they be given another string of glass beads, and they told me they planned on returning next day.

The fostering of good relations with the Indians by asking for water was but a means of achieving his real purpose: to reach the wealth of the East, which—in spite of his having seen no sign of more than a primitive civilization—must surely, he thought, lie nearby. His fog of misapprehension had still not lifted.

I wished to have all our water jars filled here, so that, weather permitting, I might coast this entire island until I have some contact with this king, and see if I can obtain any of the gold which I hear that he has. Afterwards I plan to leave for the very large island that I believe—according to the signs I've been given by these Indians whom I've taken—to be Cipangu. They call it Colba, and indicate the presence there of great ships and many sailors. I also plan to sail for another island

---

[1] Las Casas reportedly claimed that this was an iguana.

that they call Bohío, which is supposed to be very large. I'll likely see other islands in passing. If I find a source of gold or spices, I'll decide then what to do. But I'm still determined to find the mainland and the city of Quinsay,[1] where I'll present the Grand Khan with Your Highnesses' letters, request a reply, and return with it.

WEDNESDAY, OCTOBER 24, 1492 Last night at midnight I weighed anchor from the Cabo del Isleo on Isabela's north shore, where I had been resting, and sailed for the island of Cuba, which I've heard from these people is very large and full of trade, and where gold and spices and great ships and merchants are to be found. They've told me by signs to head west-southwest. I believe that if this island is as described by all the Indians of these isles, including those I carry on board (all of whom communicate with us by signs, since we cannot understand one another by words), then it must be the island of Cipangu, about which marvelous tales are told. From the globes and painted maps that I've seen, it does lie in this region.

The fleet proceeded cautiously west and south for several days, holding to a course recommended by the Indian captives, encountering on October 28 the north shore of what the Admiral believed to be Japan. It was today's Bariay Bay, in Holguín province, Cuba. They proceeded northwest along the island's northern shore until October 31, when a strong north wind forced them to turn back to the southeast, to the harbor of present-day Gibara, Cuba. Columbus wrote that the villagers of this place were more advanced than others he had seen, and in further evidence that a wish can easily become father to thought, stated his expectation that they would be even more advanced the closer to the mainland they might go. On November 2 he provisioned a landing party for six days, with the injunction to seek out the king of that land — expected to be an Oriental monarch — and to tell him that the Admiral, who wished to conclude friendship with him, awaited him with letters of introduction from the king and queen of Castile. Among the landing party — which of course had no chance of finding such a monarch — was a linguist who spoke Spanish, Hebrew, Aramaic, and Arabic. One of two Indians accompanying the Spaniards was from San Salvador and the other from Cuba. On

---

[1] Hangzhou, China, visited by Marco Polo in the late thirteenth century.

November 5, still awaiting the return of the landing party, he took the opportunity to run the flagship and caravels onto the beach to careen them.[1] On November 11, contrary winds keeping the newly careened vessels in harbor, he occupied his men with capturing more Indians. He described and gave reasons for his action in an entry for November 12, referring to these unfortunates much as one would refer to cattle.

> MONDAY, NOVEMBER 12, 1492 Yesterday a dugout with six men came alongside the flagship and five of them came aboard. I ordered them detained, since I plan to bring them back with me. I later sent to a house on the western bank of the river, and they brought seven head of women, young and old, and three boys. I seized these women because the men I'm bringing to Spain will behave better if they have their own women with them than if they go without them. Many times it happened that we brought men out of Guinea [on the west coast of Africa] to Portugal so that they could learn Portuguese, and after they went back it was thought that we might — due to the good company they had enjoyed and the good things we had given them — get some return from them in their own land, but it never worked out. . . . These men, however, having their women with them, ought to be willing to do whatever they're told, and the women could teach their language to us, a language that's the same in all these islands of India.

Over the ensuing two weeks — the Admiral's emissaries having returned without finding an Oriental monarch — the fleet proceeded southeast along the northern shore of Cuba, exploring bays and islands, Columbus periodically landing to plant a large cross on the beach. Early in the morning of November 21, Martín Alonso Pinzón, master of *Pinta*, departed without the Admiral's permission, following up, it was later suspected, on a lead to a gold field given him by a captive Indian. He would not be seen again for six weeks. Columbus, peeved, nonetheless continued to move eastward along the unknown coast in company with *Niña*. In the midst of a rhapsodic journal entry that expounded on the beauty and fertility of the lands they were seeing, and the potential for large-scale conversions to the faith, Columbus advised the Catholic sovereigns on the need to guard all this treasure for the sole use of Spain and the Church.

---

[1] To scrape off barnacles and weed from the hull, and to force new pitch into cracks and shipworm holes.

TUESDAY NOVEMBER 27, 1492 I say that all Christendom will traffic with the large populations here—most of all Spain, to whom all this should be subject. And I say that Your Highnesses should not permit any foreigner except Christian Catholics to set foot on these lands, much less traffic with their people, for this was the end and the beginning of the enterprise, namely, the increase and glory of the Christian religion. No one who is not a good Christian should be allowed to enter these lands.

Santa María and *Niña* were kept by contrary winds in today's Baracoa harbor until December 4, when Columbus ordered a move further eastward. Putting Cuba finally behind him—having lately decided that it must be an extension of the Asian mainland, but with a lingering suspicion that it might be an island—the Admiral next day sighted the mountains of today's Haiti at a distance of about forty miles. He asked himself if perhaps this new land might be Japan. On December 6 he entered a fine harbor on Haiti's northwest coast, naming it Puerto de San Nicolao, because it had been entered on the feast of St. Nicholas. On December 7 he left the harbor to sail eastward along Haiti's northern coast, stopping to catch mullet and sole in today's Baie des Moustiques. The Admiral, having noted the resemblance of the country roundabout to Spain, and having caught fish here like the fish of Castile, decided on December 9 to name this island the "Isla Española," or Spanish Island (our "Hispaniola"). The small island lying just north of Haiti he named Tortuga (Turtle). Kept in the Baie des Moustiques by contrary winds, he took the opportunity on December 12 to raise a great cross at the harbor entrance in honor of the Spanish monarchs and the Christian Church. An excursion to Tortuga showed it to be well cultivated and populous. The Admiral could scarcely contain himself at the prospects presented by these people and their lands.

SUNDAY DECEMBER 16, 1492 Your Highnesses may rest assured that there is so much good and fertile land here—and none more so than on this island of Hispaniola—that it's hard to describe. It must be seen to be believed. And this entire island as well as all the others are as much yours as Castile. We have but to make a settlement and order these people to do whatever you wish, because I and the few men I have with me could go anywhere in these islands without opposition. I've seen a group of only three of my sailors—who intend no harm—go ashore and cause a large flock of Indians to flee. They have no weapons, they're totally defenseless, they in fact know nothing about arms, and they are cowards. A thousand of them would not face three of us. And for this reason it's easy to order them about and make them work, to sow and to do whatever else might be necessary, such as having them build houses and be taught to wear clothing and to take up our own customs.

In their presumption of Indian tractability and cowardice, the Spaniards would find they were sadly mistaken.

The flagship and caravel spent December 17, and the next day as well, off present-day Port-de-Paix, awaiting the arrival of one whom Columbus referred to as the King of Hispaniola, a chief who was to bring gold with him.[1] At length the approximately 21-year-old "king" arrived, borne on a litter, and accompanied by two hundred men. The Admiral was dining aboard ship at the time. The young man—possibly the first to have given solid hope of gold—and some of his retainers were solicitously conducted aboard by Columbus's men. The Admiral was deeply moved by his young guest's grace and sophistication, and by the veneration in which he appeared to be held by his people.

TUESDAY DECEMBER 18, 1492 It would no doubt have greatly pleased Your Highnesses to see the respect in which he was held by his people, not forgetting they were all naked. When he came aboard ship and was told that I was in the sterncastle, dining, he quickly came up to me and sat down beside me without permitting me to stand up to greet him. When he came in, he made signs to his people that they should all wait outside, which they did with the greatest show of reverence, all arranging themselves on the deck except for two elders whom I took to be his counselors, and who stayed sitting at his feet. It was said that he was a *cacique*,[2] and I, thinking that he might like to eat something, ordered food such as I was eating to be set before him. When the food arrived the

[1] This "king" was a subordinate of Guacanagarí, ruler of the northwest coast of Hispaniola.
[2] *Cacique* was the Arawakan word for chief, or ruler. Columbus began to use the word, and the Spaniards applied it thereafter to chiefs even beyond Arawakan domains.

three men tasted everything, but the cacique then sent the remainder to his people, who finished it. They did the same with the drink we offered — they each took a sip, and he sent the rest to his people. They were all very serious, saying little, but the little that I could make out told me that they were all quite grave men. The two elders looked at him, speaking both to him and for him.

Following the meal, one of the principal Indians, with great reverence, handed him a belt, something like our Castilian belts, although of different workmanship. After receiving it, he presented it to me, along with two pieces of gold that were very delicately worked. I think that little gold is found here, but I believe the spot where it is found is not far away, and that in that place there is a lot of it. Thinking that he fancied the quilt that I had on my bed, I gave it to him, together with some amber beads I was wearing around my neck, a pair of red shoes, and a bottle of orange-blossom water, all of which pleased him greatly. He and his counselors appeared distressed because they could not understand me, nor I them. One thing I did understand was that if I had need of anything, the entire island was at my disposal. I then sent for a portfolio of mine where I kept a gold *excelente* with the images of Your Highnesses.[1] I showed it to him, explaining to him once again that Your Highnesses ruled over the best part of the world, and that there were none more exalted. I showed him the royal banners and the other banners with the cross, . . . and I could clearly see that he was struck with wonder at everything.

On December 19 the two vessels — *Pinta* had not been seen for a month — left Port-de-Paix and began again to work eastward along the northern coast of Haiti. By sunset on December 20 they had entered what Columbus thought to be the finest harbor in the world — Baie de l'Acul (Acul Bay), just west of today's Cap-Haïtien. It seemed a paradise, with riveting scenery, and Indians — all obviously holding the visitors in awe — coming from near and far, bearing gifts and even impressive gold pieces for trade. The high green mountains, the gorgeous anchorage, the cultivated fields, the apparent adulation of a handsome people, all impressed Columbus deeply. During a short trip to the interior by a landing party sent at the invitation of Guacanagarí,

---

[1] A coin of Castile.

the local ruler, the Indians vied with one another to carry the visitors piggyback. They were eager to please the strangers with tales of gold to be found throughout the interior of the island. On December 23, upwards of a thousand Indians approached the strange vessels, half of them in dugout canoes of various lengths, half of them swimming, although the ships were anchored a mile off shore. Many seemed to tell of gold and gold mines on the island — of gold apparently available for the taking. This was surely the high point of Columbus's first voyage — he could hardly contain his joy. Despite his failure thus far to find the Indies of his dreams, a path to a different dream appeared to be opening up. He began to love these people, bearers of such unbelievably good news.

> MONDAY DECEMBER 24, 1492 Your Highnesses may well believe that there can be no better or gentler people in the world than these. This ought to please Your Highnesses immensely, because they will all eventually become Christians, and be well instructed in the good manners of your realms. There can be no more perfect people on earth than these, with both people and land in such quantity that I don't know how to describe it.

This joy would be short-lived, because the explorers' fortunes were about to change for the worse. The ever-optimistic Columbus, however, would even then find a silver lining in what to others would have been disaster.

Sailing out of the Baie de l'Acul in light airs late on December 24, *Santa María* and *Niña* rounded Cap-Haïtien, heading east in shoal-strewn but not unknown seas, they having been explored by the ships' boats the previous day. A visit to Guacanagarí, the local king, had been planned for Christmas day. With the vessels ghosting slowly eastward over a nearly flat sea, the exhausted Admiral, around eleven o'clock at night, stretched out to sleep in his cabin on *Santa María*. The man at the tiller, anticipating no danger under present conditions, took his own opportunity to rest, turning over the helm to a ship's boy — a procedure that had been strongly forbidden by Columbus.

> TUESDAY DECEMBER 25, 1492 It pleased our Lord that at midnight, after I had gone to bed, with the sea in a dead calm — as placid as the water in a teacup — the crew also went to bed, leaving the tiller in charge of a boy. As it happened, the swells very gently moved the vessel onto a sandbar, but creating such a crash that it must have been heard a league away. The boy,

feeling the rudder dig in, and hearing the noise, began to shout very loudly. Hearing him, I leaped out of bed and rushed on deck, no one else apparently having noticed that we'd run aground. The ship's master, whose watch it had been, soon arrived. I ordered him and the rest of the crew to jump into the ship's boat that we were towing and to haul an anchor out [so that we could set it and pull the ship off against it]. They instantly jumped into the boat and I expected that they would do as ordered, but instead they started pulling hard for the other caravel [*Niña*], a half-league away. Seeing this, and seeing as well the ebbing of the tide, which put the vessel into grave danger, I tried lightening the vessel as much as possible by having the mast cut away. Still, with the ebbing tide the ship would not float. Moreover, since the ship had folded somewhat, water was now pouring through the hull's many seams, filling up the hold. At this moment the boat from the other caravel arrived. Because they had seen our people fleeing the ship and had refused to let them aboard, our men had been forced to return.

I saw that there was no way to lift her off. To save her people, therefore, I took them to the other caravel, and because the breeze was off shore and the night far advanced, and because we didn't know our way out of these shoals, I remained aboard the caravel until dawn, at which time I returned to the flagship. Prior to that I had sent the boat ashore with Diego de Arana, of Córdoba, chief constable of the fleet, and Pedro Gutiérrez, steward of Your Highnesses' table, to tell the king [Guacanagarí] what had happened for my having wanted to visit him, as he had asked me to do the Saturday previous. He was to be told that I had lost the ship on a sandbar a league and a half from his town.

When the king was told of this, he displayed great emotion and shed tears at our misfortune. He then immediately sent all his people to the ship in many large canoes, with which they and we were able to clear the entire deck in almost no time. Not only was the king of immense help, but even his brother and relatives pitched in. They displayed great solicitude, both on land and aboard the ship, that everything might be done properly. From time to time the king sent some of his relatives to me, weeping, begging me not to take this misfortune too hard, assuring me that their king would provide for us whatever he could. I can tell Your Highnesses that nowhere in Castile would better care be taken of our things, of which not a shoelace was missing. The king had all our goods stored together near his palace, until the buildings where he wished to store them could be emptied. He then set a guard of armed men over it, ordering them to keep watch throughout the night.

He and the others wept as if the misfortune had been theirs. They are such a loving, docile, peaceful people, that I swear to Your Highnesses, there can be no better people or land in the world. They love their neighbor as themselves. Their speech is sweet and cheerful, and always delivered with a smile.

Columbus, possibly under the prodding of his men, gradually came to see a way of turning disaster into opportunity. Instead of overloading his two caravels for the return to Castile (presuming *Pinta* would rejoin), he would leave a group of volunteers behind to construct a settlement, provisioning them with what had just become available from the wrecked *Santa María*. He would leave all the ship's tackle with these men, as well as all the tools, food, seeds, lumber, and weapons he could salvage from the ship. He would also leave them *Santa María's* barge. With gold fever burning hot among the men, there was no dearth of applicants to stay. Having noted the apparent timorousness and gentle nature of the island's inhabitants, the Admiral was perfectly confident that the settlers would be safe and the settlement a success, and that when he returned the following year, after having refitted and reprovisioned in Palos, Castile would have a solid foothold in this golden land.[1]

WEDNESDAY DECEMBER 26, 1492 So many things came to hand that, really, this was more a great piece of good luck than a disaster. It's clear that if I hadn't run aground, I would have sailed on by without anchoring in this place, which is tucked back in a large bay that has two or three shallow reefs. Nor on this voyage would I have dropped off any people, or—even if I had wanted to leave them—could I have supplied them with such good equipment or so many tools or provisions or

---

[1] It is widely believed that the settlement was constructed near today's Bord de Mer de Limonade, a few miles southeast of Cap-Haïtien.

materials for building a fortress. And the truth is that many of my people begged permission to stay. I've therefore ordered that a tower and fort be constructed, everything very strong, as well as a large moat, but not because I think this is really necessary against the people who live here. As I've said before, with the men I have, I could subdue this entire island — which I think is larger than Portugal and has twice the population — but they are naked and without arms and cowardly beyond belief. It's nevertheless proper that my men build this tower and that they do it the right way, being so far from Your Highnesses. The native inhabitants should be made to recognize the genius of Your Highnesses' subjects and what they are capable of, so that — from a mixture of love and fear — they might become obedient. My men will now have lumber to construct their fortifications, more than a year's supply of bread and wine, and seeds for sowing. They will also have the ship's barge, as well as a caulker, carpenter, gunner, and cooper. And among this group are many who, both to serve Your Highnesses and to please me, wish greatly to learn where the gold mine is. So everything has turned out much to the purpose that this beginning be made.

A beginning had indeed been made. The Admiral spent the next few days cementing his relationship with Guacanagarí and his people — thrilling to their ever more detailed accounts of gold just over the horizon — while he took on water and wood in preparation for an immediate return to Castile. A few days after the wreck of *Santa María*, the Indians reported to him the sighting of his missing consort *Pinta* to the east, but he made no immediate effort at contact. Exhorting the approximately forty men he was leaving at the new settlement — named La Navidad — to be diligent in their search for gold, he had the presence of mind to arrange for the firing of a lombard through the hull of the derelict *Santa María*,[1] in part to demonstrate the power of the Castilians to protect Guacanagarí's people from Carib Indians,[2] in part to demonstrate what they themselves would have to face should

---

[1] A lombard was a small carriage-mounted cannon, capable of firing a ball eight hundred to a thousand yards. A "lombard's shot" was frequently used as a measure of distance.

[2] Inhabitants of neighboring islands, reputed to hunt Arawakan people and eat their flesh.

they decide to turn against the settlers.

But Columbus knew that La Navidad could be only a temporary settlement. Its harbor was imperfect, and it lay far from the reputed gold fields. A settlement would have to be established the following year, he reasoned, further eastward—closer to Spain. Meanwhile he fretted about the possibility of Pinzón sailing home before him, getting to the monarchs first—not only receiving credit for the discovery, but also slipping out of the punishment due him for leaving the fleet without permission.

On January 4, after final good-byes, and after being guided through the shoals by her barge, Niña stood east along Hispaniola's northern coast. Columbus noted the presence of a high mountain that he named Monte Cristi, commenting that it would make a good marker for future voyages to La Navidad. Still confused about where he was with respect to the Indies, he stated his belief that Cipangu, or Japan, must be somewhere on the island of Hispaniola.

On January 6, as Niña beat cautiously eastward through the shallows, Pinta was sighted running down towards her from the east. Because widespread shoals made it dangerous to anchor, Columbus ordered Niña back to Monte Cristi so that he could meet with Pinzón. An unpleasant interview ensued aboard Niña. On January 8, while still held in port by an east wind, the Admiral explored today's Yaque del Norte River, just west of Monte Cristi. Much to his delight, he found the sediments to be sparkling with gold! Yet, so weary was he of the Pinzón brothers and some of his crewmen that he resolved to tuck this site into his memory and push homeward to Spain as planned. Still coasting Hispaniola on January 12, he registered amazement at the size of the island. On January 13, on today's Cape Samaná, he and his men had their first dustup with hostile Indians, whom he suspected (wrongly) of being Caribs, and two days later he seized four unsuspecting Indian youths from this peninsula for transport to Castile. (Three of them would die on their return from Castile on the Admiral's second voyage.) On January 16, the two vessels headed northeast from Hispaniola's Samaná Bay, in search of the reportedly cannibalistic Caribs, reputed hunters of Arawakans. But because both caravels were leaking badly,[1] and the crews becoming restive, he decided against looking further for Carib lands, and to shape a course

---

[1] Columbus complained strenuously about the caulkers in Palos, who, when asked to rectify their shoddy work, had run off.

farther northward for home.[1] On February 12, however, with most of the Atlantic now behind them, the tiny vessels encountered high winds and mounting seas — the worst weather of the trip. The two caravels, mere corks now amid towering waves, required the closest attention to avoid broaching. On February 14, with the storm still raging, *Niña* and *Pinta* became separated, the latter not to be seen by Columbus again this voyage. Vows were made throughout *Niña*, with many heartfelt promises to God of pilgrimages to various shrines if the vessel might only be kept from foundering. Columbus distilled these terrifying days into a carefully contrived recollection.

THURSDAY FEBRUARY 14, 1493 I could have endured this storm with less distress if it had been my life alone that I had placed in danger — not only because my life belongs to the Supreme Creator, but also because I have many times already found myself so close to death that the tiniest step could have been my last. But what caused me the deepest pain and anxiety was the realization that just when Our Lord had seen fit to illuminate me with the faith and confidence needed to carry out this enterprise — in which I have now been victorious — and just when my detractors have been won over, and Your Highnesses have been served by me with such glory and increase of your high estate, that just then his Divine Majesty would upset all this with my death. Such a fate would have been more tolerable if I had not brought these people with me, leading them on with promises of a prosperous outcome. Seeing themselves in such straits, however, not only do they curse the day they came with me, but they rail against my refusal to turn back, which many times they have resolved to do. But what redoubles my grief is the thought of my two children, left in school at Córdoba, friendless in a strange land, without my ever having known what service I might have performed that could have made Your Highnesses aware of them. And although I trusted that Our Lord would not permit an enterprise, which would exalt his Church so greatly and which I had completed in the face of such opposition and hardship, to be ruined, and I myself lost, I have nonetheless

---

[1] The Admiral very shrewdly calculated that he would encounter westerlies at these more northern latitudes. He was correct.

considered that my own sins may be the reason he wishes to keep me from enjoying any glory in this world.

When the storm abated, *Niña* found herself off the coast of Santa María, an island in the Portuguese-held Azores. Prior to reaching refuge there—a refuge that would prove only temporary—the Admiral finished penning to Their Catholic Majesties a précis of what he felt he had accomplished.[1] Within this optimistic, if naïve, account was the following:

> On this island of Hispaniola, in a spot most convenient and well situated for gold mining and all communications with the mainland—whether here or in the lands of the Grand Khan,[2] where a very profitable trade is expected—I have taken possession of a large town, which I've named Villa de Navidad. I've had a fort built there, which by now should be finished, and have left enough people there to accomplish this, with arms and artillery and provisions for more than a year. They also have a *fusta*,[3] as well as a skilled shipwright capable of building more.
>
> I've established a close friendship with the king of this land, so close in fact that he is proud to call me his brother and to treat me as such. But even if he changes his mind about attacking our people, neither he nor his subjects know anything about arms. They go about naked, as I have said before. They're the most timorous people on earth, and with only the few men I've left behind, their entire land could be destroyed. The island holds no danger for my men if they maintain proper discipline. **– Columbus to Luis de Santángel**

He then made a pitch for royal support of future voyages.

> In conclusion, to speak only of the results of this voyage, undertaken in such haste, Their Highnesses can see that, with very slight assistance from them now, I will give them as much gold as they require. I can also supply them with spices and cotton in whatever amount they specify, as well as mastic—

[1] This letter was actually directed to his friend and supporter at court, Luis de Santángel, for delivery to the monarchs.

[2] The "mainland" is a likely reference to Cuba, which he seems to have considered a continental spur at this time.

[3] A Spanish rowed boat, sometimes with one or two lateen-rigged masts (referring here to *Santa María's* barge).

found until now only in Greece, on the island of Chios, and purchased by us very dearly from the Genoese—as much as they order me to bring.[1] I can provide aloeswood in any amount they wish, and slaves in any number, all from the ranks of the idolaters. I believe I have found both rhubarb and cinnamon, and the people whom I've left there will find a thousand other useful things. Except when delayed by unfavorable winds, I've stopped nowhere except at the Villa de Navidad, which I had to leave well established and protected. I really would have done much more if my vessels had been more dependable. – **Columbus to Luis de Santángel**

Moving around Santa María from port to port, in search of shelter from the ever-shifting storm, Columbus strove to reprovision *Niña* with wood, water, and ballast for the remainder of the trip to Spain. His relationship with Portuguese authorities was uneasy, however, and he endured some bad moments, as when they sequestered half his crew and asked to see his authorization from the Spanish sovereigns for his present voyage in Portuguese waters (a document he was able to produce). By the end of February, his men freed, he was on his way east in manageable seas. About four hundred miles from Cabo São Vicente (Cape St. Vincent), however, on the Portuguese coast, he was buffeted by fresh storms and shifting winds and driven north toward Portugal, all sails virtually shredded. On March 4 he navigated under bare poles into the port of Lisbon, uncertain of his welcome. King João, for his part—although greatly chagrined at Columbus's reported feat—sent him safely on his way.[2] On March 13—after the Admiral had posted his February letter to the sovereigns overland from Lisbon—the newly repaired *Niña* weighed anchor, stood out to sea, and two days later crossed the bar at Saltés to tie up at Palos, her port of embarkation more than seven months before.

---

[1] Mastic is an aromatic resin issuing from the bark of the mastic tree, prized in the fifteenth century as a chewing gum and as a relatively waterproof hole-filler. The word has a common root with "masticate," or chew. It is unclear whether the material referred to by the Admiral was indeed mastic.

[2] Some of the king's advisors had counseled that this tiresome foreigner might better meet with a fatal "accident."

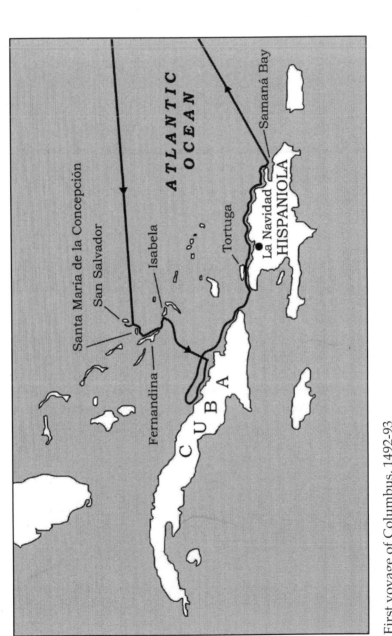

ATLANTIC OCEAN

Samaná Bay

Santa María de la Concepción
San Salvador

Isabela

Tortuga

La Navidad
HISPANIOLA

Fernandina

C U B A

First voyage of Columbus, 1492-93

3

SECOND VOYAGE, 1493-96

On his arrival in Palos in mid-March, the Admiral was concerned about the whereabouts of Pinzón, from whom he had become separated during the recent storm. He was, however, shortly to be disabused of his fears of being upstaged by *Pinta's* master, whom he imagined scurrying to the king and queen with a report on the expedition's astounding discoveries. Pinzón's caravel, it turned out—following its separation from *Niña*—had been able to reach a port in Galicia, northwest Spain. It was rumored that, although gravely ill, Pinzón had in fact made an effort to contact Their Royal Highnesses, either in person or by letter, to report on the voyage, but that they had refused to accept a report from him. The dejected and ailing Pinzón had then sailed for Palos, where he arrived on the very day of the Admiral's arrival from Lisbon. Still racked by fever, he died shortly thereafter.

Columbus—who soon found it necessary to explain away the awkward circumstance of having landed in Portugal instead of Spain—had returned to Castile with tales of vast riches to be had, and of lands and peoples ripe for conversion and subjugation. He had brought back with him a sampling of this new world's wealth—a small amount of gold, colorful parrots, monkeys, curiosities such as fishbone masks, even seven captive Indians—all of which he would eventually parade through the streets of Seville, Toledo, Barcelona, and other cities.[1]

Concerned with making his report to the sovereigns as soon as possible, as well as in showing off the human, animal, botanical, and mineral wealth he had collected, he hastened inland to Seville,[2] where he was told that the sovereigns, prior to receiving him at Barcelona (in Ferdinand's kingdom of Aragon), desired him to collect his thoughts and put down in writing his recommendations on how this great discovery, some details of which had evidently reached them, should be handled.

---

[1] Five of his captive Indians would die on the return voyage to the Indies.
[2] A very young Bartolomé de las Casas was part of Seville's welcoming throngs.

In his subsequent memorandum to the Catholic Sovereigns, composed at a monastery in Seville, Columbus argued for the establishment of a trading empire along the lines of the Portuguese in West Africa, and now beyond. This sensible suggestion was succeeded by others that demonstrated some naïveté regarding the extent to which the enterprise might be controlled. The Admiral, certain of the presence of large gold mines in his newly discovered lands (although never having seen them), advised that the collection of gold be licensed and strictly regulated, and that a portion of it should be set aside for the sovereigns and another portion for the Church. He suggested that searching for gold be prohibited at certain times of the year, so that other occupations might also be pursued. Finally, he wrote, gold should be shipped only to the port of Cádiz, with court-appointed overseers to supervise its unloading and proper distribution.

Questions of naïveté notwithstanding, he would find the queen entirely to his way of thinking in this matter.

In mid-April, Columbus arrived in Barcelona, appearing at court to make his personal report to the sovereigns. Despite the assortment of New World oddities that he had brought with him, he had no great wealth to show for his efforts or for the trip's expense — little gold, no spices. But he had proven at least part of his point: one could reach a new land by sailing west. God alone knew what treasure might be found in these new lands, he argued, and he would surely be able to find a passage beyond them.

The king and queen greeted him warmly, provided him with a public reception, and saw that he was feted throughout the city, even to riding through the streets at the side of the king. A second voyage of exploration would of course be sponsored, he was told. The sovereigns then issued — in their own ingenuous attempt to control events halfway around the globe — their instructions for this second voyage.

Uppermost in the sovereigns' minds — or in the queen's mind at least — and first in their instructions was the protection of Indian welfare and the conversion of Indians to the faith. They had recently striven to ensure such protection by prevailing upon the new pope, Alexander VI (Rodrigo Borgia, a politically savvy and very worldly Valencian) to issue a series of papal bulls ordering the humane treatment of these newfound peoples, and — likely of greater importance to the sovereigns — supporting Spain's claim to all lands discovered and to be discovered on subsequent voyages to the west.[1] In May 1493, the Spanish pope, from his still well-respected throne, decreed that Castile and Aragon would have the right of discovery of all lands lying to the west of a line drawn from the north to the south pole one hundred leagues "west and south" of the Portuguese-held Azores and Cape Verdes. The line passed through the eastern tip of today's Brazil.[2]

Paradoxically, the papal order on Indian protection—namely, that indigenous peoples should be instructed in the faith and trained in "good morals"—effectively sealed the Indians' fate as vassals of the Europeans, and did little to promote their well-being.

In their instructions to their Admiral, the sovereigns cautioned that only trustworthy people were to be taken on his second voyage, that creating and provisioning the fleet was to be done through a Crown representative (namely, Juan Rodríguez de Fonseca, royal chaplain and archdeacon of the cathedral of Seville), that a thorough record be made of every person embarking on this voyage, and that all bartering in the New World be undertaken only by an official appointed by the Crown—under the eye of a Royal Auditor, a person who would have full control over all gain from such barter. Provisions were made for a colonial administration, including judicial officers.

Importantly for Columbus, his own power as viceroy and governor of these new lands was convincingly restated.

With the energetic assistance of the queen's agent Rodríguez de Fonseca, the fleet for this second voyage was assembled at Cádiz, on

---

[1] Portugal's João II, incensed at Columbus's trespassing in what he outlandishly regarded as Portuguese waters, had been claiming the Admiral's discoveries for Portugal. Isabella had appealed to the pope as arbiter.

[2] The Portuguese king, livid at being one-upped by the young Spanish monarchs, insisted on direct discussions with Castile, and the following year, by the Treaty of Tordesillas, the line was moved nearly 1,200 miles westward, giving greater scope for exploration to Portugal. The treaty, however, could not be enforced. The Portuguese, unopposed by Spain, eventually claimed land far west of the line in today's Brazil. As Portuguese and Spanish exploration gradually moved into the Pacific, this line of demarcation was extended through the poles to the other side of the globe. Rival claims there were settled by the Treaty of Zaragoza of 1529.

the Atlantic coast south of Seville. Columbus was faced with a forest of details, not least of which was the vetting of the hundreds of adventurers clamoring to come aboard.

Columbus's first voyage had been made in the relative obscurity of a researcher carrying out an experiment. Few in Iberia knew what he was up to, or, had they known, would have cared. His second voyage, however, was undertaken more in the public eye. The word had spread fairly rapidly. Many men—mostly Castilians—who heard of it saw a voyage to this new place as a potential way of turning their lives around, perhaps of acquiring land and slaves, of becoming wealthy, and possibly of jumping far above their present station. While in 1492 the Admiral had sailed with three vessels and about ninety sullen or reluctant men, a year later he would be shepherding 1,200 or more eager adventurers of widely varying character, social station, ability, and motivation aboard seventeen vessels.

Among these passengers would be, first of all, the Admiral's 25-year-old brother Diego, whom he had summoned from Genoa on his return from his first voyage. Other passengers included Diego Velázquez de Cuéllar, who would eventually be the "pacifier" and first governor of Cuba; Francisco de Garay, who would become one of the first governors of Jamaica; Juan Ponce de León, future discoverer of Florida; Francisco Roldán, a troublemaker who would rise up against the Admiral; Alonso de Ojeda, who would also become a thorn in the Admiral's side; and one Pedro de las Casas (whose family name would become widely known),[1] with three of his brothers. All the livestock that would fit would be taken aboard, and, ominously for the future of New World peoples, many passengers would also embark their horses and large hunting dogs. With such an influx of disparately motivated men, control of his long-cherished plan would soon start to slip from the Admiral's grasp. Though it was not yet evident to him, he was at the beginning of a slow drift toward irrelevancy, eventually to be run over by the very machinery he had set in motion.

By early September it was all coming together, and on the twenty-fifth of that month, 1493, with his two young children again waving from shore, he set sail from Cádiz with fifteen square-rigged and two lateen-rigged vessels, bound for the Canary Islands, and thence again westward across the sea. A second Columbus brother, Bartholomew,

---

[1] Pedro was the father of Bartolomé de las Casas, future howling critic of Spanish atrocities in the Indies. Bartolomé was a child at this time.

would soon conduct the Admiral's children to the court at Valladolid, where, by order of the queen, they would enter service as pages to the monarchs' 15-year-old son and heir apparent, Prince Juan.[1]

We have no log of this voyage, but we do have a memorandum written by Columbus to Their Royal Highnesses with regard to the voyage, as well as first-hand accounts by two participants. These are a report to the city council of Seville by Diego Álvarez Chanca, a Seville physician under royal order to accompany the expedition, and a letter of Michele da Cuneo, a brash Genoese friend of the Admiral, who provided lighthearted treatment of even the most disturbing events.

The fleet reached La Gomera in the Canaries on October 5, and left that island for the Atlantic crossing on October 7. Land was sighted at daybreak on November 3, this time the northeast shore of an island christened by Columbus Dominica, in the lesser Antilles — far south and east of the Admiral's intended landing point on Hispaniola. Columbus chose not to land on Dominica, but on a relatively flat island just to the north, which he took possession of in the name of the Crown, christening it Maríagalante (today's Marie-Galante). After taking on water and wood, the fleet moved to a larger island further north, anchoring off shore the following day. This island Columbus named Santa María de Guadalupe (today's Guadeloupe). On it could be seen a waterfall tumbling from a high rock,[2] as well as people on the beach. The Admiral ordered a landing to be made next morning. Finding themselves now among Caribs — native peoples reputed to consume human flesh — holding Arawakan prisoners, the Europeans showed no hesitation in inserting themselves into this unknown dynamic.

> On this day that we first arrived there, we saw many men and women on the beach staring at the fleet, lost in wonder at such a novel sight. One of our boats was sent in with the object of speaking with them, our men saying repeatedly *"Tayno, tayno,"* which in their language means "good."[3] The people remained at the water's edge as long as our men did not come

---

[1] Bartholomew, thoroughly involved in his brother's calculations and vision from the beginning, had just returned from England where he had been pitching the brothers' plan to Henry VII. Unsuccessful, he returned to Castile, just missing the departure of the fleet.

[2] Carbet Falls in today's Guadeloupe National Park.

[3] Unknown to the Spaniards, it was actually the name of this people. It is now spelled Taíno.

ashore, ready to flee if necessary. In the end, however, none of the men among them could be taken either by force or persuasion—except for two who grew careless and were brought aboard forcibly. More than twenty women were taken, and later, when other natives approached freely, they too were seized. A few young boys among them sought our protection from the island natives who had evidently been holding them prisoner. **– Chanca**

Considering that the newcomers knew only a few words of Taíno, and presumably none of the related island Carib language, they seem to have had no hesitation in claiming to understand what was said to them, although it is true that what they "heard" was certainly supported by what they saw.

These people raid other islands, taking any women they can find, especially young, beautiful girls whom they keep for their service and hold as concubines. They take so many that in fifty houses we saw no males, and more than twenty of the captives were girls. These women say that they are treated with what seems unbelievable cruelty, and that their captors devour the male babies they have by them, bringing up only the babies of their own women. The men whom they capture they take to their houses, then butcher and eat them, saying there is nothing in the world like the flesh of a man. It looks like they believe this because, of the bones we found in these houses, everything that could have been gnawed was gnawed. Whatever was left was simply too tough to be eaten. In one house we found a human neck boiling in a pot. When they capture boys, they cut off their member. These boys then serve them until adulthood. Then, when the natives want to have a feast, they kill and eat them, because they say that the flesh of boys and of women is unpalatable. Of three boys who fled to us for protection, all three had had their member cut off.

– Chanca

The fleet's departure from Guadalupe was delayed by the need to search for a Spanish party that had failed to return to the ships. A large force was sent ashore to look for the stragglers in an effort that took several days. In the meantime more Indians were taken.

At this island we went ashore and stayed for about six days. We did this because eleven of our men who had formed a gang for the purpose of robbery went five or six miles into the interior, but when they wanted to return to the ships, they couldn't find their way. . . . When the Admiral saw they were not coming back, he dispatched two hundred men in four groups to look for them, each group equipped with trumpets, horns, and lanterns. But even they couldn't find them, and there were times when we feared more for the two hundred than the eleven. With God's help the two hundred men — exhausted and hungry — returned, but we were sure that the eleven had been eaten by the Caribs, according to their custom.

At the end of five or six days, however, God willed that the eleven, who had little hope of being found, built a fire on a rocky eminence. We knew it was they when we saw the fire, so we sent them the boat and got them back. But if an old woman had not, by signs, shown them the way out, they would have been lost, for we intended to sail next day.

On this island we captured twelve very plump, beautiful girls, all fifteen or sixteen years old. We also captured two boys of the same age. Each boy had had his member cut off right to the belly. We assumed this had been done to keep them from meddling with the Carib women, or possibly to fatten them up for later consumption. These boys and girls, who had been captured by the Caribs, we took to Spain with us, presenting them to the king as a sample. **– Cuneo**

Having seen to the gathering aboard of both stragglers and search party, and having informed himself as well as possible from the Arawakan captives on Guadalupe concerning the bearing to Hispaniola, Columbus ordered the fleet to weigh anchor on November 10. The vessels then threaded a path among a series of islands — some of which were named by the Admiral Santa María de Montserrat, Santa María de la Antigua, and San Martín — before heading more directly west and a little south. A few days later the vessels found themselves off a generally flat island that Columbus named Santa Cruz (today's Saint Croix). With the fleet kept in harbor there by a blow on November 14, he sent a boat ashore to capture some Indian who might be able to give him a better notion of the fleet's location with respect to Hispaniola. This island, too, proved to be inhabited by Caribs.

When this boat was about to return to the ships with the prisoner it had taken further down the coast, a canoe holding four [Carib] men, two women, and a boy came along the shore. When these people caught sight of the fleet they stopped, awestruck, holding their position for an entire hour about two lombard-shots from the ships. Their stupefaction could be clearly seen by those who were in the boat as well as by everyone aboard ship. The men in the boat began to move toward them, sticking close to shore, and the people in the canoe, totally lost in astonishment at what they were seeing, did not notice their approach until they were very close. They could not get away, although they tried hard to do so. Our men moved so quickly that no escape was possible. The Caribs, seeing this, very boldly took up their bows, the women as well as the men. I say "very boldly" because they were only four men and two women and in our boat were more than twenty-five. Two of our men in the boat were wounded, one with two arrows in the chest and the other with an arrow in his side, and if they hadn't carried leather and wooden shields, and if they hadn't moved in quickly and overturned the canoe, the rest would have been shot as well. After the canoe had been overturned, the Caribs swam about, at times finding a place to stand up in the shallows. It was difficult to take them because they continued shooting arrows as rapidly as they could. One of the men could not be taken until he was struck with a lance. He was carried thus wounded to the ships. **– Chanca**

Since we judged this Carib's wound to be fatal, we threw him overboard, but, to our surprise, he suddenly began to swim away. We therefore recaptured him, and with the grappling hook dragged him over the ship's rail and hacked off his head with an axe. The other Caribs and slaves we later sent back to Spain. **– Cuneo**

Cuneo, who had been in the aforementioned boat, on his return was awarded a prize by his friend, the Admiral.

While in the boat I captured an extremely beautiful Carib woman, whom the Admiral later gave to me. I took her with me to my quarters. She was naked, according to their custom, and I conceived a desire to have my way with her. She was of another mind. When I started on her she treated me so badly with her fingernails that I was sorry I had begun. But, to make a long story short, I took a rope to her and gave her a good whipping—her shrieking was beyond belief—and in the end, we came to such an understanding that she seemed actually to have been raised in a school of whores. **– Cuneo**

The fleet then threaded its way among today's Virgin Islands—also named by the Admiral (Santa Úrsula y las Once Mil Vírgenes)—and then sailed west, anchoring for some fishing off the western shore of today's Puerto Rico, to which the Admiral gave the name San Juan Bautista. By November 22 the vessels had finally reached the north shore of Hispaniola. Soon sighting Monte Cristi, they anchored, finally, in the bay beyond on November 25, and a landing party was sent ashore. A shocking discovery awaited them.

> As they were searching the land along the river, some of our men found two dead men near the riverbank. One had a rope around his neck and the other had his feet bound. This was on the first day. Next day they found two more corpses further upstream. One of these was in good enough condition that he could be seen to have been heavily bearded. Some of our men suspected more evil than good here, and rightly so, because Indians are beardless, . . . This harbor is twelve leagues from where the Christians had been left by the Admiral.
> **– Chanca**

The fleet moved a little further west, anchoring closer to La Navidad. Following a shipboard meeting with Indians who brought gifts to the Admiral, but who were strangely evasive on the subject of the colonists, armed landing parties were sent ashore. It soon became evident that the Indian attitude toward the newcomers had changed.

> The Admiral ordered a few men to go to the place where the settlement had been built, and they found there a palisaded blockhouse where the Christians had lived burnt down. Everything they had built or possessed was burnt and destroyed, . . . The Indians we had seen were very wary, not daring to come near us, avoiding us. This seemed a bad sign, because the Admiral had told us that on arriving in this place so many canoes would swarm around the ships that we would hardly be able to fend them off, for that's what had happened on the previous voyage. Seeing now how circumspect they were around us gave us a bad feeling. **– Chanca**

On or about November 28, the Admiral himself came ashore. The local cacique, Guacanagarí, effusively friendly toward Columbus the previous winter, was strangely absent. It had been reported to Columbus that he had been wounded and was at another village, his own having been burnt down by a rival group. Columbus, preoccupied with the situation at La Navidad, undoubtedly shelved the information about the cacique for the moment to consider the disaster. He appears to have kept his head over the deaths of his men, and brought his mind to bear on the practical questions of recovering all available gold and of rebuilding.

Next morning the Admiral and some of us landed and went to the site of the settlement, which we saw had been completely burnt, with the Christians' clothing left scattered across the ground. We found no corpses here.

Among us there was a variety of opinions. Some were certain that Guacanagarí had taken part in the betrayal or death of the Christians, but others said no, because, after all, his own village had also been burnt. The matter left plenty of room for doubt. The Admiral ordered that the site of the fortifications be searched, for he had told them to bury any gold they might find.

While this was going on, he determined to look at a spot about a league away, where it seemed to us another settlement might be built, since it was time to do so. A few of us went with him to inspect the land along the coast, and we came upon a village here with seven or eight houses, all abandoned by the Indians when they saw us coming. They had carried away whatever they could and had hidden the rest in the underbrush near their houses. These people are so like animals that they don't know how to look for a proper place to live. Those on the coast have extremely primitive houses, all covered with green or dampness. I'm shocked at how they live.
– **Chanca**

With Dr. Chanca's clucking disapproval of the village's absent population perhaps ringing in their ears, the men searched for clues about what had happened.

In those houses we found many things that had belonged to the Christians, things which we believed would not have been bartered, like a very handsome Moorish cloak that had not been unfolded since it was brought from Castile. We found stockings and pieces of cloth and an anchor from the flagship, lost by the Admiral on the previous voyage. We found other things that strengthened us in our suspicions. And, looking through the contents of a wicker basket, which was all sewn up and well concealed, we found—well hidden—a human head. We concluded it might be the head of a father or mother, or of some person much beloved. I have since heard that many of these heads had been found, which makes me think we guessed rightly. From there we returned. **– Chanca**

A second visit to the site of La Navidad, to which a few of the more trusting Indians had returned, seemed to clarify matters.

We came that day again to the spot where the settlement had been, and when we arrived we found many Indians — now very self-confident — engaged in bartering gold. They had already bartered about a mark's worth. We learned that they had pointed out where the corpses of eleven Christians lay, covered now with grass that had since grown over them. All insisted that Caonabó and Mayreni [caciques of neighboring territories] had murdered the men. But what stood out most was the complaint that the Christians had taken women — one three, another four — which made us realize that the Christians had been murdered out of jealousy. **– Chanca**

Guacanagarí sent word to Columbus, now back aboard ship, that he would like to see him, but that he was wounded in the thigh, and could not come himself to meet the Admiral. Would the Admiral please come to see him? Columbus agreed, and prepared to come ashore for a state visit.

The Admiral and all our ranking men went ashore, so handsomely dressed that they would have been noticed in the greatest of cities. The Admiral carried a few things to present to the cacique, since he had already received a substantial quantity of gold from him and it was right that he respond with the same good will. Guacanagarí himself had prepared a further present for the Admiral.

When we arrived we found him stretched out on his bed, of the kind they use, suspended above the ground, a sort of cotton net. He did not leave his bed, but from there made courteous gestures as well as he knew how. He showed great emotion, his eyes filling with tears over the deaths of the Christians. He began to talk about this, explaining as well as he could how some had died of illness, and how others, who had gone to look for the gold mine in Caonabó's territory, had been murdered there. The rest had been murdered in his own village. From the condition of the bodies, the men appeared to have been dead for less than two months.

At this point Guacanagarí presented the Admiral with eight and a half marks' worth of gold and five or six hundred cut stones of many colors. He also presented him with a headdress made of cut stones, something which it seems to me they have in great quantity. On the headdress was a jewel for which the cacique showed great reverence. It strikes me that they value copper more than gold. **– Chanca**

The sight of gold appeared to open the Admiral's heart, and he offered to the cacique the services of both his surgeon and Dr. Chanca in examining his wound. Their findings served to deepen the mystery surrounding recent events.

I and the fleet surgeon being present, the Admiral told Guacanagarí that we were knowledgeable in the illnesses of men, and asked if he would show us his wound. The cacique assented, but I remarked that it would be necessary, if he could manage it, for him to come outside, because with so many people in the house it was too dark to see well. He came out, with assistance, more out of embarrassment than good will. Once he had sat down, the surgeon began to remove his bandages. Guacanagarí then told the Admiral that he had been wounded by a *ciba*, that is, a stone. After unwrapping his wound, we began to examine him. He surely was no more wounded in that leg than in the other, although he made a cunning show of being in great pain.

Clearly no determination of what had happened could be made, the facts being still unknown. It was clear that some hostile people had attacked him. Because of this the Admiral could not decide what to do. It seemed to him, as well as to many others, that until we learned the truth we should dissemble. After we learned the truth, we could seek whatever redress we wished.

That evening Guacanagarí accompanied the Admiral to the ships, where the Admiral showed him the horses, and all that we carried aboard. He was thunderstruck by this, never having seen the like. He took supper aboard ship and later that evening returned to his house. The Admiral said that he wanted to stay here with him and build houses. He was told by the cacique that he would welcome this, but the place was unhealthy on account of the dampness, and in this he was absolutely correct.

All this conversation was conducted through two Indian interpreters who had been taken back to Castile on the previous voyage. They were the only two who had survived of the seven who had been taken. Five had died en route, these two escaping death by only a hair's breadth. **– Chanca**

On the day following this shipboard visit, in late November or early December, Guacanagarí's brother came aboard, ostensibly to barter with gold he brought. No Indian could have missed the sight of other Indians being held captive aboard the Admiral's ship.

On board ship were ten women of those who had been rescued from the Caribs, most of them being from the island of Boriquén.[1] Guacanagarí's brother spoke with them. We believe he told them that later that night they should escape, and during the first watch they began very quietly to slip overboard and swim for shore. By the time their absence was noted, they had covered such a distance that the boats could not recapture more than four, whom they seized as they were leaving the water. The women had swum a good half-league. **– Chanca**

Columbus went ashore next day to demand return of the missing Indian women, but could not find Guacanagarí. He returned to the ship and ordered the fleet to move back eastward, toward a new site that had been noticed on Hispaniola's northern coast, one offering greater possibilities for a permanent settlement.[2] On arrival off an Indian village near this point, boats were manned.

We took all the ships' boats, leaving the ships in the harbor, and rowed briskly along the coast, causing considerable anxiety among the natives. On arrival at the village we saw that all its inhabitants had fled. Moving through the settlement, we found in the undergrowth near the houses an Indian who had been wounded by a dart that was sticking out of his back. He could flee no farther. The people of this island fight with slings like those used by boys in Castile. They shoot them very far and very accurately. Clearly they can do great damage to an improperly protected person. This man told us

---

[1] Today's Puerto Rico.

[2] The new site lay on the coast about seventy miles east of the first settlement, in today's Puerto Plata province of the Dominican Republic.

that Caonabó and his men had wounded him and had burnt the houses of Guacanagarí.

With the little that we understand, therefore, and the obscure and equivocal statements that we've been given, it's been impossible to learn the truth about the death of our people. **– Chanca**

Columbus never got to the bottom of who had killed the settlers, but a prime reason for their murder seems to have been their taking of Indian women.

The Admiral spent the next several weeks in directing the construction of the new settlement, which would be called Isabela. Stone was readily available for erecting a church and other public buildings, and wood and straw for individual dwellings. But the men, sad and frustrated at being so far from home, at not having discovered the gold they had been promised, and, most importantly, at running short of Spanish food, grew surly, and some also began to fall ill. Columbus, worn out himself, had to resort to protecting the food supply with armed guards, rationing the food out. Nonetheless, men soon began to die. It became necessary for the Admiral to dispatch most of his ships to Spain for resupply, which he did, placing them under command of Antonio de Torres.[1] The purpose of sending Torres would be to inform the monarchs of recent events, and to request supplies. He wrote a lengthy memorandum to be delivered to the monarchs personally by Torres, whose sister served in the royal court as governess of young Prince Juan.

In this memorandum, following an assurance to the sovereigns that a promising amount of gold had indeed been found in the streams of this island, he apologized for not having sent more with the returning fleet. In his defense he pleaded widespread illness among the colonists—due to the dampness of the climate, lack of a concerted effort to raise crops, and dwindling supplies of food to which the men were accustomed.[2] Among the further points listed in this high-

---

[1] Dr. Chanca returned to Castile with this fleet, which sailed on February 2, 1494, and arrived in Cádiz on April 7. A number of disillusioned or ill men also returned at this time.

[2] To this list might be added widespread venereal disease. It is thought today that syphilis was a disease of the Indians, received by the Europeans in the so-called Columbian Exchange, an affair in which the Europeans provided the smallpox virus.

priority message, written in the form of instructions to Torres, were the following:

> You shall say [to Their Highnesses] that, because of the shoddy work done by the coopers in Seville—as most here affirm—much of the wine that we carried on this voyage was lost. Therefore the greatest need we have here, or that we expect to have, is of wine. We have enough biscuit and corn to last for a while, but it would be useful to have a reasonable quantity more of this as well. . . . We could also use some salted meat—bacon would be best. But any cured meat would be better than what we've brought with us. **- Torres Memorandum**

Further items are equally revealing of the level of detail to which the Admiral had to address himself.

> In order to bring some comfort and encouragement to the people here, it would be well if everything possible might be done to see that two caravels are here by May. That way our people, especially the sick, would be able to build up their health before summer arrives. We already have a great need for things like raisins, sugar, almonds, honey, and rice, all of which were to be sent in quantity, but which were not—very little has arrived. And whatever we did have has been consumed. Due to the large numbers of sick here, even most of the medicines that were brought across have been used up. As mentioned earlier, you have signed orders from me for everything needed for both sick and healthy. If the money is sufficient, all this should be collected and sent at once on the two caravels. If not, they should at least send what we need most. **- Torres Memorandum**

Thinking to do his Carib prisoners a great service, in addition to making his own task easier by having interpreters available, he had determined to send a few of them back to Spain, where they would be distributed as slaves and taught Spanish.[1]

> You shall say to Their Highnesses that, because we have no interpreter here to help us explain our holy faith to these people, as Their Highnesses and we ourselves desire, and which we have been trying valiantly to do, we're sending back in these vessels a few cannibals—men, women, and children of

---

[1] The queen would not be pleased by this.

both sexes. Their Highnesses can have them put under the supervision of persons from whom they can learn the language, employing them as servants, and little by little seeing that better care is taken of them than of other slaves, . . . If they can neither see nor speak to one another until much later, they'll learn more quickly there than here, and will become better interpreters, although every effort is also made here to see that happen. **– Torres Memorandum**

The Admiral then made a strong pitch for a steady trade in Indian slaves, presenting the idea as being beneficial to both Indians and Crown.

You shall say to Their Highnesses that the welfare of the souls of these cannibals [who are being sent to Spain], and even of those remaining here, has made people realize that the more of them that can be sent to Spain, the better. Their Highnesses would benefit in the following way: We have such a need here of cattle and beasts of burden for the support of the people who have to be here, and indeed of the people of all these islands, that Their Highnesses might grant license and permission to a sufficient number of caravels to be sent here every year with cattle and other provisions that will help us to settle and improve this land. The transporters would be paid a reasonable price here, but the payment would be in slaves from among these cannibals—a savage people, yet suitable to the purpose, well-built, and quite intelligent. We believe that, once they have lost their inhumanity—which will be more easily accomplished once they've been removed from their own lands—they will be superior to any other slaves. . . . Their Highnesses could levy a duty on such imported slaves.

– Torres Memorandum

Columbus seemed to be thinking no longer of a simple trading enterprise as he had proposed to the queen the previous year. It would instead be a Spanish settlement, one where slaves would be the currency used to purchase necessities from Spain. But from the beginning the queen was uneasy about enslavement of the Indians, and emphatic about their not being sent to Spain. By 1500 she would not only forbid their importation, but would order that all held in Spain be released and returned to the Indies. Unfortunately, she proved unable to protect them upon their return.

The Spaniards spent the next few months consolidating their position in Isabela and exploring surrounding terrain, specifically the lush central part of the island, called Cibao, where gold was indeed found and is found to this day. Leaving his young brother Diego in charge of the hungry and increasingly restive population at Isabela, Columbus himself journeyed to the Cibao in March, ordering the construction of a new fort there, to be called Santo Tomás. In early April 1494 he ordered a punishing raid against the Indians of that area. Throughout his domains, he resorted to violence, threats, and intimidation to make the colonists work at construction—many of them highborn men who had never known a day's work in their lives, men who had come not to be laborers, but to become rich. Unbeknownst to him, some of those who had returned with Torres to Spain, thoroughly disillusioned with the Admiral, were at that moment doing their best to run his reputation to the ground with the monarchs. Then in April, with affairs throughout the island in a highly unsettled and even dangerous state, he inexplicably decided to leave governance in the hands of a council headed by his young brother Diego, and to embark upon what he loved best—a voyage of exploration. He was a parent closing the door on his needy and dysfunctional family to indulge a personal passion.

His lack of interest in good administration would have the most unpleasant consequences for him and for the budding colony.

Towards the end of April he departed from Hispaniola with three caravels and about a hundred men—including his friend Cuneo—to range along the southern coast of Cuba, which he in fact explored for well over two hundred miles, at which point he turned south to investigate an island where he had heard there was much gold. In early May the caravels anchored off the north shore of this island—Jamaica—at the mouth of a river they called the Bueno.

> No sooner had we anchored than we were surrounded by about sixty canoes. Seeing this, we fired ten or twelve blanks from our lombards, and when they heard this they all fled to shore. We wanted to go ashore ourselves, but they threw stones at us, so that our boats had to return to the ships. We then equipped the boats with shields, crossbows, and lombards, and headed back to shore. They attacked us in the same way. But we immediately killed sixteen or eighteen of them with our crossbows and five or six with the lombards. This happened late in the day, and we soon retreated to the

caravels. When we went back next day, ready to confront them again, the men came to us with their arms crossed upon their chests, begging mercy and bringing us all they had, including bread in great quantities, fish, roots, and gourds full of water.
   – Cuneo

The three caravels turned north again to further explore the coast of Cuba, reaching nearly to its western capes.[1] But the daily trial of negotiating shallows and of threading their way among innumerable islands left Columbus sleepless, weak, and increasingly ill. Seeing the apparently endless extent of Cuba to the west, and factoring in the difficulties of shallow-water navigation and the growing scarcity of provisions, he ordered his fleet to turn back. The extent of Cuba had convinced him by now that this was indeed a piece of the Asiatic mainland. Driven by his deep-seated desire, his absolute need, to reach Asia, in early June 1494 he actually forced all crew members to swear an oath before a notary on a beach in Cuba's far west that this extensive land was indeed part of a mainland where civilized people would be found. He imposed a heavy fine (or scourging, or even mutilation!) upon anyone who subsequently maintained the contrary. One can imagine the furtive glances exchanged among crew members during this exercise as they raised their right hands to swear an oath of dubious validity. But Columbus's future as an important man in the Indies depended on the sovereigns' never having cause to suspect that they were financing a mere island excursion.

After riding out a tropical storm or hurricane that, many miles away, was wreaking destruction in Isabela, they once again headed south, around the west side of Jamaica and then skirted its southern coast to the east. They continued eastward along the southern coast of Hispaniola, and in late September curled up around the island's eastern capes and along the coast to anchor finally off Isabela. Columbus—suffering now from high fever, damaged vision, and seemingly impaired mental faculties—found a desperate situation there, with storm-related destruction, illness, and discontent throughout the settlement, with colonists committing daily atrocities among the Indians, and the Indians retaliating in kind. It seemed a vision of hell. While he convalesced, pondering what to do next, Antonio de Torres arrived with four caravels from Castile, laden with

---

[1] They took on wood and water at San Juan Evangelista island, today's Isla de la Juventud (Isle of Youth), in Cuba's far west.

the long-awaited provisions and new colonists. Much to the Admiral's joy, Torres also brought with him Columbus's brother Bartholomew, sent by the sovereigns to assist in island governance. The news that yet another foreigner would be set over Spanish colonists—and another Columbus, to boot—was poorly received.

Fortified now by the wine and foodstuffs to which they were accustomed, many colonists were soon well enough to take the Indian problem in hand. A large slave roundup was undertaken, presumably with the acquiescence of the Admiral, and leading no doubt to scenes of great barbarity, one of which was recorded the following February by Cuneo, departing for Spain at that time in Torres's returning ships.

> When our caravels—on which I wished to return home— were ready to leave for Spain, we assembled in our settlement 1,600 Indians, both male and female. We then chose 550 of the best to take aboard ship. This was on February 17, 1495. It was announced that, of the remaining Indians, anyone could choose the ones they wished to have, and it was done. When all demands had been satisfied, about four hundred were left, and they were given leave to go wherever they wished. Among these were many women with infants at the breast. These women, in order better to escape us, and terrified that we would recapture them, dropped their babies on the ground and fled like souls desperate for escape. They fled as much as seven or eight days' journey from our settlement at Isabela, beyond the mountains and great rivers, so far that they'll never be found again.
>
> Among the people we had captured was one of their kings, with two of his captains. It was decided that these men would be executed with arrows on the following day, and they were therefore left tied up for the night. But during the night they chewed through one another's ropes and got away. **– Cuneo**

Of the 550 Indians taken aboard, two hundred died on reaching Spanish waters and their bodies were cast overboard. Of the remainder, half were seriously ill on arrival. The queen was highly displeased.

Following the departure of this fleet for Spain—a fleet that carried back dozens of disillusioned men who would bear with them vivid tales of the foreign despot in the Indies and of the royal money being wasted by taking him seriously—Columbus set his sights on a second punitive expedition to the interior. On March 24, 1495, with two hundred men, twenty warhorses and as many dogs, and assisted by the forces of Guacanagarí, the Admiral and his brother Bartholomew engaged and defeated a much larger Indian force under several of Guacanagarí's rival caciques. The island was now more nearly "pacified," and the colonists, now beginning to receive tribute from the Indians, dug in for the long haul.

Despite the blunting of the Indian threat, affairs in the faction-rife colony remained dismal, and, because of this, Columbus may have expected eventual repercussions from the Crown. As it turned out, the monarchs were being made increasingly uncomfortable both by the wave of Indian arrivals and by the rising chorus of complaints about the Columbus brothers among Indies returnees. They determined to send an investigator, a man known to Columbus, a passenger on the second voyage, but apparently having returned to Castile with Torres the previous year. The investigator's name was Juan Aguado, and he arrived in October 1495 in one of four caravels, again commanded by Torres.

It is a tribute to the esteem in which Columbus was held by the sovereigns that when Aguado's apparently unfavorable report eventually reached them, it was pigeonholed. Nonetheless, since the monarchs were unwilling to see any of their subjects grow overmuch in importance, they may at this time have begun to see the need for a little shortening of the Admiral's sails.

By March 1496 Columbus had decided he must return to Spain himself and defend his reputation to the sovereigns. In that month he therefore departed for Castile with 225 men (along with thirty Indian prisoners) packed like fish aboard only two caravels: the intrepid *Niña*—which, now owned by Columbus, had survived a vicious hurricane shortly after Aguado's arrival—and *Santa Cruz*. The journey—a slow passage, since the Admiral this time stuck to a course too far south to receive full benefit of the westerlies he'd found on his first voyage—was marked by a skirmish with female warriors on Guadalupe. One woman in particular had thrown a Canary Islander to the ground and nearly choked him to death before being captured and put aboard ship along with the Indians from Hispaniola.

Columbus left behind his two brothers. Bartholomew, assisted by brother Diego, would serve as *adelantado*,[1] an office that he would hold for the next two and a half years. An ambitious man named Francisco

---

[1] Military governor.

Roldán would serve under Bartholomew as *alcalde mayor*.[1] The colony over which they presided contained several hundred men.[2]

The two caravels reached Cádiz in June. Once they had been offloaded, Columbus—garbed, curiously, as a Franciscan—hastened overland, his men leading mules laden with gold and botanical specimens, and with a cluster of captive Indians shuffling along behind. He headed first to Seville to rest with a priest friend, Andrés Bernáldez, and later in the summer to Burgos to make his report to the sovereigns, who were there awaiting the arrival of their soon-to-be daughter-in-law, Margarita of Austria.

---

[1] Chief justice. Although both Bartholomew's and Roldán's were royally appointed positions, Columbus made the appointments on his own authority, only later securing Crown approval.

[2] And possibly a few women.

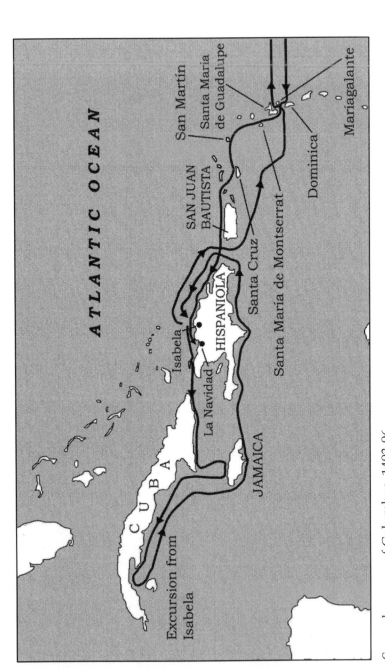

Second voyage of Columbus, 1493-96

4

THIRD VOYAGE, 1498-1500

First-person narratives of Columbus's third voyage are not abundant. A redaction of Columbus's log of this voyage by Las Casas contains little first-person material of value. We do have a letter of Columbus to the monarchs regarding this voyage,[1] as well as a letter to Juana de Torres,[2] a woman close to the queen, and one to whom the Admiral seems to have been comfortable opening his heart.

Columbus's third voyage would be notable not only for marking the first landing of Europeans upon the American continent—in this case South America—but even more for what occurred following the Admiral's subsequent arrival in Hispaniola.

In late summer 1496 Columbus headed north from Seville to Valladolid and then to Burgos, in the far north of Castile, to meet with the king and queen. Not only was he looking forward to making his report and displaying a more abundant sampling of New World treasure than he had previously presented, but he wished to see his young sons, who now lived and traveled with the court. Once he had embraced his children, however, and made his report to Their Highnesses, he began to push for a third voyage, a proposition to which the sovereigns appeared cool—not necessarily because they were against the idea, but because both their present war with France and their efforts to marry off their children to other European royal families were draining their already-strained resources. Likely the disappointing reports they had received on Columbus's administration of the new colony were also on their minds.

Over the ensuing months Columbus badgered them as often as he dared, insinuating himself into the court at every opportunity and doing his best to counter his enemies, who were portraying the Indies venture as a total fiasco and Columbus as a foreign tyrant. In April 1497 he attended the wedding, in Burgos, of the sovereigns' 18-year-old son Prince Juan to the Archduchess Margarita of Austria.[3]

---

[1] This letter, too, is available only as redacted by Las Casas.
[2] Sister of Antonio de Torres.
[3] This would turn out to be a brief marriage, since, within six months, the young prince would be dead (of tuberculosis, it is thought). Columbus's

Following the wedding, the queen appeared to find more time for her Admiral. She agreed to supply six ships and to pay for three hundred persons to embark on a new voyage.[1] She allowed that fifty more could go at their own expense. It was stipulated further that thirty women could go, but they too were expected to provide their own passage. Columbus, aware that more people were fleeing the Indies now than were emigrating there, asked that jailed criminals might also be given leave to go. In answer, the king in June 1497 issued two letters on the subject, directing that those criminals sentenced to exile or to the mines would be permitted to emigrate to the Indies and that even the death penalty would be lifted in exchange for two years of service there.[2] Columbus was told to deal with Fonseca from now on, as he had in the past. Yet when Fonseca, now bishop of Badajoz, was contacted by Columbus, he pleaded lack of funds and proved generally uncooperative. The queen's promise was one thing, he told Columbus, but the actual transfer of scarce royal funds quite another.

The funding finally came through, and by the following spring six vessels were being provisioned at quayside in Seville, virtually all supplies earmarked for relief of the colony on Hispaniola. By the end of May the six ships were riding at single anchor at the mouth of the Guadalquivir—Sanlúcar de Barrameda—where the Admiral joined, and on May 30, 1498, the little fleet departed. After traveling together to Madeira, then south to the Canary Islands, and further along the African coast to the Cape Verdes, Columbus ordered three of the heavily laden caravels to proceed, via Dominica and today's Puerto Rico, directly to Hispaniola—specifically, to the new settlement of

---

two sons, who had been serving as the prince's pages, would be taken into the service of the queen herself.

[1] Columbus—knowing that the monarchs had, the previous summer, sent 130 ships to escort their daughter Juana to Flanders for her marriage to Philip, Duke of Burgundy, and then to escort Philip's sister, the Archduchess Margarita, back to Castile—had confidently requested eight ships. He was disappointed at not being given even that relatively small number.

[2] Las Casas claimed to have known some of these transported criminals. He commented on one in particular who had had his ears cut off as punishment in Castile, affirming that his behavior in the Indies was "beyond reproach."

Santo Domingo.[1] Columbus, for his part, would take the two remaining caravels and his flagship — also laden with supplies for the colony — and set a course south and west, where he hoped to land this time not on an island but on a continent. By the first week of July the Cape Verdes were dropping astern as the three small vessels steered southwest to the latitudes of Guinea and Sierra Leone, then due west into unknown waters. This course was the closest to the equator that Columbus had yet sailed.

Despite all previous evidence he had seen to the contrary, he still expected to find the civilized lands of the East, including the domain of Marco Polo's Grand Khan. He did not yet know that, just ten days prior to his departure from Spain, the Portuguese Vasco da Gama had, by rounding the southern tip of Africa, reached the very lands of the East that Columbus sought.

In mid-July the little fleet spent a week drifting slowly in the oppressive heat of the doldrums, sails hanging limp, pitch bubbling from cracks in the deck, the ships' heads rolling through all points of the compass. The crews — never having faced such unrelenting heat and humidity before — were increasingly crank and restive, sick from the random rolling of the ships, unhappy to be so far from land. A number of wine and water casks dried and split, spilling their precious contents. After more than a week of this distress, the crews, to their immense relief, felt the breath of the southeast trades. After a further week or so of fine sailing, however, they found themselves dangerously low on water. The Admiral therefore decided to alter his course to take on fresh water among the islands he knew to lie further north, then return south.

But on July 31, the date that he reached this decision, land was sighted and the plan changed. The three rocks barely seen poking up from the sea prompted the Admiral to christen this new land Trinidad. Soon houses, people, and cultivated land were seen — "as green and lovely as the orchards of Valencia in March," wrote the Admiral. No landing was made, however, until the following day, when repairs

---

[1] In an action presided over by Bartholomew Columbus in late 1496, and approved by the sovereigns, Isabela had been abandoned in favor of a new location on the southeast coast, a settlement first called Isabela Nueva, but very soon thereafter Santo Domingo. Better harbor facilities at the new location, and better access to fresh water, appear to have been the reasons for the change.

were undertaken and fresh water replenished. The crews, tired and dirty, seized the opportunity to splash and cavort in the shallows, enjoying the feel of land under their feet for the first time in a month. A low firmament could be seen to the south — present-day Venezuela — but Columbus at this point had no inkling that this thin band was the edge of a vast continent.

On August 2 the three vessels passed easily through the normally fast-moving water of what Columbus called the Boca de la Sierpe (Serpent's Mouth) to anchor in the Gulf of Paria, off Trinidad's southwestern cape. Among the inhabitants of Trinidad, the word had apparently spread about the arrival of these strange craft.

> On the following day a large canoe carrying twenty-four young men came toward us from the east. All were equipped with bows, arrows, and wooden shields. They were well-built, and not dark — some being even lighter-complected than others I've seen in the Indies. They had nice features and well-formed bodies, with long, straight hair, cut in the Castilian style. Their heads were wrapped in a cotton cloth in the manner of an *almaizar*,[1] elaborately worked and colored. They wore a similar cloth around the body as a sort of breeches.

> When this canoe arrived, the men hailed us from a distance, but neither I nor anyone else aboard could understand them. I ordered our men to encourage them by signs to approach, and we carried on like this for more than two hours. They would approach a little, then turn aside. I had the men hold up large pots for them, and other shiny things to get them to come closer, and after a long time they came a little nearer than before. I wanted greatly to speak with them, but had no more items to attract them. I therefore ordered a tambourine to be brought up onto the poop and played, and had some of the men dance to it, thinking that this festivity would draw them in. But when they saw this they dropped their paddles, grabbed their bows, strung them, picked up their shields, and began shooting at us. I stopped the music and dancing and ordered crossbows to be fired. The Indians fled toward another caravel, hastily taking refuge under its stern. **– Columbus to the King and Queen**

---

[1] A Moorish head covering.

The Indians soon disappeared, and Columbus spent two more days observing the constantly west-setting current that passed through the Boca, very strong both at full flood and ebb. Fearing to attempt exiting the gulf against this current, he decided to continue northward in hopes of finding a more manageable point of egress to the sea. After weighing anchor on August 4, however, he and his men were struck dumb by an event thought by scholars today to have been the result of a volcanic eruption:

> And very late at night, standing on deck, I heard a horrendous roaring coming toward the ship from the south. I looked closely, and saw the sea rising from west to east, in a mountain as tall as the ship. It continued its advance toward us. On top of it I could make out a line of swirling water, the whole bearing down on us with a deafening clamor. My experience with such waves produced in me a mortal fear that the ship would break up when this wave reached us.
> **– Columbus to the King and Queen**

The huge swell passed harmlessly beneath the ships, and they continued north, landing next day on an outstretched arm of the South American continent for the first time. Since no Indians were in evidence, they saved the formal ceremony of taking possession in the monarchs' name for a landing on the following day, when they succeeded in attracting the usual audience of bemused natives.

Columbus at this time noted Indians wearing pieces of gold around their necks and strings of pearls around their arms, but was unable to discover where these treasures came from. His annoyance at not being able to acquire this information quickly was compounded not only by his chronic ill health but by his anxiety to be away, to deliver his cargo of perishables very soon to Hispaniola.

> I would like to have stopped, but the provisions that I carried — wheat and wine and meat — for the people of Hispaniola were already starting to go bad. They had caused me so much trouble, I wished to go no farther with them, only to deliver them, and to stop nowhere for any reason.
>
> I tried to obtain a few of those pearls, sending some boats ashore for them.
>
> These people are very numerous, all good-looking, of about the same color as others we've seen, and quite easy-going. The men of ours who went ashore found them very pleasant, and they were received quite hospitably. They told

me that after they had landed in their boats two principal men
of the town—I think father and son—came out to meet them
with all their people, and brought them to a very large house
with a gabled roof, not round like a field tent, as we've seen
elsewhere. In the house were many seats on which our men
were invited to sit, while they themselves sat on other seats.
They had bread and all sorts of fruit brought in, and an
assortment of wines, both white and red, but not made from
grapes—they were made in some other way from one fruit or
another. Some is likely made from maize, which is a seed that
grows into an ear of grain. I brought some back from my last
voyage and a lot of it is already growing in Castile. The best of
it they seem to consider excellent, and value it highly.

In this house all the men grouped themselves together on
one side and the women on the other. Both they and our men
were distressed that they could not understand one another—
they wanting to ask us about our country, and our men
wishing to know about theirs. After our men had dined in this
house, which belonged to the elder man, they were taken to
the home of the younger one, where they had to eat again.
They then got into the boats and returned to the ship. On their
arrival I immediately weighed anchor because I was in such a
hurry to deliver the provisions, which had cost me so much
effort, and which were spoiling. I also needed some relief from
my illness, caused by my inability to sleep. On my last voyage
to the mainland I was without sleep for thirty-three days and
went a long time without seeing well, but my eyes have never
been so damaged or bleeding, or caused me as much pain as
they do now.[1] **– Columbus to the King and Queen**

It would not be for Columbus to find the nearby pearl fisheries.
Others would discover them and receive credit for their discovery.

By mid-August the fleet was passing through the Gulf of Paria's
northern strait, the chaotic Bocas del Dragón (Dragon's Mouths), and

[1] Ferdinand Columbus, in his account of his father's fourth voyage, makes
frequent reference to the Admiral's growing incapacitation from gout. It
is believed today, however, that he suffered from—and ultimately died
from—reactive arthritis, a crippling form of the disease contracted
through bacterial infection from food. Bleeding from the eyes is known to
accompany it.

out to sea again, heading north to Hispaniola, which the Admiral believed he could hit dead-on. But he was especially preoccupied. He had been astonished to find fresh water in the Bocas, so far from its presumed source—the lowlands lying along the gulf's southern horizon—and began to believe that this lowland was indeed the edge of a continent being drained by rivers larger than any he had ever seen. In ill health, and disturbed that he had no time to explore this new discovery further, he began to think deeply about what it all signified.

This hard-headed and now very skilled navigator, who was embarked even now on an extraordinary feat of dead-reckoning, concluded on the basis of some anomalous compass readings that he was sailing on a bulge of the globe. He wrote of this belief to the sovereigns:

> I have always read that the world, both land and water, was spherical, and the authoritative accounts and research of Ptolemy and all the others—based on lunar eclipses and other phenomena which occur from east to west, and on the elevation of the pole star from north to south—serve to demonstrate this. But now I've noted an irregularity, as I've said. And for this reason I say that the earth is not round as has been written, but is more pear-shaped—round except near the stalk, where it bulges out more. You might also think of it as a round ball with one spot where there's something like a woman's nipple, and this part is higher and closer to the heavens. This elevated region lies below the equator, in this ocean, at the farthest point of the East—by which I mean where all land and islands end. **– Columbus to the King and Queen**

He further mused on the meaning of this continent he had discovered, and did so in his habitual biblical frame of reference. This continent, he decided, must be the terrestrial paradise, the Garden of Eden from which Adam and Eve had been banished, and to which the just would one day return. He continued:

> I don't find and have never found in Latin or Greek writings a clear statement about the location of the earthly Paradise. Nor have I ever seen it represented on any map of the world, except by those who argue more from authority than research. Some place it at the sources of the Nile in Ethiopia, but others have traveled these lands without finding anything in the mildness of the climate or elevation toward the sky that would confirm this. Nor have they found evidence

that the waters of the Flood, which covered such and such, reached there. Some Gentiles have argued that it was in the Fortunate Islands, namely, the Canaries, etc.[1] St. Isidore and Bede and Strabo, and the Master of Scholastic History, and St. Ambrose and Scotus and all the top theologians concur that the earthly paradise is in the East, etc.

I have already mentioned what I have found in this hemisphere, and its shape, and I believe that if I sail below the equator, and arrive at these higher elevations, I will find a cooler climate and greater diversity of stars and waters. I don't necessarily believe that there, where the elevation is greatest, the seas are navigable, nor even that there is water there, nor that one can even get up there. I do believe, however, that the earthly Paradise is there, and that no one may go there unless God wills it. And I feel that this land that Your Highnesses have sent me to discover is immense, and that there are many more such lands to the south, of which no one has yet reported a thing.

I don't think the earthly Paradise looks like a rugged mountain, as certain drawings show, but that it does sit upon a summit—the summit of what I've described as the protuberance of a pear—and that by approaching this protuberance gradually from afar, one can begin to climb toward it. **– Columbus to the King and Queen**

One pictures the king, at least, scratching his head at this startling insight into the Admiral's thought processes.

Despite these opaque musings, Columbus was in the process of performing his greatest navigational feat. The three ships would have hit Santo Domingo—the new capital—perfectly if not for strong west-setting currents of which the Admiral had no knowledge. As it was, they raised the Hispaniola coast about a hundred miles west of their intended landing point, and therefore had to work strenuously eastward against wind and current to arrive at their destination. Columbus sent Indian messengers overland to inform Bartholomew that they had arrived, but a caravel bearing the adelantado—who had heard of the presence of three Spanish vessels off the southern coast and, thinking it might be the Admiral, had come looking for

---

[1] The "et ceteras" in this paragraph are Columbus's own.

him — [1]appeared on August 21. All reached Santo Domingo ten days later, the Admiral exhausted and still suffering from an acute vision disorder.

If Columbus had left the island in disarray on his previous departure, he found it much worse this time. Supplies were short, illness was rampant (a quarter of the population was down with syphilis), and the mood was ugly. Following the 1496 shifting of the capital from Isabela to Santo Domingo, a revolt had been raised by alcalde mayor Francisco Roldán. Setting up a rival encampment in the southwestern part of the island, Roldán had sent a message to his sympathizers encouraging them to cast off rule by foreigners (namely, the Columbus brothers), demand more attention from Spain in the matter of provisions, and seek a freer hand in dealing with the Indians and hunting for gold. Like most demagogues, he promised an easy life with something for everyone. Bartholomew Columbus — having, to the chagrin of many, recently been confirmed adelantado by royal edict — had been attempting to deal with Roldán when the Admiral arrived.

The Admiral put off involvement in these issues for as long as he could. Yet in his message to the sovereigns, sent off in mid-October, he felt the need to defend himself against the personal accusations and general ridicule of the enterprise that he knew were reaching royal ears. His message, frank and direct, seemed also searching in tone.

> May it please Our Lord to forgive those who have maligned and calumniated such an excellent enterprise, and who block it and have kept it from moving forward, with no thought for the honor and glory that it brings to your royal estate throughout the world. They don't know how to argue against it, except by complaining about its cost, and pointing out the absence of vessels coming home loaded with gold. But they don't take into account how short the time has been, and the great difficulties faced here. Nor do they consider that, in the household of Your Highnesses in Castile, many earn more in a year than it would cost to finance this entire enterprise. In the same way they fail to consider that no princes of Spain have ever won land outside of Spain until now, when Your

---

[1] The three ships were actually the three supply caravels that had separated from the Admiral's three vessels off the African coast in June. They had gotten lost, and had reached Santo Domingo the day after Columbus's arrival.

Highnesses possess another world here, a place where our holy faith can grow, and from which such great profits may be had. If little gold or anything else of value has so far been shipped, one can see that it won't be long before great benefits are realized . . . .

I say all this not because I think that Your Highnesses will not pursue this enterprise as long as you live—I firmly believe what Your Highnesses once said to me personally—and not because I detect any change of mind on the part of Your Highnesses, but because I'm frightened by what I hear about these people of whom I speak, for constant dripping can wear stone. Your Highnesses responded to me with that magnanimity that is known throughout the world, telling me not to worry about this in the least, because your will was to continue with this endeavor and to sustain it, if it were to yield only rocks and stones. **– Columbus to the King and Queen**

Because of ongoing traffic between Hispaniola and Spain, the sovereigns were subjected to a rising tide of complaint against their Admiral and his family. It was by now known that there was deep unhappiness, even a mutinous faction, among the colonists. The queen's frequently stated wishes for Christianization of the Indians and her opposition to their enforced servitude were being widely disregarded. The Columbus brothers, for their part, could not decide how to deal with Roldán. Even appeasement—including the granting of large tracts of land with rights to all Indians inhabiting that land (the beginning of the highly exploitative *encomienda* system)— [1]seemed not to help.

Back in Spain, Columbus's two children at court were harassed by returning colonists and berated for their father's ignominy and failure. The king himself was set upon by disillusioned adventurers demanding back wages.

By the spring of 1499 the sovereigns had heard enough. They selected Francisco de Bobadilla, a no-nonsense member of a military order, to journey to Hispaniola and straighten things out in their name. He would supersede Columbus in fact, if not by title. The sovereigns' factotum Bishop Fonseca, for his part, now licensed an exploratory

---

[1] Under this system, the Indians "packaged" with these lands could—with minimal attention to their spiritual and corporal welfare—be worked virtually as slaves.

venture not involving Columbus—one by Alonso de Ojeda (who soon paid a lucrative visit to the pearl fisheries that Columbus had not had time to visit the previous year,[1] and followed up by fomenting further revolt on Hispaniola). Accompanying Ojeda in his voyage to the South American continent was the Florentine Amerigo Vespucci, who made his own explorations. Because of an apparent deception on the part of Vespucci,[2] it was his name, not Columbus's, that would soon be attached by cartographers to the newly discovered lands. The Admiral's lot seemed daily to be changing for the worse.

Bobadilla, the queen's emissary, was not shy about taking control. His first sight, on arrival in the port of Santo Domingo in August 1500, was of seven bodies swinging on a gibbet, victims of the Columbus brothers' most recent attempt to bring law and order to the island. After presenting his orders to Diego Columbus—who was in charge while the Admiral was elsewhere on the island—Bobadilla, incensed, ordered an immediate cessation of executions. When Diego objected, he had Diego arrested. When the Admiral and his brother Bartholomew appeared, he had them arrested as well. He then moved into the Admiral's home.

In early October 1500, all three Columbus brothers, manacled, were put aboard ship to be taken to Spain as prisoners. When the embarrassed captain of the ship carrying the Admiral begged to be allowed to remove his manacles, Columbus refused, saying he would wear them until they were removed by the queen herself.

Manacles or no, Columbus found the opportunity during this crossing to write, drafting a letter to a female friend who had the queen's ear—Juana de Torres, sister of Antonio de Torres, and former governess of the now-deceased Prince Juan. He probably posted the letter on his arrival in Cádiz in late October. The letter offers a rare insight into his suffering mind, as well as to the disturbing situation he left behind on Hispaniola—a situation for which he seemed to admit some responsibility.

---

[1] Ojeda had taken advantage of an opportunity to study—apparently without the Admiral's knowledge or permission—Columbus's chart of the coastline around Paria.

[2] It is said that Vespucci back-dated the account of his voyage from 1499 to 1497, making it appear that he had arrived on the mainland before Columbus.

I have arrived at a point where even the vilest person thinks nothing of insulting me. To refrain from doing so is actually counted as virtue. If I had seized the Indies or the land made famous by the altar of St. Peter, and given them to the Moors, I could not have been treated as a greater enemy in Spain. Who would have believed this of such a noble land?

I would like very much to withdraw from this business if it could be done with honor to my queen, but I've been made to continue by the strength of Our Lord and of Her Highness. In order to relieve her of some of the confusion that death had brought upon her,[1] I embarked upon a new voyage—to a new heaven and earth, undiscovered until now. If this is not regarded over there as highly as my other voyages, it's nothing to wonder at. But it's due to my efforts that these parts have become known. . . .

When I returned from Paria, I found nearly half the people on Hispaniola in revolt. They have made war on me right to this day as if I were a Moor. I also faced serious trouble with the Indians. Into all this walked Ojeda, who tried to complete my downfall. He claimed that Their Highnesses had sent him with promises of grants, privileges, and money. He attracted a large following, since most of the settlers on Hispaniola are rootless good-for-nothings. None have wives or children. This Ojeda gave me a very hard time. He had to be sent away, but he promised to return with more ships and men . . . .

It would be a charity to me if Their Highnesses might censure that mob that knows of my exhaustion. The slander I have suffered from these people has done me very great damage. My long devotion to the preservation of Their Highnesses' estates and dominion has profited me nothing. If my honor were restored by them, their action would be told throughout the world, because the importance of this enterprise will be proclaimed and recognized more and more every day. . . .

---

[1] Likely referring to the death of young Prince Juan three years before, and the subsequent stillbirth of the newly married couple's daughter. Three months after Columbus's departure on his third voyage the queen's own 27-year-old daughter Isabella had also died, in childbirth.

Today, with so much gold being found, it's debated which is better—to make your living by plundering or by working the mines. You can buy a woman for a hundred *castellanos*, about the same as a farm, and the trade is quite common. Many merchants are looking for young girls. Nine- and ten-year-olds are popular at the moment, but women of any age fetch a good price. . . .

I've been very much aggrieved that an investigator has been sent over here, a man who knows that if he find something damaging against me, he'll be left in charge of the government. . . . [1]

In Spain they judge me as if I'd been sent to govern Sicily, or a city or town already in good order, and where the laws are strictly kept with no fear that everything might collapse. This grieves me. I ought to be judged as a captain who left Spain for the Indies, to conquer a people numerous and warlike, a people with customs and beliefs very different from our own, a people who live in forests and mountains without fixed settlements, far from us. By God's will I have established in such places the rule of the king and queen, our sovereigns— another world, through which Spain, which once was called poor, has become very rich. I ought to be judged as a captain who for a long time, right up to today, has borne arms without laying them aside for a single hour. I should be judged by knights of conquest—men of action, not letters,[2] unless they be Greeks or Romans or their present-day equals, of whom there are so many noble examples in Spain . . . .

The gateway is already open to gold and pearls, in great quantity, and we can safely look forward to precious stones, spices, and a thousand other things. I pray that I might be preserved from fresh calamities so that I might make, in the name of Our Lord, the first voyage to open up trade with Arabia Felix as far as Mecca . . . .

I'm conscious that my errors have not been committed with the purpose of causing harm, and I believe that Their Highnesses will take my word for this. They treat with mercy even those who are malicious toward them. I feel strongly that

---

[1] A reference to Bobadilla.

[2] Columbus here refers to lawyers.

they'll show me special kindness, for I fell into error through ignorance and force of circumstance, as they will later learn completely. I am their humble servant and when they look at my service they will realize that it brings them more advantage every day. They'll place everything in the balance, just as Sacred Scripture tells us with respect to good and evil on Judgment Day. If they insist that I be tried before another judge, which I do not expect, and that my role in the Indies be investigated, I beg them most humbly to send two conscientious, honest men there at my expense. I believe they'll quickly discover that five marks' worth of gold is now collected in four hours. But however they choose to do so, it is most important that Their Highnesses look into this matter.

– Columbus to Juana de Torres

Following his arrival in Cádiz in late October, Columbus, near penniless, and still refusing to have his chains removed, hastened to the monastery of Santa María de las Cuevas in Seville. In December an order arrived from the sovereigns that his manacles be removed, and that he and his brothers proceed to Granada, where the king and queen would be awaiting them. Despite a warm reception at court, and a promise that all the Admiral's rights and possessions—peremptorily usurped or commandeered by Bobadilla—would be restored, nothing further occurred for months as Columbus languished at Las Cuevas. He filled the time by writing his strange Book of Prophecies, a work of apocalyptic scholarship seemingly in a different universe from the world of the practical mariner.

In September 1501, the appointment was announced of a new governor and viceroy of the Indies—Nicolás de Ovando, also a member of a military order. Bobadilla would be recalled. This was some consolation to Columbus, but what of the promised rights and titles, what of his money and possessions appropriated by Bobadilla? And would he ever be sent on another voyage of discovery? In fact his rights were restored officially at this time, and restitution of his goods formally ordered, but his actually securing them would prove to be another matter.

With the appointment of Ovando, Columbus despaired of ever returning to the lands he had discovered for the Crown. In February 1502 the new governor set sail from Castile in a fleet commanded again by Torres—thirty ships and 1,500 to 2,500 men, with, of course, horses and dogs. Among Torres's other passengers was a teenage Bartolomé de las Casas, a young man destined to become the conscience of the Spanish conquest.[1]

Columbus, the man who had started it all, himself seemed destined for the dustbin.

---

[1] Las Casas accompanied his father, who was returning to the Indies.

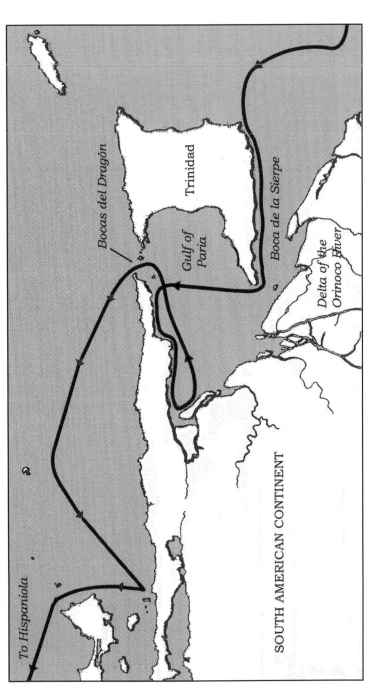

Third voyage of Columbus, exploratory portion, 1498-1500. Map adapted from S.E. Morison, *Journals and Other Documents on the Life and Voyages of Christopher Columbus*.

Bocas del Dragón

Trinidad

Gulf of Paria

Boca de la Sierpe

Delta of the Orinoco River

SOUTH AMERICAN CONTINENT

To Hispaniola

5

FOURTH VOYAGE, 1502-04

But he tried once again, approaching the sovereigns in late February 1502—just after Ovando's departure—about a fourth voyage. Its purpose, he said, would be to explore further the islands and mainland in hopes of discovering a passage to the Indian Ocean through some narrow point of the continent—possibly, he may have thought, upstaging the Portuguese in the process. To the Admiral's astonishment and delight, the sovereigns answered affirmatively, and did so within two weeks of his request. To his further surprise, they encouraged him in the strongest way to get on with this voyage as quickly as he could. Perhaps, being strapped for cash as they fought a deepening war with the French in Italy, they had decided that this New World might indeed provide them with the financial wherewithal to carry on, perhaps enough wealth even to increase Spanish power in Europe. Columbus, they may have thought, should be taken more seriously. Who knows what he might find this time around? The Admiral was granted virtually everything he had asked for, including weapons and gunpowder. He was reassured of the sovereigns' genuine anguish over his earlier arrest and detention, and of their unabated esteem for him and his family.

The king and queen, then in residence at Valencia, empowered their Admiral to take possession in their name of any islands and mainland he might discover, and went on to give him detailed instructions on how to handle gold, silver, pearls, precious stones, and spices — on how to preserve, as we might say today, a chain of custody. They provided detailed instructions on recordkeeping, with orders that all such items be delivered to the expedition's treasurer. Bartering for gold by colonists was to be strictly regulated. On the chance that the Admiral might encounter the "Portuguese captain" known to have recently embarked on his second voyage to India—namely, Vasco da Gama (whose most likely location would be the Indian Ocean)—he was given a letter of introduction to him.[1] Finally he was told,

---

[1] The Portuguese and Spanish monarchs were by now on excellent terms, the Spanish sovereigns having married their third daughter María off to the Portuguese king, Manuel I.

curiously, not to put in at Hispaniola, but to head directly for the "islands and mainland" in the region of the Indies—the sovereigns likely wishing to reduce any chance of friction with their new governor, Ovando. The notion, moreover, was growing in the royal mind of a division between explorers and administrators, and they had probably decided that the Columbus brothers should be kept exploring.

Among Columbus's requests to the king and queen had been permission to take one of their young pages with him—namely, his own 13-year-old son Ferdinand. They willingly acceded to this request, unwittingly opening a window for us onto the details of this *alto viaje*, as Columbus would refer to it—his top voyage. Young Ferdinand would keep meticulous notes along the way, and, in later years using them to fortify his memory, would produce a highly readable account of the voyage.

Bartholomew Columbus, chastened by his experience thus far in the Indies, reluctantly agreed to accompany his brother on this fourth voyage.

By late April, again with the assistance of Bishop Fonseca, Columbus had signed 140 men and assembled a fleet of four caravels: *Capitana* (his flagship), *Santiago de Palos* (nicknamed *Bermuda*), *Gallega*, and *Vizcaina*. On May 9, 1502, the little fleet departed, detouring briefly to the coast of Africa, where they had been asked by the sovereigns to assist the Portuguese in a military operation against the Moors. (It turned out that their assistance was not needed.) Then after making their customary call at the Canary Islands to take on water and wood, near the end of May they set out across the Atlantic. On June 15—having made a very fast passage—they arrived in the Indies.

Despite being forbidden to land on Hispaniola, Columbus made for Santo Domingo anyway, feeling that he had a strong reason. *Bermuda* had threatened to founder during the Atlantic crossing, and he wished to exchange her for a more seaworthy craft. Furthermore, he was sure that a serious storm was in the offing, and he did not wish to be caught at sea, especially with a vessel that could barely be kept afloat under the best of conditions. Fearing to go ashore himself, he sent one of his captains to Ovando. The captain was told by the new governor, in blunt language, that Columbus was forbidden to enter the harbor or to exchange the caravel. The governor scoffed, moreover, at the Admiral's reported concern about a large storm brewing. He was planning, he said, to send Torres out very soon with twenty-eight ships to Spain, and this fleet, nearly ready to depart, would sail on schedule. It would carry a sizable shipment of gold and a large number of men,[1] he added, among these former governor Bobadilla and Francisco Roldán.

As the eastern skies darkened, Columbus and his men, their vessels anchored just off the coast, watched the fleet leave the harbor and stand east. It was the last anyone would see of most of these vessels, since, shortly afterwards, a hurricane struck with great ferocity, sinking all but four ships and drowning hundreds of men—Bobadilla, Roldán, and Torres among them. Of this fleet, only one ship, heavily laden with gold, carried through to Spain. Columbus's own vessels were flung widely apart by the storm, but all came through it, battered but afloat, to reassemble and refit in the harbor of Azua, farther west along the island coast.

Resigned once again to playing the hand he had been dealt, Columbus left the safety of the harbor and continued westward, with fresh storms, powerful currents, and variable winds requiring the most strenuous effort to keep the vessels afloat and on course. Putting in now to a port called by the Indians Yaquino,[2] to ride out a storm, they once more stood out to sea in mid-July. Sailing south of Jamaica, then driven by a powerful current northward toward Cuba, then navigating southwest toward the mainland, by month's end they had entered today's Gulf of Honduras. Incessant rain, frequently high seas, and near-irresistible currents had made for a harrowing six weeks, but it was not yet over. At the gulf's south end the coast turned sharply eastward, and the fleet was forced to beat against a strong east wind for nearly six more weeks before arriving in mid-September at a cape where the coastline finally veered south—Cape Gracias a Dios, as Columbus named it.[3] His ships had by this time been badly mauled.

In his account to the sovereigns penned the following summer, he described this frightening period:

> For eighty-eight days I could not escape this terrifying storm. The sea was so high that I could see neither sun nor

---

[1] Gold was now being mined, with Indian labor, in the interior of Hispaniola.

[2] On the south coast of Jaragua, the westernmost province of Hispaniola.

[3] Columbus's decision to turn east instead of west ensured that he would not discover the kingdom of either the Mayas or the Aztecs. And in neither direction was there hope of discovering a passage to the Indian Ocean.

stars. The ships were leaking, with sails split, and anchors, rigging, cables, boats, and many provisions all lost. The people were very sick, all repenting their sins, and many turning to God, none without vows and promises of pilgrimages. Some even confessed their sins to one another. I've passed through many storms, but none has lasted as long or been as frightening as this one. On more than one occasion many men previously considered strong went to pieces. The distress of my son, whom I had taken with me, tore me apart. All the more for seeing him, only thirteen years old, bearing up for so long under such exhaustion. But Our Lord has blessed him with such strength that he was able to give heart to the others, and he worked as hard as if he'd been at sea for eighty years. He was my great comfort. I myself fell ill, many times to the point of death, and had to conn the ship from a little shelter I had ordered made on deck. My brother was in the worst vessel of all, the most dangerous. Knowing that I'd brought him with me against his will distressed me beyond measure.

– Columbus to the King and Queen

Apart from the vigilance normally required when sailing near a lee shore, the voyage southward from Cape Gracias a Dios was relatively easy, the four vessels being carried steadily southward by the strong easterly wind. But it was a perilous coast: on September 16, a boat that Columbus had sent ashore for water was lost with all hands. Along the length of this beautiful, heavily wooded shore, the sailors regularly interacted with Indians, some interactions friendly, others less so. Efforts were made to trade, and to show good will, yet the four crews, easily inflamed at the sight of gold and of native women, had to be kept on a tight rein.

Ferdinand reported a diversion—perhaps jarring to modern sensibilities—occurring in the first week of October, off today's Costa Rica:

> Among the animals of those parts are found some grayish monkeys,[1] quite fierce, about the size of a small greyhound, but with a very long tail. Once they grab onto something with that tail they hang onto it as if tied by a rope. These animals live in the trees, leaping from tree to tree like squirrels, and

---

[1] Ferdinand actually refers to these animals as cats, but they appear to have been spider monkeys.

when they do so, not only do they cling to the tree with their hands, but also with their tail, sometimes even hanging by it upside down, either in play or at rest. One day a crossbowman of ours shot one of these animals in the forest, knocking him out of the tree. Once the creature found himself on the ground he became so fiercely aggressive that our man was afraid to go near him. He nonetheless succeeded in hacking off one of the monkey's arms with a long knife and brought him thus wounded to the ship. We had a good dog aboard who became very frightened when he saw him, but even more frightened was one of the two wild boars that the Indians had recently given us.[1] As soon as the boar saw this creature, he tried madly to escape. This surprised us all, because previously the boar had attacked everyone in sight, including the dog. The Admiral then ordered monkey and boar thrown together. The monkey immediately wrapped his tail around the boar's snout, and with his good arm seized the boar's neck to bite him, the boar squealing in terror. **– Ferdinand Columbus**

Columbus's plan was to continue hugging the coast (which soon turned eastward again at today's Panama) until he reached the region he had briefly visited on his previous voyage—today's Venezuela and Trinidad. Strong east winds, however, and dangerously high seas— some of the worst weather the Admiral had ever seen—made this impossible. With Columbus and many of his men exhausted and ill, the ships were repeatedly driven back along today's Panamanian coast, finding shelter finally in a small harbor they called El Retrete.[2] The harbor entrance was narrow, making it necessary to moor the vessels virtually up against the shore, reducing even further the weakened Admiral's ability to keep his men on board and away from the Indians.

We spent nine days in this harbor, in very unpleasant weather. In the early days of our stay, the Indians came very peacefully to trade with us. But once they saw our sailors starting to sneak off the ships, they went back to their houses. Our mariners, a dissolute and greedy crowd, had begun to commit many outrages against them, causing the Indians quickly to lose their peaceful attitude toward us. Before long

---

[1] Native peccaries.

[2] Likely today's Puerto Escribano, Panama.

skirmishes broke out between our men and theirs. The Indians' numbers, moreover, increased to the point where we feared they might storm the vessels, moored as they were so close to shore, and do us serious harm.

The Admiral tried to placate them with patience and civility, but at length seeing their pride and arrogance, he decided to put some fear into them by firing some artillery, the roar of which caused them to shout, beat the tree branches with sticks, and hurl frightful curses at us—all calculated to demonstrate that they had no fear of this sound, believing as they did that this thunder was meant only to frighten. In order to rein in their pride, therefore, and to teach them some respect for the Christians, the Admiral ordered the gunner to fire a ball at four Indians standing on a hillock. Quickly learning that this thunder was accompanied by lightning, they fled to the forest and never came out again. **– Ferdinand Columbus**

After taking what appeared to be a favorable opportunity to push out again to sea, the fleet was enveloped once more in what seemed an endless and evil storm. Columbus later described this ordeal in vivid detail to the sovereigns:

For nine days I ran, lost, with no hope of survival. Eyes have never seen the sea so high, so ugly, so seething with foam. The wind would not allow me to move forward, not did it permit me to seek shelter behind some headland. It held me in a sea turned to blood, boiling like a cauldron on a roaring fire. The sky had never been more frightening. For a day and a night it blazed like a furnace, hurling forth fiery flames. Every time I looked I feared that masts and sails had been carried off. These bolts came with such terrifying fury that we all feared the ships would be sunk. And through it all the rains came pelting down. It wasn't just rain, but felt more like the coming of the second Flood. The people were already so broken in spirit that they begged for death, just to escape this martyrdom. The ships had twice now lost boats, anchors, and ropes, and were presently running under bare poles.

– Columbus to the King and Queen

By early December the Admiral had given up on beating eastward. He decided to let the winds carry him further west to investigate rumors that the source of gold in these parts was Veragua—the name he had given to the coasts of today's Nicaragua, Costa Rica, and western Panama. Pummeled by towering waves, however, and driven by variable winds first eastward, then westward, drenched by incessant rain, the men were given sign after sign that their doom was at hand. One of the most frightening was an enormous waterspout.

In addition to these various terrors, another danger appeared—one no less grave, but quite spectacular. It was a waterspout that, on Tuesday December 13, passed right among the ships. If we had not dissolved it by reciting the Gospel of St. John, there is no doubt that it would have swamped whatever it struck. The water was lifted in a column right up to the clouds, a column thicker than a barrel, twisting like a whirlwind. That night we lost sight of *Vizcaina*, but fortunately sighted her again after three extremely dirty days. She had, however, lost her boat as well as her anchor, which she— having anchored too near a lee shore—had had to cut away to avoid being wrecked. It was noted on this occasion that the currents along that coast follow the prevailing wind, the current running east with a wind from the west, and west with a wind from the east. **– Ferdinand Columbus**

Then came the sharks.

After facing such contrary winds and seas, with the fleet practically dismembered and the crews on the point of exhaustion, we finally experienced a day or two of quiet seas. During this period, however, the ships were surrounded by sharks, which struck fear into all, but especially into the doomsayers. For just as they say that vultures can find a dead body by its smell from very far away, some thought the sharks shared this power.

These animals can seize a person by arm or leg with their teeth, and cut it off as clean as with a razor, having, as they do, two rows of saw-like teeth. We slaughtered many of these sharks, catching them with a hook and chain, until we finally could kill no more. They are so voracious that they not only bite at carrion, but will even attack a red cloth stuck to a hook. I saw a turtle taken from the belly of one shark that not only was alive, but that we kept later aboard ship. In a shark's belly we also found the head of another shark, a head that we had cut off and thrown overboard as inedible. . . .

Although some took these sharks as a bad omen, and others as just a bad fish, everybody did them the honor of eating them, so short were we of food for having spent eight months at sea, and having consumed all the meat and fish we had carried from Spain. Moreover, with the heat and the dampness the biscuit was so full of maggots that, with God as my witness, I saw many men who refused to eat their porridge until nightfall so as not to see them. Others were not bothered by them. Although they could see the creatures, they didn't remove them, for fear that if they stopped to throw them away they might lose their supper. **– Ferdinand Columbus**

Managing to stay afloat for yet another month, the fleet, still including the fragile and worm-eaten *Bermuda*, made its way back to what would later be defined as the eastern edge of Veragua. All four ships then succeeded in dragging themselves across a sandbar into a river that Columbus christened the Río Belén (Bethlehem River).[1]

On the day of the Epiphany,[2] completely broken in spirit, I arrived at Veragua. Our Lord provided me with a river there, a safe harbor, although one whose entrance was less than eight feet deep.[3] I got in with some difficulty, and on the following day the storm returned. If it had caught me outside, I could not have gotten in because of the sandbar. It rained without ceasing till February 14, and there was no way to go ashore or to improve our situation in any way. On January 24, when I was safely moored inside the bar, the river suddenly rose very sharply, breaking mooring lines and threatening to sweep the ships out to sea. I had never seen them in greater danger, but Our Lord saved us as he always has. I don't know if anyone has suffered greater distress. **– Columbus to the King and Queen**

Initial contact with local Indians was made warily, with courtesy seeming to prevail on all sides. The cacique himself, known in these parts as the Quibián, arrived to see this startling sight of winged vessels and bearded strangers. An early reconnaissance of the area by Bartholomew Columbus, still referred to as the adelantado, showed that gold could be picked up here even from the surface of the ground, and from around the roots of trees. It appeared to be abundant—

---

[1] In today's Panama.

[2] January 6.

[3] Ferdinand Columbus notes that it was closer to ten feet deep over the bar.

finally, it seemed, they had found the riches they were seeking. This confirmed the Admiral in a decision he had made almost upon arrival: once the ships had been repaired and good relations established with local Indians, perhaps by March, his brother the adelantado would be left here with a complement of men to build a settlement and to begin gathering gold. Columbus himself would return to Spain to carry news of the discovery back and return with provisions. This would be the new Navidad. Thoughts of finding a path to the Indian Ocean were fading, as the Admiral perhaps began to wonder if he had one-upped the Portuguese after all.

As Columbus would later write to the monarchs regarding the goldfields of Veragua:[1]

> Gold is most excellent. With gold one can build treasure. He who has it can do anything he wants in the world, even to leading souls to Paradise. . . . I regard the possession of these extensive gold mines and their associated trade more highly than anything else we have accomplished in the Indies.
> **– Columbus to the King and Queen**

He longed with all his heart to see this colony—which at the moment was the culmination of his dreams—developed properly.

> This is not a child to be turned over to a stepmother for raising. I can't think of Hispaniola, or Paria, or those other lands without weeping. I believed that our approach there would serve as an example to others, but it has not. These lands are already in a state of exhaustion. Although they are not dead, the sickness is incurable and widespread. Let those who brought them to this state produce the remedy if they can.
> **– Columbus to the King and Queen**

Bartholomew now made a short journey along the coast and into the back country, seeking a good spot to build a settlement. He apparently found none better than along the Belén River, near the moored ships.

> Having walked a great distance from the ships without finding any harbor or river along that coast as broad as the Belén on which to build a settlement, on February 24 Bartholomew returned along the same route by which he had come, with many ducats' worth of gold that he had gained in barter. On his arrival he immediately gave orders that the

---

[1] Gold is still mined in today's Panama.

eighty men who were to stay with him should break into groups of ten men apiece and begin the construction of houses on the banks of the Belén. The settlement was to be about a lombard-shot from the river-mouth, beyond a gully and a small hill on the right bank, as viewed from the mouth. The houses were to be built of timber, and thatched with the leaves of palms that grew along the beach. A large building was constructed to serve as an arsenal and storehouse for powder, ordnance, some provisions, and other things necessary for the colonists' sustenance. The more important provisions, such as wine, biscuit, oil, vinegar, cheese, and several types of vegetables, they placed for greater security aboard *Gallega*, which was being left for the adelantado's use on land or sea. The men would also be left nets, hooks, and whatever else might be necessary for fishing, since fish were known to be abundant in all the rivers of that region. **– Ferdinand Columbus**

The eager men had doubtless vied with one another over who would be allowed to stay in this paradise, from which they would surely return home rich after a few months of prospecting. Gone were any thoughts of the sovereigns' chain-of-custody requirements, if indeed the would-be colonists had ever heard of them.

There seemed little doubt that the colonists would be able to coexist with the Indians, who had been amicably permitting the strangers to observe their ways.

The customs of these Indians aren't very different from those of the Indians who live on Hispaniola and its neighboring islands. But these people of Veragua and environs turn their backs on one another when they talk, and when they eat they chew some kind of herb, which we think is the reason their teeth are so worn out and rotten. Their main food is fish, which they catch with nets and bone hooks. They make these hooks from turtle shells, sawing them out with a fibrous thread, as they do on the other islands.

They employ another method of fishing for catching the very tiny fish they call *titi* on Hispaniola. In the rainy season these fish gather along the shore, chased there by the larger fish. In their rush to escape these fish, the titi rise to the surface, where the Indians scoop them up in very fine nets and on small reed mats. They can catch as many as they wish. They roll them up in leaves in the same way that apothecaries roll up their confections, and once these bundles are dried out in an oven, they keep for a long time. In a similar way they also catch anchovies in a net, since the anchovies are also in flight from larger fish. The anchovies sometimes flee in such haste and fright that they jump as much as two or three paces onto the beach, and one has only to scoop them up.

They catch anchovies in another way as well. Down the centerline of a canoe from bow to stern they build up a screen of palm leaves, a few feet high. They then paddle very noisily along the river, banging their paddles on the side of the canoe. The anchovies, to save themselves from the pursuing fish, jump over the canoe, but strike the partition and fall into it. . . . At other times — and this is marvelous to see — they catch large quantities of fish that are swarming up the river. These they also preserve by drying, and they keep well. **– Ferdinand Columbus**

The presence of maize was noted.

They also consume a great deal of maize, which is a kind of grain that grows like millet, with spike and ear. From this they make red and white wine, as beer is made in England, and they mix it in various ways according to taste. It has a pleasant flavor, like a sharp wine. **– Ferdinand Columbus**

A brusque change in the weather made it difficult for the Admiral to adhere to his plan of departing in March with *Capitana*, *Bermuda*, and *Vizcaina*, which were by now all leaking anyway.

Everything was ready. Ten or twelve houses had been built and thatched, and the Admiral was ready to depart for Castile. But the river, which had once placed us in great danger by its rapid rise, now put us in a worse condition by falling. With the January rains having ceased, and good weather returned, the mouth of the river was choked up with sand. When we had entered the river we had had ten feet of water, which even then was less than we would have liked, but when we wanted to sail out of the river, we found just over a foot, meaning that we were hopelessly locked in. It was impossible to haul the ships over the sandbar, and even if we had had the equipment to do so, the sea was not quiet enough. The slightest wave breaking over the bar would have caused the ships to be pounded to pieces in such shallows — especially our worm-eaten ships, which were more like honeycombs with snake-sized perforations.

We therefore commended ourselves to God, begging that he would send rain, just as before we had begged him for fair weather. We knew that if it rained, the river would rise and the mouth would open up, as normally happens in those rivers.

– Ferdinand Columbus

A sudden revelation about the Quibián's real intentions threw this plan entirely to the winds.

At this time we learned from our interpreter that the Quibián, the cacique of Veragua, had decided to come secretly to set fire to our houses and kill all the Christians because the Indians were very angry that we had settled on this river.

– Ferdinand Columbus

On discovering what was brewing among the Indians, young Diego Méndez, Columbus's enterprising and intelligent secretary, offered to take another man — Rodrigo d'Escobar — and find out exactly what was afoot. The Admiral said yes. At the Veragua River, about three miles southwest of the Belén, Méndez and his companion encountered some Indians whom they asked for help in getting upstream to talk to the Quibián. The Spaniards were told at this time, somewhat truculently, that although the Quibián had recently been wounded in an action with other Indians, he nonetheless intended to kill them all and burn their ships. They should not seek out the Quibián. Méndez and his companion, thoroughly vulnerable, nevertheless persisted.

I asked them to take me in one of their canoes upriver, making it clear that I would pay them. They refused, advising me on no account to go, because both I and my companion would certainly be killed on arrival.

I nonetheless prevailed upon them to do so — they took us upriver as far as their villages, which had obviously been placed on a war footing. They would not permit me to approach the hut of the cacique. But I pretended that I was a surgeon, and that I could cure him of the arrow-wound which he reportedly had in his leg. I gave them gifts, and eventually they conducted me to his royal residence, which was on a leveled-off hilltop with a large open space before it. Three hundred skulls were set around this space, the remains of men they had killed in battle.

Now when I had succeeded in crossing this plaza and arriving at the cacique's dwelling there was a great outcry from the women and children standing around the door, and they ran screaming into the cacique's palace. At that moment one of the cacique's sons rushed out, angrily shouting curses in their language. He laid his hands on me and gave me a hard shove backwards. **– Méndez**

Méndez would prove time and again to be very cool under pressure.

To calm him down I tried to explain that I was here to treat the wound in his father's leg, and I showed him some ointment that I carried for this purpose. He said there was no way I would be taken to his father. Seeing that I was not going to soothe him in this manner, I took out a comb, a pair of scissors, and a mirror, and told my companion Escobar to comb and cut my hair. When the cacique's son and the others standing around saw this, they were astonished. I then had Escobar comb and cut the Indian's hair, and afterwards presented the young man with the comb and mirror. With this, he finally relaxed. I asked if we might have something to eat, and they brought it. We then ate and drank together like old companions, in friendship and harmony. **– Méndez**

On his return to the ships Méndez reported his findings to the Admiral, who, overworked and in great pain from his chronic illness, decided to put off a decision till next day.

Next morning his Lordship called me to discuss what we should do about all this. I told him it seemed to me that we should seize that cacique and all his captains, because with them as our prisoners the people would be more tractable. His Lordship said he was of the same opinion. I suggested a ruse by which this might be accomplished, and his Lordship then ordered his brother the adelantado and me to move out with eighty men to execute this plan. **– Méndez**

By the end of March 1503 news had spread rapidly among the Indians that the strangers were assembling an armed force to advance on their village.

When the Quibián heard that the adelantado was approaching, he sent to warn him not to come near his house, which happened to be situated on a hill overlooking the Veragua River. In order to keep the Quibián from running away out of fear, the adelantado decided to go to the house with five men only, ordering the others to follow two by two, keeping some distance between each pair. When they heard the firing of the harquebus,[1] they were to surround the house and see that no one escaped.

When the adelantado arrived near the house, the Quibián sent a second messenger out, warning him not to come into the house, but saying that he—despite his suffering from an arrow-wound—would come out and speak to him outside. They're very jealous of their women, and do this to keep the Christians from seeing them. At any rate the Quibián came out and sat down in his doorway, indicating that the adelantado was to come forward alone. The adelantado, before doing so, commanded his men to move in when they saw him seize the Quibián by the arm.

Going up to the cacique, he asked him about his wound, and about some matters related to the country around. He spoke through an Indian whom we had taken prisoner in those parts more than three months earlier, and who had become a willing servant of the Spaniards. Having some affection for us, this Indian feared for our safety, knowing that the Quibián intended to kill us. Because he as yet knew little of our strength, he believed this would be an easy task, given the number of people the Quibián had at his disposal. The adelantado, however, paid no heed to his fears. Pretending now that he wished to see the Quibián's wound, he grabbed hold of his arm, and although both men were quite strong, the adelantado managed to hold on until four of his men ran up to take the cacique captive. **– Ferdinand Columbus**

The Spaniards quickly took control.

Now the harquebus was fired and all the Christians came rushing out of their ambush positions to surround the house, inside which they found fifty adults and children, most of whom were captured, and without a single wound being inflicted, since—having seen their king taken prisoner—no resistance was offered. Among the captives were wives and children of the Quibián, as well as some high-ranking Indians.

---

[1] A long and heavy smooth-bore matchlock weapon, muzzle-loading and shoulder-fired.

These latter offered a ransom, saying that they had great treasure secreted in the forest nearby, and that they would give it all in return for their freedom. The adelantado, paying little attention to this offer, decided that, before the news of this event spread and other Indians arrived, he would send the Quibián, his wife and children, and the principal Indians to be held aboard ship. He himself, with most of his men, would stay here to attempt to hunt down the cacique's subjects and relatives who had escaped. **– Ferdinand Columbus**

The captives, including the Quibián, were now taken downstream in one of the ships' boats—which had been brought upriver—for confinement in the ships.

After some discussion about who should be responsible for getting the prisoners to the mouth of the river, the assignment was given to Juan Sánchez of Cádiz, chief pilot of the fleet and a well-respected man, who had offered to take the cacique down the Veragua River, bound as he was hand and foot. Being warned not to let him escape, Sánchez responded that if the prisoner got away they could pluck the beard from his face. He took the Quibián in tow and left with him in a boat [with other Spaniards and their prisoners].

When they had proceeded to within a half-league of the river mouth, the Quibián began to complain that the ropes were too tight on his hands. Juan Sánchez, taking pity on him, untied his hands from the seat where they had been tied, taking the rope in his own hand. Shortly afterward, when the Quibián noted that Juan Sánchez was distracted, he leaped into the water, Sánchez releasing his hold on the rope so as not to be pulled in after him. As night had by now fallen, and with the commotion caused by all the other prisoners in the boat, the Christians could neither see nor hear where the Quibián had gone ashore. They lost track of him completely, like a stone fallen into the water and vanished. To keep the other prisoners from doing the same, they hurried downstream to the fleet, deeply chagrined by their carelessness. **– Ferdinand Columbus**

Pursuit of the Quibián was soon given up. The remaining prisoners—including many of the Quibián's family—were shoved aboard *Bermuda* and thrown into the fetid hold.

Columbus, in spite of his men's growing misgivings about being left behind in this hostile country, remained determined to carry out his original plan, returning to Castile as soon as the water might rise enough to allow his three caravels to exit the river. In early April the requisite rains returned.

Once all had been arranged for the maintenance of the settlement, and the statutes of governance established by the Admiral, it pleased God to send so much rain that the mouth of the river opened again. The Admiral therefore resolved to sail for Hispaniola at once, with three ships, in order to send relief as quickly as possible. We awaited fair weather so that the seas would not be breaking or beating upon the bar, and when that day arrived, we towed the caravels out of the river with the boats.

Despite our care, however, no ship got across the bar without scraping its bottom, and if it weren't for the fact that the sands were soft and shifting, even with such good weather the damage might have been great. We now hurried to load the vessels with the items we had removed to lighten them for crossing the bar, then made for the open coast. At about a league's distance from the river, however, where we had anchored to await a fair wind, God put it into the Admiral's mind to send the flagship's barge back ashore for water and a few other necessities. **– Ferdinand Columbus**

The task fell to Diego Tristán, master of the flagship *Capitana*. He selected a crew of oarsmen, and ordered water containers stowed in the barge. When all was ready, he stepped into the barge himself and the men began to pull for shore. From the cover of the forest, meanwhile, a large force of Indian warriors had been observing the division of Spanish forces, noting that some were on land, while others were now far out on the water, beyond hope of rendering assistance.

When the Indians and the Quibián saw that the caravels had left the river, they realized that the men remaining in the settlement would now have no assistance. Just as the flagship's barge was nearing shore, therefore, they attacked the settlement, having taken advantage of the forest cover to advance to within only ten paces of the houses. They charged forward with war whoops, throwing their lances at men and huts. Since the huts were covered only with palm leaves, the lances easily penetrated the walls, wounding some of those within. . . . Four or five of our men were struck before the resistance hardened.

The adelantado, a brave man, stood against them with a lance, encouraging those around him, offering a spirited resistance. With seven or eight men at his side he fought so well that he forced the Indians to retreat to the forest, which lay close by the huts. The Indians then sallied from the forest to skirmish, throwing their lances and retreating, just as in Spanish jousting. This continued until the Christians were able to come together and drive them back with swords, aided by a dog, who pursued them with a vengeance. In this action one Christian was killed and seven wounded. Among these was the adelantado, who had been struck in the chest by a lance.
– Ferdinand Columbus

Tristán, by now approaching the river mouth and witnessing the outbreak of the attack, ordered his rowers to hold offshore and wait.

Tristán . . . , although on the river near the site of the fighting, remained in the barge with his people throughout, and when asked why he didn't move in to help the Christians, he responded that he was afraid they'd rush the boat in panic if he came near the shore, and then everyone might be lost. And if the boat were lost, he added, the Admiral would run a great danger at sea. For that reason, he said, he would do only what he was ordered to do, namely to fetch water, at least until it might become plain that his assistance would have made a difference.

He decided now to fetch the water promptly and inform the Admiral of what had happened. To his men he announced that they would be going upriver some distance to a place beyond the influence of seawater. Some warned him against such a trip—it was dangerous, they said. The Indians were waiting in their canoes. He replied that they ought not to fear this danger, and anyway, it was for this reason that they'd been sent by the Admiral. They then continued upstream. In its upper reaches this river is very deep in the middle, and on both sides the trees grow right down to the water. Except for the places where fishermen's trails end or where the Indians conceal their canoes, the undergrowth along the river is so thick that it's virtually impossible to land. **– Ferdinand Columbus**

With unreasonable confidence — likely assuming that the attacking Indians had been driven back to their village — he ordered the oarsmen to continue up the steadily narrowing stream. He was too late in discovering his mistake.

When the Indians observed the barge about a league upstream from the settlement, they attacked from the thickest parts of the underbrush on both riverbanks. They came out with their canoes and with wild shouting and horn-blowing, swarming around the men on all sides. Due to the lightness of their craft — which one person can easily manage, especially the smaller fishing canoes — they had a great advantage. In this case there were three or four men in each canoe, one to paddle while the rest hurled lances and arrows against the Spaniards. (I call them lances and arrows for their size, but they're really just wooden shafts tipped with fish bone or fish tooth, since they have no iron.)

In the Spaniards' boat, along with Captain Tristán, were seven or eight oarsmen and two or three soldiers. Since they couldn't protect themselves from the shower of lances and arrows, the oarsmen had to stop rowing and pick up their shields. But so many were the Indians, darting out with their canoes and retiring at will, that most of the Christians were wounded, including the captain, who had been struck several times. Although he remained steady, giving heart to his men, it was of no use, because the boat was closely surrounded. The Spaniards could neither move nor bring their muskets into play. Tristán was finally struck in the eye with a lance, and immediately fell over dead. All the others were killed as well, except for a cooper from Seville named Juan de Noya, whose good fortune it had been to fall overboard in the thick of the fighting. Swimming under water to the riverbank without being seen, he plunged into the dense vegetation and succeeded in reaching the settlement to report what had happened. **– Ferdinand Columbus**

Despite the Spaniards' recent success against the Indians, the news of Tristán's fate proved highly unsettling.

When our men received this news they were horror-stuck. Seeing themselves so few, with so many of them already wounded, some of their comrades dead, and the Admiral at sea without a boat, now unable to send help to them, they decided to leave this place. They would have done so, too, in a mutinous and disorderly fashion had the water level allowed them to exit the river. But, with the onset of bad weather, the river mouth was again closed, meaning that not only could they not take out the caravel, but, with the waves crashing so heavily on the bar, not even a boat. There was therefore no way of getting news to the Admiral of what had happened. **– Ferdinand Columbus**

Columbus, his son Ferdinand, and the crews of *Capitana*, *Bermuda*, and *Vizcaina*, too far from shore to see clearly what was occurring, were forced to stand by impotently. What had happened to the men on shore? What had happened to the flagship's valuable barge and crew? What could be done to find out?

The Admiral himself was in equally dire straits at sea, anchored far out, without his barge, and now with reduced numbers of people, some having been lost in battle. He and the rest of us were in the same fix as the men on shore, and just as mystified. The men on shore, having experienced the attack and having seen the corpses of Tristán and his men, covered with wounds, floating downstream to a chorus of circling crows, took it all as an unlucky omen, fearing that the same would happen to them. This fear was magnified by the refusal of the Indians — haughty in victory — to give them a moment's rest, taking advantage of the vulnerable position of the settlement. They would all surely have come to a bad end had it not been decided to move to the other side of the river. Here they built a fort of barrels and assorted other materials in a large, cleared area, setting up artillery at strategic points, so as to be able to defend themselves. The Indians, knowing the damage a cannonball could do, no longer dared to come out of the forest. **– Ferdinand Columbus**

The standoff on shore lasted for several days. The Admiral and his crews, straining their eyes through daily mists and rain, still could not make out what was happening. Should another boat be sent in?

While these events were taking place ashore, the Admiral spent ten deeply anguished days, suspecting what had happened, but waiting anxiously for the weather to clear so that the other boat might be dispatched to learn why the first had not returned. But fortune was against us in everything — we couldn't learn what happened to them, nor they to us.

To make matters worse, the children and relations of the Quibián, who were being held aboard *Bermuda* for transport to Castile, succeeded in breaking out, and did so in the following way: During the night they were confined below deck. Since the hatch cover was considered too high for them to reach, and because some sailors on deck were actually sleeping on top of it, the men of the watch neglected to chain the cover closed from above. The prisoners nonetheless came up with a means of escape. Very quietly they piled up ballast stones till they nearly reached the hatch cover. Then several of them climbed on top of the pile, pressed their backs hard against the cover, and succeeded in tumbling the sleeping sailors to the deck. Climbing out quickly, some of the high-ranking Indians leaped into the water. The last Indians to exit the hold were not so lucky, since the noise attracted sailors from all parts of the ship, and they were seized. They were again put below, the cover was chained down, and a better watch was set. These Indians, however, in despair at not having escaped with their comrades, found short lengths of rope and, the next morning, were found to have hanged themselves. Since the ceiling of the hold was too low to do it properly, they were all found hanging with knees bent or legs stretched out upon the floor.

Of the prisoners that had been taken, therefore, all were either dead or escaped. While this event would have no repercussions upon those of us at sea, it might have seriously increased the danger to those on shore, for it was certain that the Quibián would have made peace with those ashore in order to recover his children. Yet seeing now that the Spaniards held no hostages, he would likely make a serious effort to wipe out the settlement.[1] **– Ferdinand Columbus**

To remove the uncertainty of the situation, a few sailors volunteered to swim ashore if *Bermuda's* barge—the only boat now remaining among the three caravels—could ferry them to the edge of the breakers.

The Admiral accepted their offer, and the men rowed the boat to within an harquebus-shot of shore, staying just outside the breakers, which were crashing on the beach. From here Pedro de Ledesma, a pilot from Seville, volunteered to swim

---

[1] It is unclear how the Quibián would have learned of the mass suicide.

in, and did so, at times buried by the great waves, but finally reaching shore. He learned the state of things in the settlement — all with one voice affirming that they refused to remain in this hopeless situation. They begged that the Admiral not leave without taking them aboard, because leaving them here was a death sentence. And by this time discipline was breaking down, some refusing to obey either the adelantado or their captains. Their whole focus was on leaving, on escaping in a canoe at the first break in the weather, because not everyone could be accommodated in the one boat they had. If the Admiral refused to take them aboard, they would take their chances on the sea in canoes. Anything, they said, but face certain death from these barbaric, butchering Indians.

Pedro de Ledesma swam back to the waiting boat, returned to the fleet, and related all he had heard to the Admiral. **– Ferdinand Columbus**

Ferdinand was at his father's side on *Capitana* as the truth became clear to all: no Spanish colony would be set up on the Belén River. The goldfields would have to be abandoned. Columbus now had to take these frightened and angry men back aboard. But how to accomplish it? The ships could not cross the shallow bar to re-enter the river. *Gallega* could not come out. The only boat remaining to her was small, totally unsuitable for these seas. And rescue by *Bermuda's* barge, large enough for the task, was out of the question until the weather improved. To make a bad situation worse, a strong east wind was blowing, and only their bow anchors prevented the caravels' being driven shoreward and shattered in the surf. How long would the anchors hold?

Columbus decided to wait.

When the Admiral learned of the defeat, desperation, and breakdown of discipline among the men left on shore, he resolved to take them aboard. Waiting for them, however, would not be without danger — the fleet was riding at single anchor not far off the coast, totally exposed, and destruction was inevitable if the weather turned bad. But eight days later it pleased Our Lord to bring fair weather, which meant that the men ashore could begin packing their gear into the boat, as well as into some large canoes that had been lashed together for greater stability, and start moving it out. Every man was so bent on not being the last to leave that, within two days, nothing remained behind—nothing, that is, but the hulk of *Gallega*, which was so worm-eaten as to be useless. **– Ferdinand Columbus**

It had been Diego Méndez, stuck ashore with the stranded defenders, who had pulled the men together for the escape attempt.[1]

This situation lasted for four days, during which time I ordered many sacks to be made from the sails of the ship that was left us in harbor. Into these sacks we put all our remaining biscuit. I then took two canoes and bound one to the other to make a pair, holding them together with poles lashed across the tops, and into these we loaded all the biscuit, as well as the casks of wine and oil and vinegar tied into bundles. When the sea grew calm, we towed this cargo to the ships with canoes. We made seven trips. The men who were with me were also taken out a few at a time, and I remained to the last with five men. When night fell, I left with the final boatload. **– Méndez**

Columbus, impressed at young Méndez's leadership, and overjoyed at his success, promoted his secretary to the now-vacant captaincy of the flagship.

The Admiral was delighted at this, and he embraced me heartily, kissing my cheeks for the great service that I had performed. He then asked me to assume the captaincy of *Capitana*, to take command of its people, and to oversee the voyage. To oblige him I accepted this charge, which seemed to me a great responsibility—as indeed it was. **– Méndez**

The three caravels, with all remaining men aboard—about 130 in all—departed the disastrous scene on April 16. Columbus, now understanding something of the prevailing easterly winds and the westward set of current in these waters, charted an easterly course along the coastline, explaining that, because of the prevailing winds and currents, if they were to strike Hispaniola a long eastward leg would be necessary before heading north. He was apparently opposed by his pilots, however, and even by the men, who believed he was attempting a run directly to Castile with these leaking and poorly provisioned vessels.[2] Barely afloat, the little fleet nonetheless pressed on to the east, the men pumping day and night. One week out of Belén,

---

[1] The adelantado Bartholomew had presumably been incapacitated by his wound.

[2] This does indeed seem to have been his intention.

however, *Vizcaina*—hopelessly shipworm-riddled and sinking—had to be abandoned, and on May 1 the Admiral, likely under increasing pressure from his men, ordered a change of course to the north. The two remaining caravels swung away, finally, from the isthmian coast.

Columbus had proven correct, however, in his insistence upon more easting: they missed the port of Santo Domingo by more than seven hundred miles, landing far to the west, in Cuba.

> We left Veragua . . . with three ships, thinking we could sail straight for Castile. But with the ships worm-eaten and leaking, we could not stay afloat. So after sailing thirty leagues we abandoned one of them, cramming ourselves aboard two others that were in worse shape than the one we had abandoned. We scarcely had enough hands to man the pumps and empty the pots and kettles of water that poured in through the worm-holes. In this way, with enormous labor and danger, we sailed for thirty-five days . . . . But at the end of this period we found ourselves off the southernmost tip of Cuba, in the province of Homo, where the town of Trinidad now stands. . . . As I've indicated, the ships were in terrible condition, unseaworthy, and we were almost out of supplies. – **Méndez**

Méndez failed to mention that not only were the two caravels on the point of foundering as they approached Cuba, but *Bermuda* ran afoul of *Capitana* in a storm, badly staving her own stern and cracking the flagship's stem. After getting clear of one another, and managing to avoid a series of rock-strewn shoals, they put in briefly at an Indian village on the south coast of Cuba before again standing out to sea to begin a difficult eastward leg. The exhausted hands continued to pump around the clock. By mid-June, however, eight weeks after leaving the Belén River, they were almost out of provisions and the water inside *Capitana* had risen nearly up to the deck. At length realizing that their ships would sink before they could reach Hispaniola, on June 25 they purposely ran both ships aground in the shallows off the north coast of Jamaica.[1] They would have to survive there until rescued. There was no other option.

> Having succeeded in getting in, with the ships barely afloat, we ran them into the shallows as far as we could, side by side and close together. To keep them from listing, we quickly propped them up with plenty of supports on both

---

[1] It is thought that this grounding took place in today's St. Ann's Bay.

sides. Because the making tide continued filling the hulls almost to the deck, cabins were constructed for the men's lodging on deck as well as on fore- and sterncastles. These would, we hoped, also provide protection from Indian attacks, the island not yet having been settled or subdued by Christians. **– Ferdinand Columbus**

Indians soon appeared, but to these destitute men, they were a welcome sight.

> We thus established and fortified the ships about a crossbow-shot away from land. The Indians, who proved to be a kind and gentle people, soon came in their canoes to trade their food and other items with us, appearing to have a strong interest in the things we possessed. That no dispute might arise between our men and the Indians, and that they might not cheat us nor we them, the Admiral appointed two men to take charge of the trading, and of whatever might be gained by the Christians. This was to be divided by lot on a daily basis among the people, because at that time no one aboard ship had anything to eat. Most of the provisions had been consumed already, much had gone bad, and the rest had been left behind in the men's flight from the Belén River, so great had been their haste to get away from that place. **– Ferdinand Columbus**

Columbus and his men had reached relative safety, but the men were no longer isolated aboard ship. They were on land now, with Indian-owned resources at hand—notably food, clothing, and women. He would try to hold them aboard the grounded caravels and deal civilly with the Indians, but he likely suspected that such confinement would be difficult to enforce over the long haul.

> It had pleased Our Lord to bring us to this island, abounding in food and quite well populated. The Indians seemed interested in trading with us, since they came from all over to bring what they had. To keep the men from wandering in bands around the island, the Admiral had decided to fortify himself aboard ship rather than on shore. Spaniards being by nature a disobedient lot, no punishment or command would have sufficed to control them, nor would it have kept them from running around the country and into the huts of the Indians, taking whatever they could find, upsetting their women and children—a scenario that would surely have resulted in quarrels and a general explosion, turning us into

enemies. If we took food from them by force, we'd have an even greater problem.

But none of this occurred because the men were required to secure permission to leave the ship, and even to sign out. The Indians were pleased by our restraint, and brought us everything we needed at ridiculously low prices. For one or two hutias, which are like rabbits, we'd give them a piece of wire. For rounds of cassava bread, made from a grated plant root, we'd give them two or three glass rosary beads, green or yellow. If they brought us a large quantity of something we gave them a hawk's bell. To the caciques or important men we might give a small mirror, a red cap, or a pair of scissors, things they seemed to appreciate. This arrangement worked out nicely — we were well supplied with all the food we needed, and they lived quite agreeably with us as neighbors.
– Ferdinand Columbus

Once a supply of food had been assured and the Indian attitude toward the shipwrecked sailors had been judged non-threatening, the Admiral turned his mind to how they would get off the island and return to Castile.

Since some means had to be found of returning to Castile, the Admiral held several meetings with his captains and other respected men to discuss how they were going to get out of this prison and at least back to Hispaniola, because it was vain and unreasonable to expect that a ship might find them here. It was, moreover, impossible to think of building their own ship since they had neither the tools nor the artisans required to do it properly. Possibly something could be fabricated, they agreed, if time didn't matter, but such a vessel would likely be incapable of dealing with the winds and currents among these islands, which all run westward. Building a vessel would therefore seem to be a waste of time, and more likely to cause our ruin than to prevent it. **– Ferdinand Columbus**

The plan decided upon — virtually the only option — was daring indeed.

After many discussions, the Admiral decided we must get a message to Hispaniola informing them that we were marooned on this island, and that they should send a ship with ammunition and provisions. To carry out this mission he selected two courageous and competent men in whom he had great confidence. Courage was clearly a necessity for the mission because it was rash to consider paddling a canoe between these two islands. The canoe, however, was the only means at their disposal. These canoes are made by excavating out a great log, and when they're heavily laden, the freeboard is no more than a few inches. For this mission it was, moreover, necessary that the canoe be medium-sized, because the smaller ones were too dangerous, and the larger ones too heavy and slow for such a long voyage. **– Ferdinand Columbus**

One of the men chosen for this high-risk gambit was the redoubtable young Diego Méndez.

Two canoes were finally selected, both suitable to the purpose. In July 1503 the Admiral directed that Diego Méndez of Segura, secretary of the fleet, go in one with six Christians and ten Indians, the latter to paddle. In the other he sent Bartolomeo Fieschi,[1] a gentleman of Genoa, with a similar crew. Once Diego Méndez had reached Hispaniola, he was to head straight for Santo Domingo, 250 leagues from where we were at present. Fieschi was then to return to inform us whether Méndez had arrived safely, to alleviate our fears of his having suffered some misfortune. We already feared this greatly, seeing how unsuited such a craft was to the open sea, and especially as it was carrying Christians. Had only Indians been making the journey, the danger would have been less, because they are highly skilled in hanging onto a swamped or capsized canoe, righting it, and getting back in, even in the open sea. **– Ferdinand Columbus**

The men would be required to cross more than a hundred miles of open sea in hollowed-out logs supplied by local Indians.[2] There was no other option. Without rescue, all would eventually perish, either from starvation or from inevitable clashes with the Indians. Columbus, ailing as usual, penned a lengthy letter to the king and queen, not only recounting the events of the voyage to that point, but requesting immediate assistance in returning to Castile. Courageous, and a congenital optimist, he wasted little ink in bemoaning his plight, but briskly told the monarchs what was needed, and why. Méndez would carry the letter with him in his unstable and vulnerable craft.

---

[1] Fieschi had been captain of the now-abandoned *Vizcaina*.

[2] Fieschi was expected to do it twice.

If it should please Your Highnesses to render me some assistance, please send me a vessel of at least sixty-four tons, with two hundred quintals of biscuit and some other provisions, so that I and my people can get back to Spain. As I've said before, it's less than twenty-eight leagues between Hispaniola and Jamaica, but I would not have gone to Hispaniola even if the ships were fit to do so, since I was told by Your Highnesses not to go there. God knows if these orders served any purpose. I'm sending this letter with Indian messengers.[1] It will be a great miracle if it gets there.

– Columbus to the King and Queen

Meanwhile, Méndez, Fieschi, one or two other Spaniards — likely volunteers — and the Indians prepared their canoes as best they could.

I pulled my canoe out of the water, rigged a false keel, and pitched and greased it. At both bow and stern I nailed on some boards to keep out the seawater, which, owing to the low freeboard, was sure to come in. I also erected a mast and sail, and loaded whatever provisions I could for myself and another Christian and six Indians. We were eight men in all, with no room for a thing more. **– Méndez**

After bidding good-bye to the Admiral and their comrades, the Spaniards, accompanied by the adelantado and a small armed party, then hiked some sixty coastal miles to the cape nearest to Hispaniola, the canoes likely being paddled by Indians along the shore. Here all rested, awaiting a calm that they prayed would hold for a few days. Eventually it came.

After the Indians had filled their gourds with water and loaded them into the canoes — along with some of their food, including cassava bread — the Christians climbed in with their swords, shields, and provisions, and the canoes were launched. The adelantado, who had accompanied the men to the island's eastern cape in order to keep local Indians from interfering with the voyage in any way, stayed there until nightfall, at which time the canoes were lost to view. He and the others then made their way slowly back to the ships, attempting to persuade any Indians they met to remain our

---

[1] Columbus was undoubtedly aware that the message would not get through without Indian assistance.

friends and to continue trading with us. **– Ferdinand Columbus**

Méndez in his later years recalled the details of the voyage.

Seeing that the sea was calming down, I very sadly took leave of my escort and they of me. I commended myself to God and Our Lady of Antigua, and then sailed for five days and four nights without the steering oar ever leaving my hand, while my companions paddled. With the help of our Lord God we arrived after five days at Cape San Miguel on the island of Hispaniola.[1] Having run out of food, we had neither eaten nor drunk for two days. We beached our canoe on a very beautiful coast where we found many people. They brought us a variety of things to eat and we rested with them for two days. Taking six Indians from this village, and leaving my companions, I began to paddle along the coast of the island toward the city of Santo Domingo—a voyage of 130 leagues.[2] I headed there because there I expected to find the governor . . . .

After traveling eighty leagues along the coast, not without considerable labor and danger—because this island had still not been fully subdued or pacified—I reached the province of Azua, which lies twenty-four leagues from Santo Domingo.[3] There I was informed by the Comendador Gallego that the governor had left to pacify the province of Jaragua, fifty leagues from there.[4] On learning this, I left my canoe and set out overland to find the governor. **– Méndez**

If Méndez had had the punishing task of navigating more than a hundred miles of ocean in a dugout log, then to paddle nearly another three hundred miles along the coast toward Santo Domingo, only to be told the governor was in the province where he had originally landed, Fieschi's promised lot was possibly worse—returning across a hundred miles of open sea to tell the Admiral that Méndez had made

---

[1] This is Cape Tiburón, in Haiti, the island's farthest southwest point. Méndez, in command of a hollowed-out log, had performed a remarkable feat of seamanship.

[2] The distance is about 330 miles by sea.

[3] About sixty miles. He had traveled 270 miles by canoe along the coast.

[4] His landing from Jamaica had actually been in Jaragua, the westernmost province of Hispaniola. He now had to return there.

it. Probably to his own good fortune, if not the Admiral's, he could convince no one to go with him, so he remained on Hispaniola.

> After resting two days, Bartolomeo Fieschi, driven by his honor as an hidalgo, proposed to return in a canoe to the Admiral as ordered. But his companions, including both Indians and sailors, were so exhausted and ill from their recent exertion and from having drunk so much seawater that he could find no one willing to attempt a return trip. Three days and three nights they'd been in the whale's belly, the Christians told him, like the prophet Jonah. God had delivered them, and they had no intention of going back. **– Ferdinand Columbus**

The tireless Méndez abandoned his canoe far to the east and struck out overland, back to the west, in search of the governor, the only man who could authorize a rescue. Lives depended on his effort.

> Diego Méndez, . . . although suffering from a quartan ague contracted during his dreadful passage over sea and land,[1] now made his way over rugged mountain paths to the western province of Jaragua, where he found the governor. His arrival was greeted with a show of pleasure on Ovando's part, but his departure was delayed by the governor for a very long time. **– Ferdinand Columbus**

Méndez and Fieschi had left the marooned men in July 1503. Because of being stalled now by Ovando—who had no love for Columbus, and who besides was presently engaged in the brutal suppression of Jaragua—Méndez was unable to secure a ship for the men's relief until May 1504.

> The governor kept me with him there for seven months while he had eighty-four ruling caciques burnt or hanged, and in addition to them killed the lady Nacaona, the greatest cacique of the island, whom all the others obeyed and served. When this business was over I left on foot for Santo Domingo, seventy leagues away, and I stayed there awaiting the arrival of ships from Castile, which had not been seen for more than a year. While I was there it pleased God that three ships came in. I purchased one of them and loaded it with supplies—bread, wine, meat, pork, mutton, and fruit—and I sent it to where the

---

[1] A malarial fever recurring every fourth day.

Admiral was,[1] so that he and all his men might come to Santo Domingo and from there return to Castile. I myself returned with the other two ships to report to the king and queen all that had happened on this voyage. **– Méndez**

He still carried with him Columbus's letter to the sovereigns.

In Jamaica, meanwhile, the Admiral and his stranded men, their hopes of rescue dimming by the week, gradually lost weight, and many saw their health deteriorate. Moreover, with little of a constructive nature to occupy their time, the more truculent among them began to cast around for a scapegoat for their predicament. They saw no reason to look beyond their odious Genoese Admiral.

After the canoes had left for Hispaniola, the people in the caravels began to get sick, as much from their change of diet as from the hardships they had endured in getting here. By this time their Spanish food had run out. There was no wine, and no meat other than the flesh of the occasional hutia, obtained in trade. Soon even the healthy men, confined as they were aboard ship with no end in sight, began to murmur against the Admiral, who, it was said, had no intention of returning to Spain, having been banished from there by the king and queen. He had even less intention of going to Hispaniola, it was alleged, because on leaving Castile he had been forbidden to land on that island. The real reason he had sent Méndez and Fieschi by canoe, they said, was not to seek ships or other relief for them, but to enable the two men to get to Spain where they could mend the Admiral's relationship with the king and queen. While his case was being presented to the Catholic Sovereigns, he would observe the banishment order by sitting right where he was. If this were not true, then where was Fieschi? Why hadn't he returned as he was supposed to? And what if Méndez and Fieschi had drowned? In that case there'd be no help for the marooned men at all, except what they could figure out for themselves. As for the Admiral, he couldn't be counted on to help them escape, not only for the above-mentioned reasons, but because of his arthritis,[2] which was so

---

[1] Méndez used funds kept in Santo Domingo by the Admiral.

[2] In light of modern opinion that Columbus suffered from reactive arthritis, Ferdinand's references to gout as the cause of his father's suffering have been altered to read "arthritis."

bad that he could hardly get out of bed, much less endure the hardships of a canoe voyage to Hispaniola. **- Ferdinand Columbus**

The bravery of the dissatisfied men, gathering furtively and angrily in the ships' corners, mounted daily. It was at length decided among them to exit the ships and make for Hispaniola on their own.

Their only remedy, therefore, was to take matters into their own hands while they were in sound health, and not fallen ill like so many others. The Admiral would be unable to stop them, and, because of the hatred and enmity that Governor Ovando, the Knight Commander of Lares, bore toward him, their reception on Hispaniola would be all the better for having left the Admiral in such danger. Going on to Castile, moreover, they would doubtless find favor with Don Juan de Fonseca, as well as Morales, the Royal Treasurer, who—because his mistress was a sister of the brothers Porras, ringleaders of the shipboard conspiracy—would surely see that they were well received by the Catholic Sovereigns. To the sovereigns it would be made clear that the entire blame lay with the Admiral, just as it had been during the Roldán business on Hispaniola. They would then surely take immediate action to strip him of whatever titles he had, freeing themselves of their commitments to him. **- Ferdinand Columbus**

By New Year's Day 1504, nearly six months after the departure of Méndez and Fieschi, affairs had come to a head.

Their boldness increasing from the repetition of these and similar arguments, and under the prodding of the brothers Porras—one of whom was captain of *Santiago*, and the other comptroller of the fleet—forty-eight men signed a mutineers' pact, in which Francisco de Porras was named captain. They then prepared for the day and hour on which they had decided to act.

With everything ready, and all rebels armed, on the morning of January 2, 1504, Francisco de Porras strode onto the sterncastle of the Admiral's ship, where the Admiral was lying abed, and said to him, "Sir, why do you make no effort to proceed to Castile, and insist on keeping us all here until we are dead?"

Hearing him speak so insolently, far from his usual manner, the Admiral suspected what was afoot. Feigning ignorance of this, however, he very calmly replied that they had no means of proceeding to Castile until the men he had dispatched in canoes sent a ship on which they could sail. No one had a greater desire than himself, said the Admiral, to get away from this island, not only for his own well-being, but for that of all the men for whom he was responsible. But if Captain Porras had a better idea, said the Admiral, he would call another meeting of the captains and other ranking men, and Captain Porras could present his idea to them. He would, he said, call as many meetings as necessary to ensure that the matter was thoroughly discussed.

The time for talk was past, replied Porras. It was now time for either escaping or staying here with God. Saying this, he turned on his heel and called out, "I'm for Castile! Who's joining me?" He was answered by the cries of his henchmen, "We're with you!" Then, in great disorder, some of his men rushed to one part of the ship and others to another, taking over the vessel fore and aft and climbing into the tops, all with weapons in hand. Some were shouting, "Kill them!" others, "To Castile, to Castile!" and still others, "Captain, what should we do?"

Although the Admiral was prostrate in his bed with arthritis, being hardly able to stand, he rose from bed and hobbled into the midst of the melee. But no sooner had three or four of his most stalwart servants seen him than they rushed forward and gathered him in their arms to keep him from being killed by the out-of-control mob, and with great effort dragged him back to his bed. They then ran out and seized the adelantado, who, lance in hand, had been offering a spirited resistance to the mutineers, taking the lance away from him by force and leading him away to where his brother lay. They then begged Captain Porras just to go with God, and to do nothing that could only bring harm upon all. No attempt, they said, would be made to prevent him from leaving. **– Ferdinand Columbus**

Columbus was no longer molested, and the men departed the beached caravels, helping themselves along the way to the vehicles of their intended escape.

Once things had quieted down a little, the mutineers took ten canoes that had been tied alongside the ships. The Admiral had had the island scoured for these canoes, purchasing them not only to make use of them in case of necessity, but also to keep them from the Indians' use in any attack. The mutineers set out in these craft as gaily as if they were paddling around some Castilian harbor. Seeing this, many who were not part of the mutiny, yet who were desperate to avoid being left behind and abandoned by the greater and healthier part of the force, also piled into the canoes. The few loyal men who remained with the Admiral, and the many sick, were deeply distressed by this, imagining themselves doomed to perish there — and without a doubt, if all had been healthy, not twenty men would have stayed with the Admiral. He himself, in so far as the situation allowed, went around speaking words of consolation to those who remained behind.

The rebels under Porras paddled along the coast to the eastern tip of the island, where Diego Méndez and Fieschi had embarked for Hispaniola. Wherever they landed along the way they inflicted outrages upon the Indians, stealing their food and whatever else struck their fancy, telling them that the Admiral would take care of payment, and that if he didn't, they were free to murder him. They could do with him whatever they wished, the Indians were told, for not only was he loathsome to the Christians, but he was the cause of all the woes suffered by the Indians of that other island [Hispaniola], and he would treat them in the same way if he were not eliminated. The Admiral indeed intended, they said, to remain and build Spanish settlements on this island. **– Ferdinand Columbus**

The mutineers, unprepared either mentally or physically for such a daunting enterprise as an escape by sea, found themselves in terror of the ocean, their panic leading them to barbarity in their desperate attempt to return to the island.

On the first calm day after reaching Jamaica's easternmost cape, the mutineers set out for Hispaniola. They brought Indians with them to paddle, but because weather conditions were unsettled and the canoes overloaded, they made little progress. Less than four leagues from shore the wind turned against them, frightening them so much that they decided to head back to Jamaica. But since they were so inexpert in handling canoes, they began to take on water, and in order to lighten the load threw many of their belongings overboard, save only their arms and enough food to last them till they reached shore. But then the wind picked up even more, and they realized they were in great danger.

To lighten the canoes further, they decided to knife the Indians and throw them overboard as well, and did so with some. Other Indians, confident in their swimming ability, jumped overboard to save themselves, but when they could swim no more they returned, exhausted, to hang onto the sides of the canoes and catch their breath. The Spaniards, in response, struck at them with their swords, hacking off their hands and wounding them in other grievous ways. They killed eighteen Indians in this way, leaving only enough unmolested to manage the canoes, for the Spaniards themselves had no idea how to do it. If they had, these Indians would surely have been slaughtered too. This was the Indians' reward for having allowed themselves to be duped into helping the Spaniards embark on this important voyage.

Once they reached shore, the Spaniards were of various opinions on what to do next. Some were for going to Cuba, taking advantage of the west-setting currents and winds to get them there. They considered that the run from Cuba to Hispaniola would then be easy, being apparently ignorant of the fact that it was a seventeen-league trip. Others said it was better to return to the ships and either make peace with the Admiral, or take by force whatever arms and goods were left to him. Still others were of the opinion that, before attempting any of these things, they should wait for fair weather or calm seas and try crossing to Hispaniola again.

Since this opinion carried the day, they stayed there in a village called Aomaquique for more than a month, awaiting the right conditions, all the while wreaking havoc on the land around. When the weather improved, they tried twice more to set out for Hispaniola, but were turned back by contrary winds. Disconsolate and downcast, they then headed back toward the ships on foot, at times eating whatever they could find along the way, and at other times—depending on the strength of defending Indian forces—seizing whatever they needed from the Indians. **– Ferdinand Columbus**

The Admiral now faced seemingly insurmountable difficulties. Most of the men who had remained loyal to him were sick, and by February—likely as a result of the poisonous notions sown among the Indians by the mutineers—the Indian attitude toward the men had begun to change.

Once the mutineers had departed, the Admiral made every effort to see that the sick received all the biscuit they required to regain their strength, and that the Indians were well treated, so that they might continue to bring us food for barter. He worked at this so assiduously that in a short time the Christians grew strong again and the Indians, for some days at least, continued to bring us provisions.

But these people have little interest in cultivating large fields of grain, and we consumed in one day what they ate in twenty. Their desire for our trading goods, moreover, had by now begun to wane, and they considered carrying out what the mutineers had suggested. Observing that a large number of our own men had turned against us, they became lazy about bringing us food, which put us into a serious bind. If we were to take food from them by force, we'd have to leave the ships to fight them ashore. This would place the Admiral, who was gravely ill with arthritis, in great danger back aboard ship. To wait for them to bring us food voluntarily was to opt for daily privation and to pay ten times what we had paid before, for they knew their business, and believed they had the advantage of us. We ourselves had no idea what to do. **– Ferdinand Columbus**

For all his faults and aggravating ways, Columbus sometimes showed flashes of brilliance, as he did now.

But since God never forgets those who commend themselves to him, as the Admiral always did, he caused the Admiral to strike upon an idea by which we could get all the food we needed. The Admiral remembered that in three days' time, just after dark, there would be an eclipse of the moon. He therefore sent an Indian we had with us from Hispaniola to summon the ranking Indians of the region, inviting them to a feast where he wished to speak to them.

Arriving during the daytime, before the eclipse was to occur, the caciques were told through the interpreter that we were Christians, which meant that we believed in a God who dwelt in the heavens and whom we served. This God took care of good people and punished the wicked. Having seen the mutinous Christians, said the Admiral, God had not permitted them to cross to Hispaniola, as he had done for Diego Méndez and Fieschi, and had caused them to suffer many hardships and deprivations, as was well known throughout the island. But God had now seen, he continued, the lack of interest the Indians had in trading with the Christians for food. He was in fact angry with them, said the Admiral, and planned to send them great famine and pestilence. Since they obviously did not believe in him, however, he would give them a sign from heaven to help them clearly recognize that their punishment had to have issued from his hand. If they paid close attention to the moon tonight, he said, they would see it rise angry and swollen, in sign of their coming chastisement.

When he had finished, the Indians departed, some frightened, others scoffing. But when the moon rose, they paid close attention, since the higher it rose, the darker it became, as the blackness crept over it. So astonished and frightened were they that they hurried toward the ships from every side, loaded down with victuals, wailing and crying out, begging the Admiral to ask God not to send his wrath upon them, promising that they would in future bring everything that the Spaniards required.

To this the Admiral replied that he would have to take counsel with God, and he secreted himself in his cabin as the moon darkened further, with the Indians crying out for his help. When the Admiral saw that the eclipse would soon end and the moon brighten, he came out and explained that he had spoken with his God, offering petitions on their behalf, and that he had promised in their name that they would be good in the future, and bring the Christians whatever food and other items they required. God had pardoned them, said the Admiral, and as a sign of his pardon, the moon would now lose its angry swelling. When the Indians saw that this in fact was occurring, they thanked the Admiral profusely, and sang the praises of his God. They carried on with this until the eclipse had passed.

From then on they took great care to provide us with whatever we needed, praising the Christian God unceasingly.

They believed now that the eclipses they had witnessed in the past had been harbingers of punishment. They had no knowledge of the cause of eclipses nor or their occasional appearances, nor could they grasp that any man on earth could comprehend what occurred in the heavens. They were therefore fully convinced that the Christians' God had revealed this eclipse to the Admiral. – **Ferdinand Columbus**

By March, the Spaniards had become divided into two fairly permanent camps—the Columbus loyalists aboard the stranded ships, and the mutineers, camped a short distance to the east. Of course, unknown to either camp, Fieschi was not returning, and Méndez—finally released by the governor—had only just succeeded in reaching Santo Domingo. It would be two more months before he could arrange for a ship large enough to take off all the stranded men. Méndez was possibly unaware of a token, face-saving effort about to be made by Governor Ovando.

Eight months had now passed since the departure of Diego Méndez and Bartolomeo Fieschi, and the Admiral's people, having heard no word from them, lived with heavy hearts, suspecting the worst. Some were certain they had drowned, others, that the Indians of Hispaniola had killed them. Still others thought they had died of illness or of hardships suffered along the way, since the shortest distance from the Hispaniola cape nearest Jamaica to the town of Santo Domingo was more than a hundred leagues, with travel across the island impeded by rugged mountains, and coastal sea travel made hazardous by conflicting and contrary winds and currents. Their sense of foreboding was strengthened by some Indians' claiming to have seen a capsized ship being carried by the currents down the Jamaican coast—likely an idea planted by the mutineers to dash the hopes of those who had remained with the Admiral.

With many now taking it for certain that no relief would be coming, yet another mutinous conspiracy was born—this one led by a Valencian apothecary named Bernal and two companions, Camacho and Villatoro, and into which were drawn most of the men who had been sick. But Our Lord, seeing the great peril into which the Admiral was falling, blunted the effect of this second mutiny by causing a tiny caravel to be sent from the governor of Hispaniola. This vessel anchored one afternoon near the grounded ships, and its captain, Diego de Escobar, was pulled across to the Admiral's ship, where he extended to the Admiral the cordial greeting of the governor, Nicolás de Ovando. Explaining the present impossibility of sending a ship large enough to take everyone off, Escobar affirmed that the governor had nonetheless sent this ship in token of his concern. With it, he had sent a cask of wine and a side of salt pork.

That very night, following delivery of the wine and salt pork, Escobar's caravel departed without even taking letters from anyone. **– Ferdinand Columbus**

Among the men in the ships (not the mutineers, who knew nothing of the caravel's arrival or departure) it was at once a moment for good cheer, disbelief, and suspicion. Yet, to the men's immense relief, it was at least now clear that Méndez had succeeded in his mission. Their stranding was known. They would be rescued. But why could not some of them have been taken in the caravel? Was the relationship between the governor and the Admiral somehow affecting their rescue?

With the people much comforted by this visit, the conspiracy that had been hatching quieted down. Some suspicion, however, still lingered around the haste and secrecy with which the captain had departed. This was interpreted as indicating the governor's wish not to see the Admiral return to Hispaniola. When the Admiral became aware of these rumors, he told the people that he himself had been responsible for sending the caravel away. He didn't wish to depart from there unless with everyone, he said, and that particular caravel was not large enough. And, he added, if the caravel had remained, it would only have caused further problems with the mutineers.

The truth was, however, that the governor feared that the Admiral, once arrived in Spain, would be restored to his former office by the Catholic Sovereigns, displacing himself. For that reason, the Admiral had to be left on Jamaica, and not be given the means to reach Hispaniola. The caravel had been sent to spy on him and secretly to take stock of his condition so as to determine the best method of destroying him.

The Admiral knew all this from a letter sent in that caravel by Diego Méndez, a letter in which Méndez described not only his voyage but also what had happened to him afterward.
– Ferdinand Columbus

In May, Columbus decided that, with rescue undoubtedly imminent, he would make an effort to placate the mutineers, who had no knowledge of the caravel's brief visit.

Since the Admiral and his company — now greatly relieved at the news of Diego Méndez's safe arrival, as well as by the coming of the little caravel — were virtually assured that they would all be rescued, the Admiral decided to carry this news to the mutineers in hopes of bringing them back to obedience. He therefore sent two men of standing, men who had some friends among the mutineers. Knowing that they would not have believed a caravel had come — or even that they might have denied it — he sent them some of the salt pork that the captain had given him.

When the two emissaries arrived at the mutineers' camp, Porras — in an effort to keep his men from being persuaded that they had committed a crime and were now being offered a general pardon, which was in fact the case — came out to meet them alone. But the men could not be prevented from hearing of the caravel's arrival, or of the good health and spirits of the Admiral's men, or of the offer that had been made. After lengthy discussion among them, it was decided that they would place no faith in the safe conduct or pardon offered by the Admiral, but that they would depart from the island quietly if, on the arrival of two ships, the Admiral would give them one, or on the arrival of a single ship, half would be assigned to them. In the meantime, they insisted, because all their clothing and trading goods had been lost at sea, what was held by the Admiral's people should be shared with them.

The two envoys, explaining why these were unreasonable demands, were interrupted by threats: if these concessions were not given freely, force would be used to obtain them. At this point the envoys were dismissed, and the mutineers' followers were told that the Admiral was a cruel and vindictive man. While the leaders themselves, it was explained, had no fear that he would damage them — because they enjoyed such favor at court — it was not unreasonable that he might carry out a vendetta upon others, under color of punishment deserved. It was for this reason that Roldán and his followers on Hispaniola had had no faith in his offers. And everything had turned out well for them—they had seen the Admiral sent back to Castile in chains. The men here, it was said, should have no less hope of success.

To dispel whatever impression might have been caused by the news of Diego Méndez's safe arrival being brought by the caravel, the men were told that in fact no caravel had arrived—that it was a chimera, a product of black magic, of which the Admiral was an expert practitioner. If there had been a caravel, the men were told, why did the crew not mix in with the Admiral's men at all, and why did the caravel leave so quickly? And why, it was asked, did not the Admiral and his brother and son sail away in it?

With these and other arguments the leaders of the mutiny hardened the resolve of their followers, egging them on to march upon the ships and seize whatever they found there—in the process taking the Admiral prisoner. – **Ferdinand Columbus**

Columbus, in chronic poor health himself, now had to face what he had strenuously tried to avoid—a pitched battle between the two factions among his crew. Bloodshed was clearly in the offing. Bartholomew would have to take matters in hand.

Persisting in their plan of aggression, the mutineers moved forward to an Indian village named Maima—later the site of a Spanish settlement called Seville—only a quarter-league from the ships. The Admiral, being informed of their advance, ordered his brother the adelantado out to talk sense to them, but only in company with a party strong enough to deal with them if they caused trouble. The adelantado therefore took fifty men with him, well-armed and ready to fight.

When they had arrived to within a crossbow-shot of the Indian village, the two envoys dispatched previously were sent forward again, principally to offer peace, and to ask whether the two chiefs might hold a quiet discussion. But the mutineers' ranks were as strong as our own, and their men—mostly sailors—equally courageous. Unfortunately, however, they viewed our men as inferior to them, and cowardly. They therefore refused to allow the envoys to speak, and with lances and drawn swords, rushed without warning at the adelantado and his party, crying "Kill them, kill them." Six of the rebels, regarded as the bravest, had formed a company sworn to murder the adelantado himself, considering that, with him dead, the rest of the force could be easily dealt with.

But God willed that events turn out differently, since at their first charge five or six of them fell—among them several of those who had sworn to kill the adelantado. He himself was fighting like a man possessed, quickly dispatching Juan Sánchez of Cádiz, the one who had let the Quibián escape. Then he mortally wounded Juan Barba, who had been the first to draw his sword at the time of the mutiny. Many others on their side fell badly wounded, and Captain Porras was taken prisoner. Those who had not been killed or wounded fled as fast as they could run. The adelantado, bent on pursuing them, was restrained by his captains. "This has been a good lesson for them," they said, "but let's not go any further with it. If we kill too many of them, the Indians, who are standing around waiting to see what happens, might then attack us."

The adelantado took this advice to heart, rounding up the prisoners and leading his men back to the ships. The Admiral and those who had stayed behind with him were overjoyed at the outcome of the venture, all crediting God for the victory. The rebellion had finally been put down, and with bearable losses—the adelantado himself having been wounded in the hand, and one of the Admiral's stewards having died from a slight lance-wound in his side.

Getting back to the mutineers, Pedro de Ledesma, the pilot who had . . . been the one to swim through the breakers at the Belén River, had fallen over a cliff that day, wounded, and had lain there undiscovered by us till evening of the following day. The Indians, however, had known he was there. Curious to see the effect of our swords, they had prodded open his many wounds with twigs. Through the slash on his head they could see his brain. They inspected his wounded shoulder, from which his arm dangled, and the cuts on his thigh, which were to the bone, as well as another on the sole of his foot, from which a slab of flesh resembling a slipper had been sliced off from heel to toe. Despite his condition, Ledesma protested strenuously at this intrusion, snarling at the Indians and threatening them: "Leave me alone, because if I have to get up I'm going to . . . !" His threats actually succeeded in frightening them off.

Once we found out about him, we brought him back and laid him inside a palm-leaf hut near the ships, where the mosquitoes and dampness alone should have done him in. Since no turpentine was available to treat his many wounds, they were cauterized with hot oil. The surgeon who treated him swore that he found new wounds every day for a week, but, while the lightly-wounded steward of the Admiral had died, the very grievously wounded Ledesma survived. **– Ferdinand Columbus**

Thanks to the adelantado's determined action, the mutiny was broken. The Admiral then followed up with an imaginative personnel-management stroke.

The next day, which was Monday May 20, the mutineers who had fled sent to the Admiral, humbly begging his mercy. They repented of all their misdeeds, they said, and wished to be taken again into his service. In reply the Admiral issued a general pardon, the only proviso being that Captain Porras remain in irons to keep him from creating some new disturbance.

But the Admiral saw the difficulty of now lodging so many men aboard the grounded ships. In the first place there would be little room for all of them with their possessions, not to mention an insufficiency of food, and even a total lack of peace and quiet. Beyond this was the likelihood of quarrels breaking out between the two groups over half-forgotten injuries, and of new tensions arising. To avoid this occurrence he decided to send them a captain with merchandise to trade. Men could accompany this captain around the island, supporting themselves in honest trade until the arrival of the ships— which were looked for daily. **– Ferdinand Columbus**

In late June, nearly a year after the departure of Méndez and Fieschi, the rescue ship arrived, and all the men with their meager goods clambered aboard.

With the mutineers now reduced to obedience and the Indians therefore better disposed to trade with us for food, we soon reached the anniversary date of our landing on Jamaica, and it was at this time that a ship paid for and provisioned by

Diego Méndez in Santo Domingo—with the Admiral's funds—sailed into view and anchored. On June 28 we all embarked, friends and enemies alike. The journey to Santo Domingo was difficult, what with the contrary currents and winds, but on August 13, 1504, with an overwhelming desire to simply rest, we sailed into the river at Santo Domingo.

Governor Ovando had arranged a grand reception for the Admiral and had even made his house available to him, but it was a scorpion's peace. He freed Porras, for example, and attempted to punish those responsible for imprisoning him. He also tried to inject himself into judicial matters that were the purview only of the Catholic Sovereigns, who had sent the Admiral out as captain-general of their fleet. The governor's stroking of the Admiral was all carried out with deceitful smiles. Things went on like this until we got our ship refitted and had chartered a second vessel. The Admiral, his family members, and his servants would embark on this vessel, with most of our other companions having chosen to remain on Hispaniola. **– Ferdinand Columbus**

Columbus, his son Ferdinand, and his brother Bartholomew spent four weeks in Santo Domingo, not sailing for Castile until mid-September, and then in company with only one other vessel. The Admiral, however, remained dogged by bad luck, as became evident on this, his final ocean crossing.

We sailed out of the river on September 12, and had gotten only two leagues out to sea when the mainmast of the vessel accompanying us split right down to the deck. The Admiral ordered her back to port and we held our course for Castile. The weather was fine for nearly a third of our course, but we were soon hit by a violent storm that made us fear for our lives. On Saturday October 19, the day after the storm, with a calm sea and all of us recuperating, our mainmast fell apart, breaking in three places. The adelantado, with the advice of the Admiral—who was prostrate with arthritis—then rigged a jury mast from a lateen yard, strengthening it with ropes and boards torn out of the ship's fore- and sterncastles. A second storm later broke our mizzenmast. It was God's will that we sail some seven hundred leagues in this condition, at the end of which we arrived at the port of Sanlúcar de Barrameda, and from there went to Seville, where the Admiral was able to rest somewhat from his labors. **– Ferdinand Columbus**

Columbus had arrived in Castile on November 7. Less than three weeks later the news rippled across the land that Isabella, Queen of Castile, was dead. With the loss of his great patroness, with his own advancing age and precarious health, with the eternal chorus of vituperation surrounding him both in Spain and in the infant colony, he would lead no further voyages of discovery. He in fact lived only a year and a half longer, spending most of that time in a campaign to have his rights, privileges, and possessions – lost at the time of his arrest – restored by a less than sympathetic king.[1]

Columbus passed away in a monastery at Valladolid on May 20, 1506. He was fifty-four years old. Among those keeping vigil at his deathbed were two men who had shared with him some of his darkest hours – Diego Méndez and Bartolomeo Fieschi.

Columbus had served as a bridge between two worlds. Like a bridge, it was his fate to be trodden upon. It is difficult to see him in the full joy of discovery. Everything he grasped seemed to turn sour in his hand. Perhaps our most poignant picture of Columbus was supplied by his own pen in the last letter he ever wrote to the sovereigns – the letter written from his seemingly hopeless isolation on a Jamaican beach, to be carried across the sea on a modified log by Méndez, and at length almost miraculously to reach them in Castile.

> I myself have profited little from twenty years of laborious and dangerous service. Today in Castile I have no roof over my head. If I need a meal or a bed, I must go to an inn or tavern, and I frequently have no money with which to pay the bill. . . .
>
> The lands here that obey Your Highnesses are more extensive and richer than any Christian lands. Yet after I, by the will of God, had brought them under your royal and exalted rule, and was on the point of securing very great revenue, suddenly, while waiting for ships to take me into your royal presence to tell of victories, and bearing great news of gold, secure and content in myself, I and my two brothers were arrested and thrown onto a ship. We were weighted

---

[1] In fairness to Ferdinand, he was involved in far more pressing matters at the time, notably his wars in Italy. He had, moreover, through the death of his queen, lost all authority in Castile.

down with chains, stripped, and treated very badly, with no legal process. Who could believe that a poor foreigner would dare to rebel in such a place against Your Highnesses, without cause and without the support of some other prince, standing alone among your vassals and subjects, and with all his children at your royal court?

I came to serve at the age of twenty-eight [sic], and now there's not a hair on my head that's not gray. I'm sick and worn out. Everything that I and my brothers ever had has been taken from us and sold, right down to our coats, without our being heard or seen, and with great dishonor to me. It's impossible to believe this was done by your royal command. The restoration of my honor, the restitution of my property, and the punishment of the one who caused all this will redound to your royal honor. . . .

The honest devotion that I have ever brought to the service of Your Highnesses, and the unjust offenses that I have suffered, don't allow me to keep silence, even if I should wish to. I beg of Your Highnesses to pardon me. I am so ruined, as I have said. I've always wept for others, but now may heaven have mercy upon me, and may the earth weep for me. Concerning material goods, I don't have a penny even for a spiritual offering. And here in the Indies I have stopped observing the prescribed forms of religion—remaining alone in my distress, sick, expecting death every day, and surrounded by hostile savages, cruel beyond belief. I have been so separated from the blessed sacraments of the Holy Church that my soul will be forgotten if it leaves my body. Weep for me, whoever has charity, truth, and justice.

– Columbus to the King and Queen

In 1504, the year of Columbus's final return to Spain, the next major actor in this developing drama decided to book passage to Santo Domingo and try his luck in the New World. His name was Hernán Cortés.

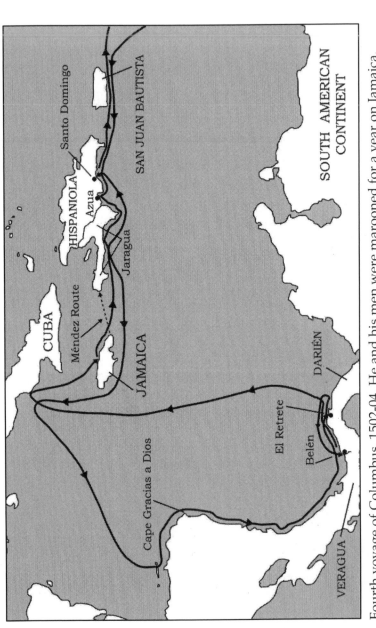

Fourth voyage of Columbus, 1502–04. He and his men were marooned for a year on Jamaica.

HERNÁN CORTÉS

The Conquest of Mexico

CHAPTERS

1. To the Indies 131

2. The Cortés Expedition 143

3. Establishing a Foothold 153

4. Cempoala and Villa Rica 163

5. The Road to Tenochtitlan 179

6. Into the Aztec Capital 203

7. The Seizure of Montezuma 223

8. Setback and Calamity 237

9. La Noche Triste and Escape 257

10. Cortés Resurgent 267

11. The Siege of Tenochtitlan 283

12. Aftermath 301

MAPS FOLLOWING PAGES 141, 177, 221, 265

1

TO THE INDIES

On August 13, 1521, heroically defended by Cuauhtémoc, Tlatelolco fell to the power of Hernán Cortés. It was neither a triumph nor a defeat, but the painful birth of the mestizo people that are the Mexico of today.

– Translation of Memorial Plaque in Tlatelolco, Mexico City, on the site of the final battle for Tenochtitlan

Of the five conquistadors treated in this book, Hernán Cortés — notwithstanding his capacity for calculated and cruel excess — was the most urbane and perhaps most intelligent of all. A clever man in every respect, indefatigable in the pursuit of his ends, he was an especially astute psychologist, adept in the use of fawning servility, gentle coaxing, brazen lies, or outright terror to achieve his ends.

He was born in 1485 in Medellín, Extremadura, to Martín Cortés de Monroy and Catalina Pizarro Altamirano (thought to be a distant cousin of the future conqueror of Peru, Francisco Pizarro). He was born into a family of hidalgos — the minor nobility — whose men customarily made their way in life by military service. Yet Cortés, as he advanced from childhood to youth within this family, gradually became aware of another path he might take. Apparently not keen on the idea of fighting in Europe's ongoing wars, he paid attention to a recurring topic of conversation among his parents and neighbors — namely, the Indies that had been first reached by Spanish sailors when he was seven years old, and the opportunities that must exist there.

As a child he was sickly, and his parents — perhaps feeling that he was not suited to military life — sent him in his mid-teens to Salamanca to study. What he studied is not known, but in his two years there he seems to have picked up at least a smattering of Latin and some knowledge of the law.

In early 1502, having finally rejected the idea of joining an army, the 17-year-old Cortés decided to ship out to the Indies with the fleet bearing the new governor Nicolás de Ovando to his post. An injury reportedly sustained while making a hurried exit from the bedroom of a young married woman made it necessary for him to postpone this plan.

But by 1504, the year of Columbus's return from his fourth and final voyage, the 19-year-old Cortés found himself aboard ship heading at last for Hispaniola, where he quickly prospered. With the assistance of Governor Ovando, a family acquaintance, he began to acquire property and Indians, and was before long appointed notary — a position of some prestige among his countrymen — in the settlement of Azua, on the island's south coast.

In the meantime the chronically poor Castilian government had been searching for ways to control and profit from this promising discovery that had been thrown so unexpectedly into its lap. In 1503, the year Columbus found himself marooned on Jamaica, Bishop Fonseca,[1] under the direction of Queen Isabella, had formed the *Casa de Contratación*, or House of Trade. In the face of Columbus's disastrous administration of the Crown's burgeoning holdings across the sea, the queen had seen the need to establish direct royal control over them. Among the new agency's purposes were to be regulation of commerce and collection of taxes and duties. Importantly, all voyages to or from the Indies, whether for trade or exploration, would henceforth require licensing by this agency. The Crown at a minimum sought to ensure that the "royal fifth" — namely, twenty percent of all treasure from the Indies — would flow into government's painfully empty coffers instead of into the pockets of its subjects. In 1524 the House of Trade would become part of the Royal Council of the Indies, which would, for many years thereafter, make all decisions regarding the Indies.

The death of the queen in 1504 shook the Crown's already tenuous hold upon its overseas colony. More importantly, it caused a power vacuum in Castile that lasted for the next five years, as Ferdinand struggled with his increasingly unstable daughter Juana — heir to the Castilian throne — and her husband Philip, Duke of Burgundy, for the right to rule Castile. In 1509, in the culmination of a tawdry sequence of events punctuated by the shocking death of Philip, 30-year-old Juana, mother of four future queens and two emperors — but herself queen of Castile in name only and considered too mentally unbalanced to rule — was quietly remanded to a convent near Valladolid. Ferdinand, now acting through Cardinal Francisco Jiménez de

---

[1] The official who had been charged by the Crown with outfitting Columbus's voyages.

Cisneros, a man palatable to the Castilian nobility, would rule Castile as regent for his daughter until his death in 1516.

Also in 1509, Ferdinand, reportedly fulfilling a deathbed wish of Queen Isabella, ordered Ovando recalled from the Indies. Named to take Ovando's place as governor—probably to the disappointment of many who remembered the Columbus brothers—was 29-year-old Diego Columbus, the Admiral's eldest son.[1] In 1511, Diego, his path likely smoothed by his wife's family relationship with the king, was further elevated to the office of Viceroy of the Indies. During the same year, in an effort to gain greater control over its new colony, the Crown established the three-man *Real Audiencia*, or Royal Audience, of Santo Domingo, a body with both legislative and judicial powers.

Viceroy Columbus soon turned his attention to the very large and so far unexploited island lying just to the west—Cuba—ordering suppression of its natives by a veteran of the Crown's Italian campaigns named Diego Velázquez de Cuéllar. The 26-year-old Cortés eagerly joined this campaign, in which the island population was quickly and easily subdued. Because of his service in the pacification of Cuba, Cortés came to the notice of Velázquez, who had by now been named governor of the island, and good things began to flow his way.[2] He was appointed secretary to the governor, and later *alcalde* of Santiago,[3] one of the first Spanish settlements in Cuba. He began to acquire land, cattle, gold mines, and Indians. Cortés eventually had a falling out with Velázquez that resulted even in a brief imprisonment, but it did him no lasting damage.

As Cuba was being settled, Velázquez was turning his attention beyond the island, and scheming to increase his influence by sponsoring voyages of discovery and settlement to the west. His hands were tied, however, by his position with respect to Diego Columbus and by the need for approval of all voyages of exploration by the House of Trade, in far-off Seville.

---

[1] The Admiral's youngest son, Ferdinand, who had shared with his father the dangers of the fourth voyage, never returned to the Indies, choosing a life of scholarship over one of action.

[2] Good things also came to his contemporary Bartolomé de las Casas, including an *encomienda*, whereby in return for caring for and educating an allotment of Indians in the faith, he would receive rights to their service on his lands.

[3] The *alcalde* served both as town administrator and judge.

The Spanish footprint was at this time being rapidly enlarged throughout the Indies. In 1508 Juan Ponce de León had landed on today's Puerto Rico, and by 1513 he would lay claim to the Florida peninsula for Castile.[1] During this same year Vasco Núñez de Balboa would cross the rugged spine of today's eastern Panama to sight the vast Southern Sea, or what would come to be known as the Pacific Ocean, claiming it and all lands touching it for Castile.[2] Jamaica was being colonized, and towns were being established throughout Cuba.

As Cortés had observed this process, calculating how best he could profit from it, an acquaintance of his, young Bartolomé de las Casas, had also contemplated it. The atmosphere in the Indies was infernal. Hundreds of greedy and aggressive men (not to mention adventurous women) were arriving—men who, because the residents of this land were "primitive" and weak, considered them to be of no account and thoroughly expendable, and treated them accordingly.

Both of these young men had been deeply involved in this exploitation from the beginning—both owned lands and Indians—but one of them would gradually become uncomfortable with it.

Las Casas, although prospering in business, had set his feet upon an ecclesiastical path. After a few years on the island—without yet having laid aside his business interests or lands or slaves—he returned to Spain to take up theological studies, and sometime between 1507 and 1510 was ordained a Catholic priest either in Spain or Italy. He returned to the colony as a "gentleman-cleric" soon afterwards.

Around the time of Las Casas's return, in 1510, the archbishop of Seville sent four Dominicans to the Indies to find out and report back on what was being done to the Indians. Appalled at what they found on Hispaniola, the Dominicans began publicly to decry Spanish

---

[1] He had previously lent his hand to the slaughter of many Indians on Hispaniola.

[2] Balboa was unaware that even as he was taking possession, the Portuguese were sailing this ocean, and had already located the Spice Islands sought by Spain (today's Maluku Islands, in Indonesia). Balboa would eventually fall afoul of Pedrarias Dávila, the new governor of Castilla del Oro, as today's eastern Panama and certain neighboring regions were then called, and—despite having recently been offered the hand of one of the governor's daughters in marriage—would be beheaded. Among those assisting in his apprehension would be Francisco Pizarro, future destroyer of the Peruvian empire (treated in Volume II).

abuses. In December 1511, Las Casas was present in Santo Domingo when a Dominican, the fiery Antonio de Montesinos, fearlessly tongue-lashed his countrymen from the pulpit for their treatment of the Indians. The outraged colonists, with the assistance of their thoroughly annoyed governor and viceroy, Diego Columbus, then succeeded in having the Dominicans recalled. When the king himself looked into the matter, however, he sided with the Dominicans. The result of the royal disgust was the promulgation of the Laws of Burgos of 1512, an earnest effort to dictate humane treatment of the indigenous peoples, but a statute that came to be honored more in the breach than in the observance.

By 1514 Las Casas, having witnessed firsthand the murder, torture, and general abuse of Indians on a near-daily basis in both Hispaniola and Cuba, had become overtly hostile to the Spanish overseas enterprise. He had abandoned his business pursuits, given up his lands and Indians, and in the following year returned to Spain to plead with the king over what he referred to as the destruction of the Indies. The death of the king in 1516, however, made it necessary for him to deal with Cardinal Jiménez de Cisneros, now serving as regent for the confined queen, Juana. The cardinal became concerned enough by Las Casas's pleading that he appointed a commission of three Hieronymite friars to look into the question of Indian abuse. These three friars would soon become the de facto governors of the Indies, superseding even the (corrupt) Royal Audience, and operating independently of Diego Columbus. But even these three supposedly upright men would prove not to be the Indians' saviors.

Upon the king's death, his daughter Juana—still locked up in a convent—had become nominal queen of Aragon as well as Castile. Yet Juana had a son Charles, who, through the blood of his parents and grandparents, was, astonishingly, heir to thrones across the face of Europe, including the throne of Castile, with its burgeoning overseas possessions. On the death of Ferdinand the 16-year old Charles—born in Ghent and fairly ignorant of Spain, Spaniards, or the Castilian language—claimed the thrones of Aragon and Castile, which he planned to rule jointly with his mother. The members of the Castilian royal advisory council, or *Cortes Generales*, made it clear that they were unimpressed with this northern boy's claim to the Castilian throne, and only when they had exacted certain promises from the claimant— such as the twin necessities of getting rid of his Flemish advisors and of learning Castilian immediately—did they reluctantly accept him as Charles I, king of Castile. Following this he was accepted in Aragon, and in 1519, after the application of heavy bribes (much of the money for which was extracted from Castile and Aragon), Charles I of Spain was elected Holy Roman Emperor as Charles V.[1] Now ruling lands from the Netherlands to Italy, including Austria and Hungary, not to mention Castile, Aragon, and Castile's new possessions across the sea, this rather unattractive young man had become the most powerful monarch in European history. His attention, however, would be most immediately drawn not to his possessions overseas, but to his European empire, with its threat of renewed war against France, and its incipient religious fracturing by a German monk named Martin Luther.

It is during the period between the death of Ferdinand and the accession of Charles to the thrones of Castile and Aragon that the first steps toward the conquest of Mexico took place.

In 1517 the settlers on Hispaniola and Cuba still knew little of what lay beyond their islands. Was the land discovered by Ponce de León, called by him *La Pascua Florida*, an island or mainland? How far did the land explored by Columbus on his third and fourth voyages, and penetrated by Balboa, extend northward? If La Pascua Florida— modern Florida—was in fact not an island, was the land to the south and west of Cuba—the land explored by Columbus, Balboa, and others—possibly connected to it?

In Cuba, in early 1517, a number of men impatient for action— some of whom had sailed with Columbus—petitioned Governor Velázquez to send them on an expedition to hunt slaves. Since sponsoring this sort of voyage was clearly within the purview of the governor, he acceded, permitting them to outfit three caravels,[2] and placing this fleet under the command of a wealthy landowner named Francisco Hernández de Córdoba. In late May, following three weeks of heavy weather, the expedition found itself off the northeastern tip of what later became known as Yucatán, where they saw signs of an Indian civilization far more advanced than anything seen in the islands. In subsequent days they alternately parleyed with and fought

---

[1] He would receive the German crown the following year at Aachen, and the imperial crown in 1530 at Bologna.

[2] Some sources say two caravels and a brigantine, others say four caravels.

these Indians as they moved west and then southwest down the large peninsula's western shore. Skirmishing on nearly a daily basis, they finally suffered a serious defeat at Champotón. Casualties were by this time so high (Hernández himself would die from his wounds) that they no longer had the necessary manpower to manage three caravels. Moreover, their water casks were leaking and replenishment was hindered greatly by the attacking Indians. So the beaten and dehydrated survivors set fire to one of the vessels and returned to Cuba in their remaining vessels, reporting on the new civilization they had found—a people who built stone temples, wore cotton clothing, cultivated maize, sacrificed humans to their idols, and were highly capable fighters. Importantly, they announced, these Indians had gold. They had discovered the Maya.

Velázquez saw an opportunity. By the following spring, 1518, he had assembled four ships and about 250 men under the command of a kinsman, 29-year-old Juan de Grijalva.[1] Grijalva was to return to the area of the previous expedition—with more and better-armed men—and attempt to trade with the natives. Departing on May 1, the fleet made its first landfall on the island of Cozumel, off the eastern coast of Yucatán. Then, following the course of the previous expedition—namely, around and down the western side of the peninsula—the soldiers and crew met the same stiff Indian resistance at Champotón, but this time the native defenders were routed. Proceeding westward along the curving coast now, they encountered thousands of hostile Indians at the mouth of today's Grijalva River in the state of Tabasco, southern Mexico, but succeeded in coming to terms with them without fighting.[2] Having been told by these Indians of a great culture to the north, a people called the Mexica with a powerful ruler named Montezuma,[3] they sailed as far north as the Banderas River,[4] on the

---

[1] Velázquez had sought and received permission for this voyage from the three Hieronymite friars, whose commission made them independent of Diego Columbus.

[2] Grijalva's interpreter was a cross-eyed Mayan named Melchor, captured during the Hernández expedition, and taught rudimentary Spanish since.

[3] The spelling of this name among chroniclers varies from Mutezuma to Moctezuma, to, most correctly, Motecuhzoma. For simplicity, the incorrect yet commonly understood Montezuma will be used here, except in the Aztec material, where the chronicler's usage will be preserved.

[4] Today's Jamapa River.

south edge of today's Veracruz, Mexico. On landing, the Spaniards were astonished to find three Indians awaiting them on the beach with gifts from the great Montezuma, who had already been told of their victory over the Maya at Champotón and of their peacemaking with the Indians in Tabasco, and who wished to pay the strangers homage—doubtless in hopes that they would leave his lands. The visitors were given foods of all kinds and were treated with the utmost respect, including being enveloped in clouds of fragrant incense. Best of all, the Indians of the region took care to load the Spaniards' pockets with gold and other valuables in return for the cheap trinkets they were offered in trade.

After six days of this love-fest—during which time the Spaniards had taken formal possession of the land for Castile—[1]the fleet moved further north, near nightfall sighting an island that showed evidence of human habitation, about a mile off the coast of present-day Veracruz, Mexico. Bernal Díaz del Castillo, a young soldier who had been with Hernández and who would soon accompany Cortés, recalled what they found there.[2]

> Juan de Grijalva and a number of us soldiers rowed in to see the island, because we had seen smoke rising from it. We found two houses of mortared stone, very well made, with some steps inside leading up to something like altars. On those altars were some evil-looking idols, their gods. We discovered that on that very night they had sacrificed five Indians. Their chests had been ripped open and their arms and legs hacked off. The walls of the houses were liberally smeared with blood.

---

[1] This was done by the time-honored *requerimiento*, the charade by which Spaniards read a proclamation (in Spanish) to usually bemused Indians that they were laying claim to their lands. The formula included a brief history of the world since creation and a description of the establishment of the papacy and of the granting of these lands to Spain by Alexander VI. The Indians were then told of their need to submit to the Crown and accept the Catholic faith or face slavery and death. Importantly to the Spaniards, the proclamation gained its legal force by its being witnessed by a notary. Las Casas reportedly said he didn't know whether to laugh or cry at the concept.

[2] Díaz, a simple foot-soldier, would become an important chronicler of the Cortés expedition.

We were mesmerized by all this. We called this island the *Isla de Sacrificios*, as it is in fact now called on marine charts. – **Díaz** Next day, further evidence of idol worship and human sacrifice was found on a second island nearby. Grijalva landed here with thirty soldiers – Díaz again among them – encountering four dark-cloaked Indian priests, hair matted with dried blood, in a prayer house.

That day they had sacrificed two boys, opening their chests and offering their hearts and blood to that accursed idol. And those priests came over to us to burn the same incense before us that they burn to their Tezcatlipoca . . . .[1] We refused to allow it. We had been greatly moved by the death of those two boys and by the sight of such consummate cruelty. The general asked our Indian Francisco, whom we had brought from the Río de Banderas and who seemed to understand them somewhat, why they had done such a thing. By signs . . . he replied that the chiefs of Culúa had ordered the sacrifices. Because he spoke lazily, saying "Ulúa, Ulúa," and because our captain was named Juan and because it was the feast of St. John,[2] we named this island San Juan de Ulúa. – **Díaz**

By this time it was clear that they could not remain on this humid and mosquito-infested coast – a coast inhabited by an apparently cruel people at that – without further assistance from Cuba. The tattered force, its diet now reduced to weevil-infested and moldy bread, and in daily danger of being overwhelmed, was further burdened by a number of wounded and feverish men. But the stubborn Grijalva wanted to hang on at least for the short term. Therefore after an agreement had been reached among expedition leaders that a beachhead be established among the dunes of the mainland until help arrived, the sick and wounded were rowed out to *San Sebastián*, which was then dispatched under command of Pedro de Alvarado to Cuba with a request to the governor for resupply.[3] To help ensure a favorable response, Grijalva sent the governor whatever gold and jewels had been gained in barter from the Indians.

Following the departure of this ship, Grijalva and his men – perhaps still unable to find a tolerable campsite – pulled up stakes and sailed 180 miles farther up the coast to Cabo Rojo, between today's

---

[1] A central deity of the Aztecs.

[2] June 24.

[3] Alvarado would become one of Cortés's highest-profile captains.

Tuxpan and Tampico. But having endured a further Indian attack along the way, with winter rains setting in, and now encountering powerful contrary currents around the headland of Cabo Rojo, Grijalva and his captains agreed to call it quits and head back to Cuba. Turning south again—stopping to trade for gold at Coatzacoalcos in southern Veracruz state—and finally retracing their course up and around the Yucatán coast, the soaked and exhausted men threaded their way into Santiago Bay in October 1518.

Shortly after this fleet's departure the previous spring, Velázquez, possibly because Grijalva was a relative, had become anxious over this second expedition to the west, and had consequently dispatched a ship under command of Cristóbal de Olid to track it down. Olid, however, had encountered a severe storm and returned to Cuba without finding Grijalva. In the midst of the governor's fretting over the fate of Grijalva's fleet, Alvarado arrived from that fleet with news of a mainland to the west, a mainland with an apparently high civilization and abundant wealth, of which he was able to show convincing evidence. Velázquez, excited by this news, immediately shipped a large sampling of the Mexican treasure to Seville, and with this treasure went his application for a license to conquer and colonize the newly discovered land.[1] Almost as soon as this ship had been dispatched, he began plotting this new expedition, one aimed not only at finding Grijalva, but one that would take up where that captain had left off. He devoted considerable thought to the question of who might lead such an expedition.

In the meantime the governor of Jamaica, Francisco de Garay, had been licensed to make his own exploratory probe with the purpose of finding a sea passage to Balboa's Southern Sea. He had selected Alonso Álvarez de Pineda to lead an expedition that would begin at the southwestern tip of today's Florida and work its way north and westward, mapping whatever coast might be found as far west and south as the lands that had been encountered in previous expeditions,[2]

---

[1] Velázquez was attempting to bypass Diego Columbus as Cortés would strive to bypass Velázquez. The governor eventually received this license, but too late to stop Cortés from usurping his rights.

[2] By this time the eastern coasts of both North and South America had been surveyed nearly in their entirety, the Caribbean Islands and Bahamas had been explored, and the isthmus of Panama crossed. Much of the

and searching for a sea passage through these lands to the true Indies. He would be mapping, in other words, the southern coast of the present United States, and much of the coast of Mexico. Word of Garay's intention seeped back to Cuba around the time of Alvarado's arrival, and the governor—and perhaps Cortés—took notice.

---

northern coastline touching the Gulf of Mexico, however, remained unvisited and uncharted.

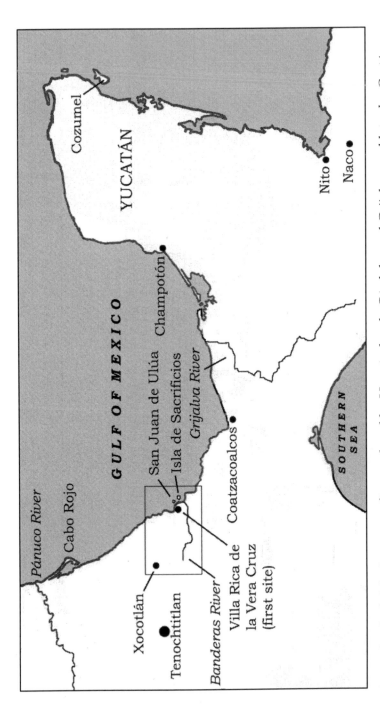

Area of today's Mexican coast first explored by Hernández de Córdoba and Grijalva, and later by Cortés. Rectangular area is detailed on the following map. Nito is in today's Guatemala, Naco in Honduras.

2

THE CORTÉS EXPEDITION

The 33-year-old Cortés had been living well in Cuba, with his Indians, his mines, his lands, his livestock, his women. He was wealthy, spending large sums on finery and high living, although he routinely outspent his income. Apart from his large debts, the only fly in the ointment for him had been his recent and apparently unsought marriage to Doña Catalina Suárez Marcaida — a requirement of the lady's family, and an event that put a temporary end to his many dalliances.[1]

Like Las Casas, Cortés felt that Spain had gone about colonization of the Indies in the wrong way. He thought a better start might be made in the lands discovered by Hernández and Grijalva than had been done on Hispaniola and Cuba. Warfare and conquest might be necessary, but warfare and conquest would have to be followed up by a responsible and intelligent colonizing effort. He itched for the chance to put his ideas into practice.

As Governor Velázquez considered that summer of 1518 whom to name captain-general of a third expedition, the governor's present secretary, Andrés de Duero, and the royal accountant, Amador de Lares, began to press him to choose his former associate Cortés, adducing the supposedly perfect set of skills that Cortés possessed for leading such an expedition. Velázquez was in fact of Cortés's mind — or at least seemed to be — on the importance of a proper colonization effort, but conquest and colonization would have to await permission from Seville.[2] With regard to Cortés, the governor had trouble seeing his former secretary's "perfect set of skills" for such an undertaking. He knew from experience, moreover, that Cortés could not be trusted.

During the summer, however, swayed by the arguments of Duero and Lares, and against his better judgment, the governor asked Cortés to lead the new expedition as captain-general. He would be charged

---

[1] Velázquez himself had been among those insisting that Cortés "do the right thing" and marry Catalina.

[2] He did, however, show extreme annoyance, on Grijalva's eventual return the following October, that a settlement had not been established in this new land.

with finding Grijalva and working together with him to establish trade with the natives of this new land. Conquest and colonization were not to be the objects of this voyage (likely since the governor planned to lead such an expedition himself when properly licensed). The governor would supply six ships.

Members of the governor's family, understanding the ambitious Cortés all too well, and the danger of his quickly freeing himself from Velázquez's control, were appalled, and urged him to reconsider. Velázquez persisted, promising Cortés the command if he would help raise the money. Cortés eagerly assented and entered enthusiastically into his new role, fully aware of the need to act quickly, since all could change in a moment. With Grijalva having returned by October, and with his four ships now assigned to Cortés, the new captain-general would have adequate resources and no requirement for cooperation with anyone.

As he began to recruit men and gather supplies, arms, and horses (paid for almost entirely by pawning possessions or begging from friends), he went out of his way to behave unctuously toward Velázquez, fawning upon the governor, even accompanying him on his rounds. But his position was precarious, with the governor having ample stimulus to reconsider his choice, as noted by Díaz in a particular incident:

> One Sunday Diego Velázquez was walking to Mass. Because he was the governor, he was accompanied on his route by the highest-ranking citizens of the city. To honor Hernando Cortés, he had seen to it that Cortés walked at his right hand.
>
> Now in front of Diego Velázquez cavorted a buffoon named Cervantes the Lunatic, making all kinds of faces and ribald jokes. He was presently crying, "Hurrah, hurrah for my master Don Diego! Oh Diego, Diego, what a captain you've chosen, a man from Medellín in Extremadura! A brave captain! But Diego, I'm afraid he might sail away with your fleet, for everyone says he knows how to take care of himself." He kept up this inanity, all with a touch of malice, until Andrés de Duero, who was walking with the governor, got tired of it and gave him a couple of slaps.
>
> "Shut up you crazy drunk," he said. "Don't be such a troublemaker. We know that this nastiness you pass off as humor isn't even coming from you, but from someone else."

Cervantes kept it up and was slapped again, but the more he was slapped the more he cried out: "Long live Don Diego, long live my master Diego and his brave captain. But let me tell you my Diego, I'd rather sail off to those rich lands with your captain than see you weep over the bad bargain you've made today." . . . And all that he said came true. **– Díaz**

As the enthusiastic yet methodical Cortés moved from town to town around the island—which happened to be in the throes of a smallpox epidemic that was wiping out hundreds of Indians daily—[1]gathering men and supplies, the warnings of doom finally had their effect on Velázquez and he revoked Cortés's commission, ordering even that Cortés be arrested and sent under guard to Santiago. But Cortés alternately wooed, threatened, or diverted virtually all the men sent to bring him in, either neutralizing them or enlisting them in his behalf. He knew, however, that his only hope of avoiding eventual arrest was a speedy exit.

Moving ever more quickly now as the winter rains came pelting down, Cortés purchased an eleventh ship (on credit), sending two vessels to Cuba's north shore to load horses and other supplies, and retaining nine vessels on the south shore at Trinidad. Crossbowmen and artillerymen were instructed to have their weapons in perfect working order, even to test their range before embarking. Cassava, salt pork, and other foodstuffs were loaded for some five hundred men. Blacksmiths were ordered to make helmets. Cotton armor was fabricated, and mangers built on board for the sixteen horses of varying quality that had been purchased or otherwise acquired.

In February 1519, not without confusion, the fleet weighed anchor and shaped a course for the coast of Yucatán, known to be the nearest point of land to the west. Cortés, having been thoroughly focused on expediting preparations so as to exit the island before he could be arrested, had not yet had time even to count his men or evaluate his resources. He knew only that he had escaped and that the future must take care of itself. His force, he knew, contained a sizeable contingent of Velázquez men, whose loyalty to him was in doubt, but they, too, could be dealt with later. He knew that the most capable men, such as Gonzalo de Sandoval and Andrés de Tapia—both in their early

---

[1] European diseases, principally smallpox, are thought to have eventually wiped out more than ninety percent of the population of the New World — tens of millions of people.

twenties—as well as the slightly older Cristóbal de Olid and the blustering, blond-bearded Pedro de Alvarado of Grijalva's expedition, could be thoroughly counted upon.[1]

On arrival at Cozumel Cortés ordered an inspection and found that he had 508 men (including a few black Africans), not counting the hundred mariners. Among the soldiers he counted about thirty crossbowmen and a dozen musketeers.[2] He had fourteen artillery pieces and sixteen horses. Cortés immediately got off on the right foot with the Indians by ordering Alvarado, who had arrived at Cozumel before him, to return or pay for all possessions that his men had already stolen, giving his captain a tongue-lashing in the bargain.

Something had been working at the back of Cortés's mind, and at this point he summoned Díaz and another soldier who had been with the Hernández expedition and asked them about it. He had heard, he told the men, that they had met Indians at Yucatán who had greeted them with cries of "Castilán, Castilán." What did they think this signified? Could there be Spaniards here among these Indians? It was decided to question the Indians about this through Melchor, the Indian who had been taken during the Hernández expedition, and who now knew a little Spanish. In response to Melchor's questioning, the Indians said, yes, there are two of your kind living across the strait, on the mainland, as slaves. Cortés was delighted and prepared letters to be taken to them. On the advice of his informants, he also sent a quantity of beads to ransom them from their owners.

While Cortés awaited the outcome of this gambit he looked at the evidence of idol worship around him, and became gradually more disturbed by it. Daringly, he ordered his men to break up the idols and roll them down the temple steps. The Indians were astounded. He then caused a cross to be made, and ordered a mason to construct an altar on which he placed an image of the Virgin. Through his Indian interpreter, he began to preach Christianity to the dumbfounded

---

[1] Alvarado, of great courage but capable of enormous cruelty, would be called The Sun by the Aztecs, possibly as much for his explosive temper as for the color of his hair.

[2] These men in Cortés's army are sometimes referred to as musketeers and sometimes as harquebusiers. In either case they were men who specialized in the use of a long and heavy smooth-bore matchlock weapon, muzzle-loading and shoulder-fired. The heavier models required a fork rest for stability.

Indians of Cozumel. Under their wide-eyed gaze, one of the two expedition priests, Juan Díaz, celebrated Mass at the new altar.

Meanwhile one of the two Spaniards living on Yucatán—Jerónimo de Aguilar—now ransomed, was in a canoe, racing across twelve miles of water from the mainland to catch up with his deliverer on Cozumel, having used some of Cortés's beads to hire Indian paddlers. When the large dugout carrying seven Indians was seen grounding upon the beach, Andrés de Tapia was sent to find out what they wanted. He was soon made to realize that one of these Indians was a Spaniard. Bernal Díaz witnessed the encounter.

As Tapia was bringing the Spaniard to Cortés, a few of the men were asking him, "Where is this Spaniard?" They were actually walking right next to him, but thought he was an Indian. He was naturally dark, and his shoulder-length hair was chopped off in the manner of an Indian slave. He was carrying a paddle on his shoulder, with one old sandal on his foot and the other tied to his belt. He was wrapped in a disgraceful old blanket and worse breechclout that covered his privates. Inside his blanket he carried a bundle that proved to be a very worn breviary.

When Cortés saw the group approach, he was as much deceived as the others. "Where is this Spaniard?" he asked Tapia. The Spaniard, who understood him, sat on his haunches, Indian fashion, and said, "I am he."

The captain then ordered that he be given clothing—shirt, jacket, breeches, cloak, and rope sandals, since he had no other clothes. The captain then questioned him about his life, what his name was, and when he had arrived in this land. The man told him, although pronouncing badly, that he was Jerónimo de Aguilar, that he was from Ecija, and that he was in Holy Orders. He and fifteen men, with two women, had been wrecked on these shores eight years ago on a voyage from Darién to . . . Santo Domingo.[1] **– Díaz**

Only he and one Gonzalo Guerrero remained of this group, he said, the others having died. Guerrero had refused to rejoin the Spaniards.

Aguilar thanked God for his liberation, and Cortés assured him he'd be well looked after and compensated. The captain

---

[1] Darién is today's eastern Panama.

then asked him about the land and peoples roundabout. Aguilar replied that, since he'd been held as a slave, the only things he knew were carrying wood and water and working in the maize fields. His longest trip had been four leagues away from his village, he said, when he'd been made to carry a load so heavy that he collapsed under its weight. But as far as he knew, there were plenty of villages in the region.

Cortés then asked him about Gonzalo Guerrero. Aguilar said that Guerrero was married and had three children. His face was tattooed, and his ears and lower lip pierced. He was a seaman from Palos, said Aguilar, and the Indians considered him quite brave. A little over a year ago, he explained, when a captain and three ships arrived at Cape Catoche (apparently referring to our expedition under Francisco Hernández de Córdoba),[1] he was the instigator of the attack against them. He was actually there, in company with a cacique from one of the larger villages.[2]

When Cortés heard this he said, "I'd love to get my hands on him and show him what's what." – **Díaz**

But in Aguilar Cortés now had a man who was fluent in Spanish and Chontal Mayan. He could now communicate with the natives of these parts, an advantage possessed by neither of his predecessors.

The fleet proceeded along the northern and down the suffocatingly humid western Yucatán coast as had the previous two expeditions, arriving at the Grijalva River in Tabasco in mid-March. Thousands of Indians awaited them on the beach. Non-threatening to Grijalva, they looked in no mood to parley with this expedition. Cortés had Aguilar speak in a kindly manner from the ship to some who were approaching in a canoe, but it did no good. They wanted to fight, and had a great numerical advantage.

Cortés succeeded in landing a party farther up the beach undetected, ordering them to hide and, on signal, to enfilade the village from front and back. When the battle came, the Spaniards gave a good accounting of themselves with crossbows, muskets, and cannon. In the lull following the first round of fighting, Cortés

---

[1] Cape Catoche, at the northeastern tip of the Yucatán peninsula, was the Hernández expedition's first landfall.

[2] *Cacique* is an Arawakan word for "chief" learned by the Spaniards in the Caribbean. They continued to use it in Mexico.

performed the ceremony of *requerimiento*, of taking possession of this land, not for Diego Velázquez, but for Charles, the King of Castile. This was his first major act of insubordination toward Velázquez, a subtle declaration to the Velázquez partisans among his force that he planned to answer directly to the king, not the governor. But it was clear that hundreds more Indians were on the way, and a great battle was shaping up for the following day. Cortés ordered the horses taken off the ships, with results that at first did not bode well.

> When Cortés saw that the Indians intended to attack, he ordered the horses taken off the ships at once, and all musketeers, crossbowmen, and soldiers — including the wounded — to be ready with our weapons. When we got the horses ashore, they were sluggish and afraid to move, having spent so many days aboard ship, but by the following day they had recovered. **– Díaz**

Some of the men, too, were unfit to fight.

> A strange thing happened that day — six or seven young, healthy men were suddenly struck with back pain. They couldn't stand up, but had to be carried piggyback. No one knew why this had occurred. Some said it was because . . . they had lived well in Cuba and were unused to a rigorous life, or to such heat. Cortés decided they should not remain on shore, and they were taken back to the ships. **– Díaz**

The ensuing bloody battle in the steamy heat was more than the Spaniards had bargained for. Horses and artillery, however, enabled them to carry the day.

> When it was over we pressed rags over our wounds, for that was all we had. The horses' wounds we cauterized, then treated with fat from the body of a dead Indian that we had cut open for that purpose. Walking the field to inspect the dead, we counted more than eight hundred, the majority of them stabbed, but many hit by cannon-fire, musketry, or crossbows. A number of them were lying half dead. Wherever the horsemen had gone there was a large harvest of the dead, with many still groaning from their wounds. This battle lasted over an hour, and we had a difficult time until the horsemen engaged. We captured five Indians, two of them captains. Since it was late and we were hungry and exhausted from fighting, we returned to camp where we buried two soldiers, one of whom had died from a thrust in the throat, and the other

from one in the ear. We continued to treat the wounds of men and horses, then set the watch, had our supper, and lay down to rest. – **Díaz**

Next day Cortés received a delegation of thirty Indians who had come to burn or bury the corpses of their fallen warriors. A higher-level delegation would be sent tomorrow, they said (through Aguilar), to arrange the peace. They then departed. Cortés, master of psychological warfare, made plans to impress this expected peace delegation.

Cortés was very astute in everything. One day when a few of us were standing around laughing and talking with him in front of his quarters he said, "You know, men, it seems to me that the Indians are really terrified of our horses. I think they suspect it's actually the horses that are fighting against them, as well as our cannon. I have an idea that may really convince them of this. Let's bring Juan Sedeño's mare, who the other day foaled aboard ship, and tie her here, where I'm standing. Then we'll bring Ortiz the musician's stallion, who is quite randy, let him get a sniff of her, then lead both mare and stallion away separately, hiding them in places where they can't be seen or heard until the Indians are here talking with me."

So it was done—they brought the mare and the stallion and he got a sniff of her at the spot where Cortés was standing. But that wasn't all. Cortés then ordered that the biggest cannon they had should to be made ready to fire a good ball with plenty of powder.

By noon, forty Indians had arrived, all caciques, dressed most handsomely and behaving politely, to greet Cortés and the rest of us. They brought their incense with them and went about burning it wherever we were standing, begging pardon all the while for what they had done, and promising better conduct in the future.

Cortés's response to them was quite solemn, even angry, and through our interpreter Aguilar, he reminded them of how many times he had tried to make peace with them, and how therefore the fault lay with them, and that what they and their people really deserved was to be simply slaughtered in their villages. He then told them that we were subjects of a great king, the emperor Charles,[1] who had sent us here to help and favor those who wished to enter his royal service. To merit this, he said, they must be peaceful and good, and if they were not, something would jump out of our *tepuzques* and kill them (tepuzque is their word for iron). Some of the tepuzques, he said, even now were angry at them for what they had done to us. He then quietly sent word to fire the cannon that stood ready, and a monstrous roar soon followed. The ball went whistling through the trees, and in the calm of midday it made a thunderous sound. The caciques were astonished. Since they had never heard such a thing, they believed that what Cortés had told them about it was true. But Cortés assured them, through Aguilar, that all was well and they should have no fear because he had ordered the tepuzques to do no harm.

At that moment they brought out the stallion who had sniffed the mare and tied him near the spot where Cortés and the caciques were talking, the spot where the mare had been tethered earlier. Catching the scent, the stallion began to stamp and paw the ground, and to neigh and snort threateningly, his eyes fixed on the Indians and on the spot where he had caught the scent. The Indians were frightened out of their wits. When Cortés saw this he rose from his chair, walked over to the stallion, and told two of his orderlies to lead him away. He returned to the Indians, assuring them that he had told the animal not to be angry, because these were good men who had come in peace. **– Díaz**

The following day was spent in receiving Indians who tried to outdo one another in the gifts they brought to the strangers: finely worked gold ornaments, golden sandal-soles, rough cloaks, and — to the delight of Cortés's men — twenty women. Cortés thanked them effusively, not immediately understanding the incalculable value of the gift he had received in the person of one of these women. He in fact gave her initially to a friend from his hometown of Medellín, Alonso Hernández Puertocarrero. All twenty women were baptized before being distributed.

---

[1] Charles had not yet been elected Holy Roman Emperor. This likely represents a slip in the memory of Díaz, who was in his seventies when he wrote his account.

Having been told by the Indians that all the gold they possessed had come from the north, from a place called Culúa, or Mexico,[1] Cortés soon gave orders to prepare the fleet for departure, but not before he had given the Indians further instruction in the faith, caused Palm Sunday Mass—complete with traditional procession—to be celebrated, and forced them to accept Christian images in place of their idols. To the undoubted relief of the natives, their strange visitors embarked the day after this celebration (albeit with their twenty women) and set sail northward.

On board ship, the men previously struck by back pain now claimed to feel better.

Word of the battle and of the strangers' movement north would reach the great king of the Mexica before mid-April, when the ships arrived at Grijalva's San Juan de Ulúa island. On Good Friday, 1519, the Spaniards disembarked among the dunes of the mainland, at the site of present-day Veracruz, Mexico.

---

[1] Mexico was the land inhabited by the Mexica, or Aztecs, a people who had migrated to this high valley in the mid-1300s, well after the peak civilizations of the Olmec, Maya, and Toltec. As newcomers they were shunted off to the worst land, the fetid shores and swampy islands of Lake Texcoco, the largest of the valley's several lakes. Through hard work and sturdy self-defense, they had slowly enlarged their island domain, and very quickly developed a well-functioning, militarily aggressive, and clearly structured society with considerable wealth, albeit one based on rule by terror. Shortly before the birth of Columbus, the Mexica of Tenochtitlan, the southern part of the principal island, allied themselves with two other states—Texcoco on the eastern lake shore and Tacuba to the west—to form what is today called the Triple Alliance, over which their ruler presided. Two decades before Columbus's arrival in the Indies they annexed the rival Mexica state of Tlatelolco, which occupied the northern part of the island. It is thought that by the early 1500s the rule of Tenochtitlan extended over 25 million people from coast to coast, from the southern portion of today's state of San Luis Potosí in the north, deep into Oaxaca in the south (with a few unconquered enclaves).

3

ESTABLISHING A FOOTHOLD

B y now Cortés had learned that the woman he had given to Puertocarrero was the key to unlocking the Mexican empire. This handsome and intelligent Indian not only knew the language of the Tabasco Maya, since she had been given away to the Maya as a child, but she was originally from Coatzacoalcos and therefore also spoke Nahuatl, the language of the Mexican empire. Cortés must have almost danced with joy. Doña Marina, as she became known after her baptism, could speak to the Totonacs — some of whom spoke Nahuatl — on the coast, and, more importantly, to the Mexica. She could translate their response into Chontal Maya for Aguilar, and he in turn could translate into Spanish for Cortés. Doña Marina, soon to be called by the Indians Malinche,[1] and — inexplicably to modern Mexicans — the willing accomplice of the Spaniards, was a codebreaker.

On being informed of the strangers' approach, Montezuma, from his palace at Tenochtitlan sent observers to the coast. The Aztec account of this mission has been preserved for us through the efforts of Franciscan priests who learned Nahuatl in the 1520s and early 1530s, and recorded the remembrances of Nahuatl-speaking eyewitnesses, in some cases fewer than ten years after the conquest.[2]

> A few days later a *macehual* [common man] came to the city from Mictlancuauhtla. No one had sent him, none of the officials; he came of his own accord. He went directly to the palace of Motecuhzoma and said to him: "Our lord and king,

---

[1] Possibly a play on her Nahuatl name. Due probably to her closeness to Cortés, he too became known as Malinche.

[2] Most of these Aztec accounts date from the 1550s and beyond, although some date from as early as 1528. The Franciscan Fray Bernardino de Sahagún was highly instrumental in the effort to create and preserve them. Despite the marvelous window they provide into the Aztec world, they are, due to the Spanish role in their translation, approached by scholars with some caution. The selections used here are from a twentieth-century translation from Nahuatl to Spanish and then from Spanish to English.

forgive my boldness. I am from Mictlancuauhtla. When I went to the shores of the great sea, there was a mountain range or small mountain floating in the midst of the water, and moving here and there without touching the shore. My lord, we have never seen the like of this; although we guard the coast and are always on watch." – **Aztec account**

Montezuma ordered men to the coast to investigate.

When they arrived in Cuetlaxtlán, the envoys spoke with the official in charge there, a man named Pinotl. He listened to them with great attention and then said: "My lords, rest here with me, and send your attendants out to the shore." The attendants went out and came back in great haste to report that it was true: they had seen two towers or small mountains floating on the waves of the sea. The grand emissary said to Pinotl: "I wish to see these things in person, in order to learn what they are, for I must testify to our lord as an eyewitness. I will be satisfied with this and will report to him exactly what I see." Therefore he went out to the shore with Cuitlalpitoc, and they saw what was floating there, beyond the edge of the water. They also saw that seven or eight of the strangers had left it in a small boat and were fishing with hooks and lines.

The grand emissary and Cuitlalpitoc climbed up into a broad-limbed tree. From there they saw how the strangers were catching fish and how, when they were done, they returned to the ship in their small boat. The grand emissary said: "Come, Cuitlalpitoc." They climbed down from the tree and went back to the village, where they took hasty leave of Pinotl. They returned as swiftly as possible to the great city of Tenochtitlan, to report to Motecuhzoma what they had observed.

When they reached the city, they went directly to the king's palace and spoke to him with all due reverence and humility: "Our lord and king, it is true that strange people have come to the shores of the great sea. They were fishing from a small boat, some with rods and others with a net. They fished until late and then they went back to their two great towers and climbed up into them. There were about fifteen of these people, some with blue jackets, others with red, others with black or green, and still others with jackets of a soiled color, very ugly, like our *ichtilmatli.*[1] There were also a few without jackets. On their heads they wore red kerchiefs, or bonnets of a fine scarlet color, and some wore large round hats like small *comales*,[2] which must have been sunshades. They have very light skin, much lighter than ours. They all have long beards, and their hair comes only to their ears."

Motecuhzoma was downcast when he heard this report, and did not speak a word. **– Aztec account**

Montezuma was downcast not only because of what his scouts had reported, but because of his mounting belief that, in the person of these strangers, the great deity Quetzalcoatl had come from the east to put an end to his kingdom.[3] He called his advisors to himself, and ordered that gifts be collected—finely worked gold, rich plumage, a collar holding a golden disk, jaguar skins, shells, a turquoise mask and mosaic, mirrors, little bells, a golden shield—and that it all be packed into baskets and carried the nearly two hundred miles to the coast for presentation to the strangers, among whom he was convinced was Quetzalcoatl, the plumed serpent.

The Spaniards spent Good Friday setting up camp among the mainland dunes. Cannon were placed where they would do the most good, horses and dogs were brought off the ships and exercised,[4] wood was gathered for the construction of huts, and an altar erected for Easter Sunday Mass. Coastal Indians—Totonacs, who assisted them in unloading and setting up—told them that important emissaries would soon be coming to greet them. On Easter Sunday these two emissaries—men named Tendile and Pitalpitoque—arrived with their heavy baskets of gifts, bowing deeply in greeting to Cortés and all his men. Cortés greeted them warmly, but held off discussions

---

[1] Rough cloaks.

[2] Dishes for baking tortillas.

[3] That this was in fact Montezuma's belief is doubted by many scholars. Since, however, the affirmation that such was his belief is made throughout the Nahuatl accounts, it will be accepted here without further comment.

[4] As the Spaniards had done throughout the conquest of the Indies, Cortés brought with him a pack of war dogs: deerhounds, wolfhounds, greyhounds, mastiffs. These ninety-pound animals were, in the words of Las Casas, "trained to tear Indians to pieces and of such ferocity that the Indians feared them more than the very devil."

until a sung Easter Mass had been celebrated in their presence. He then explained, through Aguilar and Doña Marina, that he represented the great king Charles, who wished to be friends with their prince, and who had sent Cortés to implement this friendship. He made no mention of the middle man, the governor of Cuba, who had actually granted him his commission.

Young Bernal Díaz stood by watching as Cortés began subtly to assume authority over these emissaries and, through them, over Montezuma himself.

As we later learned, this Tendile and Pitalpitoque were governors of some provinces called Cotustao, Tuxtepec, Guazpaltepeque, and Tatalteco, as well as of some provinces recently conquered [by the Aztecs]. Cortés then had someone bring an armchair, richly carved and inlaid, as well as some semi-precious stones that had been intricately worked and packed in cotton with musk, to give them a nice odor. He also had them bring a string of twisted glass beads and a crimson cap with a medal engraved with St. George on horseback slaying a dragon. He told Tendile he was sending the chair to his prince Montezuma—for we already knew his name—so that when we went to see and speak with him he might sit in it. He might also want to put the cap on his head, said Cortés. The stones and all the other things were gifts of our lord the king, who sent them in friendship, for he knew that Montezuma was a great prince. Now all we need to know, added Cortés, is when and where the great Montezuma would wish us to meet him.

Tendile accepted the gifts, remarking that his lord Montezuma would be most pleased to know our great king. He would present him with our gifts very soon, he said, and hurry back with his reply. – **Díaz**

The Spaniards were doubtless surprised at what happened next.

Tendile brought with him some of the skilled painters they have in Mexico. He had them paint realistic, full-length portraits of Cortés and of his captains and soldiers. They also created images of the ships and sails, the horses, and both Doña Marina and Aguilar, as well as two greyhounds, artillery pieces, cannonballs—indeed the whole army. All these paintings he took back to his lord Montezuma. – **Díaz**

Cortés could not let Montezuma's two ambassadors go without a sharp display of Spanish power.

> Cortés then told the gunners to load their lombards with a good powder charge,[1] so the firing would make a thunderous noise. He then told Pedro de Alvarado that he and all the horsemen should saddle up to give Montezuma's minions a sight of horses at the gallop. They were to attach bells to the horses' breast-collars. Cortés himself then mounted and said, "If we could gallop in these dunes it would be good, but they'd see that even on foot we'd get bogged down in the sand. Let's go out on the beach when the tide goes out and gallop there, two by two." He gave command of the horsemen to Pedro de Alvarado, whose sorrel mare was extremely fast and quick on the rein. The cavalry then galloped on the beach in front of Montezuma's ambassadors.
>
> In order to ensure that the Indians did not miss the lombard shots, Cortés pretended that he wanted to speak again with some of the principal men, and then, in the midst of a great stillness, the lombards were fired. The balls sailed overhead and crashed on the nearby hills with a resounding thump. The governors and all the Indians with them were astonished at such new things. They ordered it all to be painted by their artists so that their lord Montezuma might see it.
>
> – **Díaz**

The Aztec version of this meeting has a considerably different emphasis. It is clear from it that the Indians considered Cortés to be Quetzalcoatl returned.

> When they came up to the ships, the strangers asked them: "Who are you? Where are you from?"
>
> "We have come from the city of Mexico."
>
> The strangers said: "You may have come from there, or you may not have. Perhaps you are only inventing it. Perhaps you are mocking us." But their hearts were convinced; they were satisfied in their hearts. They lowered a hook from the bow of the ship, and then a ladder, and the messengers came aboard.
>
> One by one they did reverence to Cortés by touching the ground before him with their lips. They said to him: "If the god

---

[1] A lombard was a small, carriage-mounted cannon.

will deign to hear us, your deputy Motecuhzoma has sent us to render you homage. He has the city of Mexico in his care. He says: 'The god is weary.'"

Then they arrayed the captain in the finery they had brought him as presents. With great care they fastened the turquoise mask in place, the mask of the god with its crossband of quetzal feathers. A golden earring hung down on either side of this mask. They dressed him in the decorated vest and the collar woven in the petatillo style—the collar of *chalchihuites* with a disk of gold in the center.[1]

Next they fastened the mirror to his hips, dressed him in the cloak known as "the ringing bell" and adorned his feet with the greaves used by the Huastecas,[2] which were set with chalchihuites and hung with little gold bells. In his hand they placed the shield with its fringe and pendant of quetzal feathers, its ornaments of gold and mother-of-pearl. Finally they set before him the pair of black sandals. As for the other objects of divine finery, they only laid them out for him to see.

The captain asked them: "And is this all? Is this your gift of welcome? Is this how you greet people?"

They replied: "This is all, our lord. This is what we have brought you." – **Aztec account**

The Indian account contains details not even hinted at by Díaz.

Then the captain gave orders, and the messengers were chained by the feet and by the neck. When this had been done, the great cannon was fired off. The messengers lost their senses and fainted away. They fell down side by side and lay where they had fallen. But the Spaniards quickly revived them: they lifted them up, gave them wine to drink and then offered them food. – **Aztec account**

Mixing apparent bonhomie with a smiling threat of violence, Cortés now made a proposition to these likely soft-bodied officials, a proposition calculated to terrify them.

The captain said to them: "I have heard that the Mexicans are very great warriors, very brave and terrible. If a Mexican is

---

[1] *Chalchihuites* were jadeite stones, much valued by Indians and Spaniards alike.
[2] Indians of a region of modern Mexico between the Sierra Madre Oriental mountain range and the Gulf of Mexico.

fighting alone, he knows how to retreat, turn back, rush forward and conquer, even if his opponents are ten or even twenty. But my heart is not convinced. I want to see it for myself. I want to find out if you are truly that strong and brave."

Then he gave them swords, spears and leather shields. He said: "It will take place very early, at daybreak. We are going to fight each other in pairs, and in this way we will learn the truth. We will see who falls to the ground!"

They said to the captain: "Our lord, we were not sent here for this by your deputy Motecuhzoma! We have come on an exclusive mission, to offer you rest and repose and to bring you presents. What the lord desires is not within our warrant. If we were to do this, it might anger Motecuhzoma, and he would surely put us to death."

The captain replied: "No, it must take place. I want to see for myself, because even in Castile they say you are famous as brave warriors. Therefore, eat an early meal. I will eat too. Good cheer!"

With these words he sent them away from the ship. They were scarcely into their canoes when they began to paddle furiously. Some of them even paddled with their hands, so fierce was the anxiety burning in their souls. They said to each other: "My captains, paddle with all your might! Faster, faster! Nothing must happen to us here! Nothing must happen . . .!"

Then they left in great haste and continued to the city of Mexico. **– Aztec account**

Many miles away, in Tenochtitlan, Montezuma was pacing the floor of his palace.

While the messengers were away, Motecuhzoma could neither sleep nor eat, and no one could speak with him. He thought that everything he did was in vain, and he sighed almost every moment. He was lost in despair, in the deepest gloom and sorrow. Nothing could comfort him, nothing could calm him, nothing could give him any pleasure.

He said: "What will happen to us? Who will outlive it? Ah, in other times I was contented, but now I have death in my heart! My heart burns and suffers, as if it were drowned in spices . . .! But will our lord come here?"

Then he gave orders to the watchmen, to the men who guarded the palace: "Tell me, even if I am sleeping: 'The messengers have come back from the sea.'" But when they went to tell him, he immediately said: "They are not to report to me here. I will receive them in the House of the Serpent. Tell them to go there." And he gave this order: "Two captives are to be painted with chalk."[1]

The messengers went to the House of the Serpent, and Motecuhzoma arrived. The two captives were then sacrificed before his eyes: their breasts were tom open, and the messengers were sprinkled with their blood. This was done because the messengers had completed a difficult mission: they had seen the gods, their eyes had looked on their faces. They had even conversed with the gods! – **Aztec account**

Montezuma ordered that the messengers be brought before him to make their report.

When the sacrifice was finished, the messengers reported to the king. They told him how they had made the journey and what they had seen, and what food the strangers ate. Motecuhzoma was astonished and terrified by their report, and the description of the strangers' food astonished him above all else.

He was also terrified to learn how the cannon roared, how its noise resounded, how it caused one to faint and grow deaf. The messengers told him: "A thing like a ball of stone comes out of its entrails: it comes out shooting sparks and raining fire. The smoke that comes out with it has a pestilent odor, like that of rotten mud. This odor penetrates even to the brain and causes the greatest discomfort. If the cannon is aimed against a mountain, the mountain splits and cracks open. If it is aimed against a tree, it shatters the tree into splinters. This is a most unnatural sight, as if the tree had exploded from within."

The messengers also said: "Their trappings and arms are all made of iron. They dress in iron and wear iron casques on their heads. Their swords are iron; their bows are iron; their shields are iron; their spears are iron. Their deer carry them on their backs wherever they wish to go. These deer, our lord, are as tall as the roof of a house.

---

[1] A prelude to being sacrificed.

"The strangers' bodies are completely covered, so that only their faces can be seen. Their skin is white, as if it were made of lime. They have yellow hair, though some of them have black. Their beards are long and yellow, and their moustaches are also yellow. Their hair is curly, with very fine strands.

"As for their food, it is like human food. It is large and white, and not heavy. It is something like straw, but with the taste of a cornstalk, of the pith of a cornstalk. It is a little sweet, as if it were flavored with honey; it tastes of honey, it is sweet-tasting food.

"Their dogs are enormous, with flat ears and long, dangling tongues. The color of their eyes is a burning yellow; their eyes flash fire and shoot off sparks. Their bellies are hollow, their flanks long and narrow. They are tireless and very powerful. They bound here and there, panting, with their tongues hanging out. And they are spotted like an ocelot."

When Motecuhzoma heard this report, he was filled with terror. It was as if his heart had fainted, as if it had shriveled. It was as if he were conquered by despair. **– Aztec account**

Montezuma resolved to propitiate these fierce gods, no matter what the cost. He sent out another delegation.

It was at this time that Motecuhzoma sent out a deputation. He sent out his most gifted men, his prophets and wizards, as many as he could gather. He also sent out his noblest and bravest warriors. They had to take their provisions with them on the journey: live hens and hens' eggs and tortillas. They also took whatever the strangers might request, or whatever might please them.

Motecuhzoma also sent captives to be sacrificed, because the strangers might wish to drink their blood. The envoys sacrificed these captives in the presence of the strangers, but when the white men saw this done, they were filled with disgust and loathing. They spat on the ground, or wiped away their tears, or closed their eyes and shook their heads in abhorrence. They refused to eat the food that was sprinkled with blood, because it reeked of it; it sickened them, as if the blood had rotted.

Motecuhzoma ordered the sacrifice because he took the Spaniards to be gods; he believed in them and worshiped them as deities. That is why they were called "Gods who have come from heaven." . . .

Then the strangers ate the tortillas, the eggs and the hens and fruit of every variety: guavas, avocados, prickly pears and the many other kinds that grow here. There was food for the "deer" also: reed shoots and green grasses.

Motecuhzoma had sent the magicians to learn what sort of people the strangers might be, but they were also to see if they could work some charm against them, or do them some mischief. They might be able to direct a harmful wind against them, or cause them to break out in sores, or injure them in some way. Or they might be able to repeat some enchanted word, over and over, that would cause them to fall sick, or die, or return to their own land.

The magicians carried out their mission against the Spaniards, but they failed completely. They could not harm them in any way whatever. – **Aztec account**
The Aztec emissaries returned to Tenochtitlan.

During these conversations, Cortés had sent ships farther up the coast to scout out a more salubrious location for a settlement. At the same time he was coming to grips with discontent among the large Velázquez faction in his army. These men, thoroughly aware of his intention to cast off control by the governor, accused him of deceit, claiming he had no authority to settle, but only to trade, and demanded an immediate return to Cuba. Cortés offered soothing words in return, putting off a confrontation for as long as possible.

4

CEMPOALA AND VILLA RICA

Five Totonacs now arrived from Cempoala, an inland city about thirty miles to the north. They had heard of the strangers, they said. Their chief was extending them an invitation to visit his village, and possibly to perform a service for him. Cortés was soon made to understand what that service might be: defense against Montezuma. This was exactly what he wished to hear—he was not facing a monolithic Indian society after all, but a society that had cracks. Cracked edifices could be torn down. He promised the emissaries that he would come soon.

The pilots sent up the coast had returned, reporting on a more suitable site for a base camp thirty-six miles north near a fortified place called Quiahuiztlán. They also reported a very fine harbor there. Prior to moving to this place, however, Cortés decided it was time for a bold stroke, one intended to formalize his break with the governor of Cuba. He orchestrated a "demand" by the majority that their present camp be established as a town, to be called Villa Rica de la Vera Cruz. This town would be chartered under the authority not of Diego Velázquez, but of the king. Gracefully acceding to the majority's demand, Cortés appointed officers of the town council, and then resigned his commission under Velázquez. He was pleased then to accept an appointment from the town council to the same position—captain-general and chief justice—but now to serve under the direct authority of the Crown. The Velázquez men were outraged at this transparent charade, and their anger and loudly expressed desire for an immediate return to Cuba threatened seriously to undermine Cortés's effort to create a unified force. Needing every able-bodied man, he brought some of them around to his way of thinking with gifts of gold, and briefly arrested others. His supporters stood ready to protect him and to execute any directive with respect to the Velázquez partisans.

With his usual mix of cunning and latent menace, Cortés had won another skirmish. He had absolutely no authority to act in this manner, and no idea how his actions would be viewed by the Crown. He depended only upon his as yet unproven success against the great Aztec empire—and the remittance of its reputed wealth to the royal treasury—to eventually validate his conduct. It was a very long shot.

Cortés and his men then marched up the coast toward Quiahuiztlán, the ships proceeding there as well, but on the way they encountered further Indian emissaries from Cempoala. These explained to Cortés that their village in fact lay on the road to Quiahuiztlán, and that their cacique would very pleased to welcome the strangers to his village. Since, however, the cacique was too fat to come out in person to meet the strangers, they explained, they had been sent to conduct them into his presence.

The Spaniards were led to an attractive settlement, prosperous and luxuriously vegetated. Like other Indian villages of this land, it boasted a high, truncated pyramid where human sacrifices were carried out. The men were at length brought into the presence of the fat cacique, who offered them baskets of plums, maize cakes, and a small gift of gold jewelry and cloth. Cortés accepted all with his usual graciousness and flattering remarks, and promised the services of his men in return.

> Cortés told him, through Doña Marina and Aguilar, that he would repay this gift in services, that if the cacique would only tell him what needed to be done, we would do it, for we were vassals of a great lord, the emperor Charles, who ruled over many kingdoms and lands, and who had sent us to right wrongs, to punish evildoers, and to see that human sacrifices ceased. He also told them many things about our holy faith.

> On hearing this, the fat cacique heaved a great sigh and began to complain bitterly about the great Montezuma and his governors, explaining that, a short while ago, the Mexicans had brought his people into subjection. All their golden jewelry had been stolen and they had been oppressed so heavily that the only thing they could do was obey. Montezuma was, after all, lord of great cities and lands, with countless vassals and great armies.

> Cortés, knowing he could do nothing to help at the moment, assured the cacique that all these wrongs would soon be set right. **– Díaz**

Cortés explained to the fat cacique that he would be leaving next day for his ships anchored off Quiahuiztlán, a short march north. The fat cacique cemented Cortés's good will by having four hundred porters ready to carry the Spaniards' baggage the following morning.

Next day, after a friendly reception from the inhabitants of Quiahuiztlán, the Spaniards were treated to the same litany of complaints that they had heard from the Cempoalans. But as Cortés chatted with their caciques, breathless messengers arrived to tell him that the fat cacique himself was on his way to Quiahuiztlán. He was in fact arriving at that very moment on a litter borne by heavily sweating Cempoalan dignitaries.

On his arrival the fat cacique immediately joined the other caciques and principal men of that town in complaining about Montezuma. They described his far-reaching power with great emotion, so that Cortés and all we who heard it were deeply affected. In addition to telling us how they had been defeated, they described how every year the Mexicans demanded a number of their children for sacrifice, as well as other children to take into their houses and fields as servants and workers. They had so many complaints that I can't remember them all. They said that Montezuma's tax-gatherers took away the most beautiful of their women and girls and raped them, and did the same throughout the more than thirty villages where the Totonac language was spoken.

Cortés, through our interpreters, attempted to console them as much as he could, promising that he would help in any way possible, that he would put an end to all these crimes. For this very reason, he told them, our lord the emperor Charles had sent him. They should have no fear, he assured them. They would soon see how we would fix this.

His hearers seemed somewhat comforted by these words, but they had in no way lost their mortal dread of the Mexicans.
– Díaz

At this point—as happened frequently in Cortés's life—fate intervened to give him an advantage.

While they were engaged in this conversation, some of the village Indians rushed in to tell the caciques who were talking to Cortés that five Mexicans, Montezuma's tax-gatherers, were on their way. The caciques, on hearing these words, blanched and began to tremble. They left Cortés and hurried out to greet the Mexicans. Then very quickly a room was decorated with flowers, food was put on to cook, and a large quantity of chocolate—the finest drink they have—was prepared.

When the five Indians came to where we were, because ours and the cacique's lodgings were together, they passed by us with an air of great arrogance and disdain, speaking neither to Cortés nor to any of us who were standing about. They wore beautifully embroidered cloaks and loincloths (in those days loincloths were still worn). They had shining hair, tied up high on their heads, and each one carried a few roses which he sniffed from time to time. The five men were attended by servants with fly-whisks to keep insects away. Each man carried a kind of shepherd's crook in his hand. The group was accompanied by the head men of other Totonac villages, who stayed with the officials until they reached their lodgings, where they were fed most excellently.

Once the officials had dined, they summoned the fat cacique and the most important chiefs. They then scolded them for having us as guests in their villages, since now they would have to meet and speak with us. Their lord Montezuma would not be pleased by all this, they said. Without his royal license no one could trade in golden jewels. They continued to reproach the fat cacique and the others over this matter. "In fact," they concluded, "we'll need twenty of your people, male and female, to appease our gods for the wrongs that have been done here." **– Díaz**

Cortés, sensing what was happening, decided the moment had come to go all in. After having the facts clarified for him by Doña Marina and Aguilar, he made a private suggestion that utterly shocked his hosts.

Cortés asked Doña Marina and Aguilar why the caciques had been so agitated since these Indians arrived—and who were these Indians anyway? Doña Marina, who knew very well what was going on, explained it all to him. . . . As soon as Cortés understood all this he reminded the caciques of what he had told them on other occasions, namely, that our lord the king had sent him here to punish evildoers, and to put an end to human sacrifice and other crimes. And because of the demands made by these tax-gatherers, they should simply be arrested and imprisoned until their lord Montezuma could be told of their robbery, their taking of Totonac women and children as slaves, and their other violent affronts.

When the caciques heard this they were appalled at his daring. To order the maltreatment of the great Montezuma's ambassadors was too frightening—they dare not do such a thing. But Cortés insisted and they did it—they seized the tax-gatherers and imprisoned them. They locked them into collars fixed to poles, according to their custom, in such a way that escape was impossible. One of them, who would not submit to being detained, they beat with sticks. Cortés now told the caciques to pay no more tribute to Montezuma and to obey him no longer, and to publicize their refusal among friends and allies. And if tax-gatherers should show up in other villages, he was to be notified and he would send for them.

The news spread quickly across the region, because the fat cacique now sent messengers all over. Moreover the chiefs who had accompanied the tax-gatherers on their rounds, having now seen the officials arrested, dispersed and went each to his own village to . . . tell of these events. **– Díaz**

Having moved boldly against the Velázquez men earlier, Cortés had now made a bold move against Montezuma. The first of his cards were on the table, but the game, he knew, would be complicated.

In order to keep the prisoners from ever telling what had been done here, the caciques and all the village wanted to sacrifice them. When Cortés heard this he ordered them not to do it, saying that he himself would take charge of the prisoners, and he set a guard of soldiers over them. At midnight he summoned one of these soldiers and said, "Select the two most intelligent of these prisoners and bring them to me. Don't let anyone in the village see you."

When the two had been brought before him he asked them through our interpreters where they were from and why they were being held, as if he knew nothing about the matter. They replied that the caciques of Cempoala, with the help of our men, had seized them. Cortés responded that this was a pity, and that he had known nothing about it. He had food brought to them, and, with many flattering words, told them to go back to their lord Montezuma, and to tell him that he and the Spaniards were his friends and servants, that he had sent them home so that nothing further would happen to them, and that he had quarreled with the caciques of Cempoala over their seizure. He would, he said, very willingly do whatever was necessary to serve their great prince Montezuma. He promised to see the other three Indians released, and told these two to be on their way quickly and not to return, for they might well be rearrested and killed.

The two Indians thanked him profusely, but said they would have to pass through hostile Cempoalan territory to arrive home, and were afraid of being recaptured. Cortés therefore ordered six seamen to row them four leagues up the coast that very night, and to put them ashore beyond the boundaries of Cempoala.

Next morning when the caciques found the two prisoners missing, their determination to execute the other three was redoubled. Cortés, feigning anger that the two prisoners had escaped, ordered a chain brought from one of the ships. He shackled the remaining three with it and had them brought aboard ship, telling the caciques that since they couldn't seem to keep a good watch over prisoners he would see to it himself. Once he had the three aboard ship he removed the chain, and with friendly words promised the men that they would soon be sent back to Mexico. **– Díaz**

Cortés's audaciousness in seizing the Mexicans did not, however, magically put starch into Cempoalan backbones. They greatly feared Montezuma's reaction. With his long-term goal of recruiting these men into his army, Cortés very happily promised them protection from this threat.

After these events, all the caciques of this village and of Cempoala, and of all the other villages where the Totonac language was spoken, asked Cortés what was to be done now, for all the might of the Mexicans would surely be unleashed against them, and their destruction and death would be inevitable. Cortés told them to cheer up, that he and his comrades would be there to defend them, and that we would kill anyone who attempted to injure them.

The caciques therefore all promised to join the Spaniards in a single alliance against Montezuma, and to be commanded by them in everything. In the presence of the notary Diego de Godoy, they swore allegiance to His Majesty, sending news of their action around to all their villages. Since they no longer had to pay tribute and since Montezuma's tax-gatherers no longer bothered them, they were beside themselves with joy at having cast off the Mexican tyranny. **– Díaz**

Now assured of the loyalty of these coastal Indians, Cortés took advantage of their good will by asking their help in constructing a new Spanish settlement at this place—near Quiahuiztlán—a town to be called, like the earlier settlement, Villa Rica de la Vera Cruz.[1] A church, a marketplace, arsenals, and a fort would be constructed. Cortés himself took the lead in carrying stone and digging. The men, assisted by the now-indebted Indians, worked quickly. As the work progressed, emissaries arrived from Montezuma with a renewed demand for tribute from the coastal Indians. Cortés patiently explained that they were his Indians now, and that no man can serve two masters. No further tribute would be forthcoming, he said. He added that this matter could be arranged to everyone's satisfaction when he arrived in Mexico to speak with the great Montezuma personally. The disgruntled emissaries were asked to relay this message to their prince.

The fat cacique, by now entirely confident in the strangers' good will, and even referring to them as *teules*, or gods, asked Cortés to go to a mountain town — Cingapacinga — two days march from Cempoala and deal with the Mexica Indians who were destroying Cempoalan crops in that area. After dramatically stamping out yet another rebellion against him by the Velázquez faction, Cortés took horses, cannon, four hundred Spaniards, and two thousand Cempoalans through Cempoala to the cliffs of Cingapacinga. On arrival, he was informed by the Cingapacingans that Mexica troops were no longer there, and that he had stepped into an old feud between themselves and the Cempoalans, whose purpose in coming was to loot them with the Spaniards' protection. After hearing their testimony, Cortés turned sharply upon the Cempoalans, lecturing them sternly on the lies they had told him about these their neighbors. The Cingapacingans admired his evenhandedness enough to swear obedience to far-off King Charles. They also begged the strangers' protection against the Mexicans.

The Spanish force, followed by two thousand now-chastened Cempoalans, turned back to Cempoala. The fat cacique, quickly informed of what had taken place, was awaiting them with apologies and food near some huts outside the town. He had prepared a further gift calculated to renew his bond with these powerful and confident strangers.

> We spent the night in these tiny huts, then all the caciques came out and brought us to lodgings within their village. They clearly did not want us to leave their lands, since they were

---

[1] The earlier coastal settlement was abandoned.

deathly afraid that Montezuma would send his warriors out against them. They told Cortés that, since we were now their friends, and they wished us to be their brothers, we should take their daughters and nieces and have children by them. To encourage us in this they brought out eight girls, all daughters of caciques, and presented one of them—the fat cacique's niece—to Cortés. Another—the daughter of a cacique named Cuesco—they presented to Alonso Hernández Puertocarrero. All the girls were dressed in richly embroidered long shirts, and each wore a gold collar around her neck and gold earrings in her ears. They were all accompanied by female servants. The fat cacique, when he presented the girls, said to Cortés, "*Tecle* (which in their language means lord), these seven girls are for your captains, and this one, my niece, is for you. She is highborn, a ruler in her own right." **– Díaz**

Cortés saw in this gift yet another way to advance his aims.

Cortés received the gift of the women very graciously, and expressed his deep gratitude. But, he said, in order to accept the girls and to become brothers in the manner suggested, it would be necessary that they cease believing in and worshipping these idols, and that they cease making human sacrifices. When he saw those accursed idols thrown down on the ground, he said, and human sacrifice at an end, their brotherhood would be cemented much more firmly. He announced that these girls would have to become Christians before we could accept them. The caciques, he continued, would also have to outlaw sodomy. He had seen numerous young men dressed as women, offering services in that line for a fee. Furthermore, he knew that they were sacrificing three, four, five Indians every day, offering their hearts to their idols, plastering the victims' blood on the temple walls, hacking off arms and legs, and then eating their flesh as we in our country would consume beef from the butcher. (I believe they were actually taking this human flesh to the *tianguez*, or market.) He told them that if they desisted from these filthy practices, not only would we be their friends, but we would give them even more provinces to rule.

All the caciques, *papas*,[1] and other dignitaries replied that they could not possibly forsake their idols and sacrifices, for their gods gave them health and good harvests and all else that they needed. As for sodomy, they promised to put measures in place to stop it. **– Díaz**

The captain-general found this reply not only weak but offensive. He turned to his men for support.

When Cortés and the rest of us heard this insolent reply, having witnessed so many cruelties and obscenities in the past, we could take it no longer. Cortés reminded us of the doctrines of our holy religion, asking us how we could hope to accomplish anything worthwhile unless we honored God by putting an end to these human sacrifices. The idols must come down today, he said, and if they mean to prevent us we must be ready to fight if it cost us our lives.

Since we were, as usual, already well armed and ready to fight, Cortés told the caciques at once that the idols had to come down. When the fat cacique realized what was happening, he alerted his own captains to be ready to fight in the idols' defense.

Before we could climb up the high *cue*,[2] their temple — which had I don't know how many steps — the fat cacique and other dignitaries, furious and agitated, demanded to know why we wished to destroy their gods. If their idols were desecrated or thrown down, they said, they would all perish, and we with them. Cortés responded angrily that he had told them many times not to sacrifice to these evil images. He had done this, he said, to keep them from being further duped by false beliefs. He vowed that if they did not remove the idols themselves, and immediately, we intended to climb up there ourselves and roll them down the steps. He added that we no longer regarded the Cempoalans as friends, but as mortal enemies, since they had rejected all our good advice.

Fully aware that their troops were formed up and ready to fight, Cortés shouted that he was angry with them all and that they would pay for this with their lives.

---

[1] Indian priests.

[2] The truncated pyramid on top of which sacrifices were carried out.

Hearing Cortés's fearsome threats—and our interpreter Doña Marina not only knew very well how to translate them, but also how to add on her own the threat of leaving them all to Montezuma's tender mercies—the caciques began to back down. They were unworthy, they said, to approach their gods, but if the Spaniards wished to do so—though it be without their consent—we could climb up and throw the idols down the steps, or do whatever else we wished.

No sooner had the words left their mouths than more than fifty of us soldiers scaled the cue and rolled the idols down, smashing them to bits. **– Díaz**

A group of Cempoalan warriors, in a rage at this effrontery, drew back their bows in threat against the Spaniards. In reply Cortés seized the fat cacique and a few papas, threatening to kill them, and tempers began to cool.

Once the caciques and papas and all the other dignitaries had calmed down, Cortés commanded that all the pieces of the idols that we had smashed be taken out of sight and burned. Eight papas therefore came out of their quarters, picked up the pieces of their idols, carried them back to their house, and burned them.

These papas wear a close-fitting robe that reaches to their feet—something like a priest's soutane or a student's gown. They also wear a sort of hood, some of these hoods being long like a canon's, and others shorter, like those of the Dominicans. Their hair they let grow down to the waist, some even to the feet. Their hair is so tangled and matted with blood that it can't be pulled apart. Their ears they chop up in a spirit of sacrifice. They smell of sulfur and decaying flesh. As they told us, and as we ourselves soon noticed, these papas, the sons of high-ranking men, do not have women, but they engage in the foul practice of sodomy. They observe fast-days. The only thing I've ever seen them eat is a little pith or seed of cotton when it's being cleaned. Possibly they eat other things that I haven't seen. **– Díaz**

In control once again, Cortés sought to mollify his hosts, little by little tightening his grip upon them.

Cortés now told them, through our interpreters, that this was the moment when we might become brothers to them. We would now be able to help them in every way possible against

Montezuma and his Mexicans, whom we had already warned not to make war upon these provinces, nor demand tribute of them.

Now that the cues had been emptied of idols, said Cortés, they must install there an image of a great lady, the mother of Our Lord Jesus Christ, whom we believe in and worship. He prayed that they too might regard this lady as their advocate and intercessor. He spoke eloquently on these topics, holding their attention, explaining our holy faith as well as any churchman might have done. He then ordered them to bring all the masons they could find, as well as large quantities of lime. They were to scrub the blood away from the walls of the temple at the top of the cue, then whitewash the walls and construct an altar there.

When the altar had been built, it was covered with fine cloths and adorned with the most beautiful and fragrant roses that could be found. Cortés ordered the room to be filled with flowers and fresh greenery, and to be kept swept and clean.

To take charge of this chapel he appointed four papas, whom he made to cut off their long hair and to dress themselves in white robes instead of their customary clothing. They were to keep themselves clean, he warned, and see to it that the chapel with the image of Our Lady was kept clean and well adorned. To oversee this operation he appointed an old lame veteran named Juan de Torres, from Córdoba. He was to remain here when the rest had gone, to ensure that the papas fulfilled their duties as ordered.

When all this was done, Cortés had our carpenters fabricate a cross and set it upon a pedestal that had recently been mortared together and whitewashed. **– Díaz**

Since the Cempoalans were by now thoroughly cowed, Cortés had no fear of pushing them further.

Next morning Mass was celebrated on the new altar by Fray Bartolomé de Olmedo.[1] The Indians had been ordered to burn their local incense before the holy image of Our Lady, and before the holy cross, and we had shown them how to make

---

[1] A priest of the Order of *Merced* (Mercy), frequently referred to by Díaz as the Mercedarian friar. He was used by Cortés for diplomatic missions, and seems to have had some influence over his captain-general.

candles out of local wax—they had never tried to do this before—ordering them to keep these candles burning before the altar.

A large number of caciques were at the Mass, many from other villages. The eight Indian girls, still living with their families, were also there. They were to be baptized at this Mass. They were told that they were no longer to make human sacrifices to idols, that all they had to do was believe in Our Lord God. A number of things regarding our holy faith were explained to them, and then they were baptized. The fat cacique's niece, who was quite ugly, was given the name of Doña Catalina. Her hand was placed in the hand of Cortés, who received her very amiably. The daughter of Cuesco, a powerful chief, was given the name of Doña Francisca. Very beautiful for an Indian, she was given to Alonso Hernández Puertocarrero. I don't remember the names of the other six, but Cortés gave them to various soldiers.

Following these events, we headed back to Villa Rica. We took our leave of all the caciques and dignitaries, who from then on had the warmest affection for us, especially since we had received their daughters so tenderly and taken them with us, and because Cortés had reaffirmed his intention to assist them in any of their future needs. **– Díaz**

Cortés now finished a letter he had been composing to the king, gathered up all the treasure he could find, loaded it upon a caravel, and, in late July 1519, dispatched it to Castile. The ship was commanded by two men in whom Cortés placed great trust, one of them Puertocarrero.[1] Nearly waylaid by Velázquez during a stop in Cuba, the men nonetheless made it to Spain, where Cortés's account of events was eventually (March 1520) made known to the young king and emperor.[2] Along with Cortés's letter another was delivered to the king from the officials of the new town of Villa Rica, giving their

---

[1] Puertocarrero of course had of necessity surrendered the invaluable Doña Marina, who became inseparable from Cortés—at his side through countless battles, his translator in every contact with friendly or hostile Indians, and eventually his mistress. In 1522 she would bear him a son.
[2] This letter, doubtless carefully written to present the writer in the most favorable light, has never been found.

supporting version of events. Perhaps most importantly, the messengers presented the monarch with the so-called royal fifth — twenty percent of all gold and jewels acquired so far. Producing awe throughout the court, this treasure no doubt raised Cortés considerably in the estimation of the 20-year-old monarch, but did not yet lead to royal approval of his expedition. Velázquez had powerful friends in Spain — notably Bishop Fonseca — who were working strenuously to see that this did not occur. In Cuba, meanwhile, Velázquez himself was scrambling to recruit enough men to bring his rebellious captain-general back by force.

Shortly after sending the envoys off to Spain, in the summer of 1519, Cortés had to quell yet another rebellion by the Velázquez faction, men who were increasingly angry at being kept in this land against their will. It came to light that they had been preparing to steal a ship, sail it to Cuba, and report to Velázquez. On learning of the plot, Cortés saw that a soft approach would no longer do. He had the ringleaders arrested and sentenced two of them to be hanged.[1] Another was to have his feet cut off, and several sailors from Gibraltar were to be given two hundred lashes apiece. With the possible exception of the floggings, the sentences do not seem to have been carried out, perhaps because Cortés was reminded by his captains that he would need every man he could get for the march inland. The time had come to get these men away from the coast, away from the temptation of a return to Cuba, and to begin moving toward Tenochtitlan. To Cortés it was clear that most of the men were ready. But both Cortés and his supporters knew that, in order to absolutely remove the possibility of a return to Cuba, one thing remained to be done.

> We were standing around Cempoala one day, discussing military affairs with Cortés, including the rough road that lay ahead. We who were his friends advised him strongly against leaving a single ship in port. He must destroy them all, we said, so as to leave no cause of trouble behind, for if the ships remained, rebellion might break out as it once already had. A further advantage of destroying the ships, we argued, would be the addition of their officers and crews to our force, nearly a hundred men. Far better, we said, for them to be helping us

---

[1] One of those arrested was the priest, Juan Díaz.

fight than to be sitting around in port. Others of our company spoke against this idea.

From what I could judge, Cortés had had the same idea, but he wanted to hear it from us. The reason: if payment were later required for the loss of these ships, he could say that their destruction was our idea, and we would have to share in the repayment.

He now sent his great friend Juan de Escalante—who was not only a brave man and the chief constable, but also an enemy of Diego Velázquez (because he had never given him any good Indians in Cuba)—to bring ashore all the anchors, cables, sails, and anything else of value from the ships, and then to destroy them, leaving only the boats. He ordered further that any seamen unfit for battle should remain at Villa Rica. They were to be left with the two nets they possessed, for there were always fish in that harbor, though not many.

Juan de Escalante carried out this order, after which he came to Cempoala leading a company of seamen, some of whom turned out to be excellent soldiers. – **Díaz**

As Cortés was sending men back to Villa Rica to scuttle the ships, the fuming Velázquez, in Cuba, was finishing the assembly of a military force to send against his former secretary. These troops were not only to halt the progress of his illegal expedition, but to bring him home in chains.

As for Montezuma, his informants on the coast now brought him the news that the strangers, still intent upon meeting the great prince of the valley of Mexico, were preparing to head inland.

When Motecuhzoma heard that they were inquiring about his person, and when he learned that the "gods" wished to see him face to face, his heart shrank within him and he was filled with anguish. He wanted to run away and hide; he thought of evading the "gods," of escaping to hide in a cave.

He spoke of this to certain trusted counselors who were not faint-hearted, whose hearts were still firm and resolute. They said: "There is the Place of the Dead, the House of the Sun, the Land of Tlaloc, or the Temple of Cintli. You should go to one or another, to whichever you prefer." Motecuhzoma knew what he desired: to go to the Temple of Cintli. And his desire was made known; it was revealed to the people.

But he could not do it. He could not run away, could not go into hiding. He had lost his strength and his spirit, and could do nothing. The magicians' words had overwhelmed his heart; they had vanquished his heart and thrown him into confusion, so that now he was weak and listless and too uncertain to make a decision.

Therefore he did nothing but wait. He did nothing but resign himself and wait for them to come. He mastered his heart at last, and waited for whatever was to happen. – **Aztec account**

The ships having now been scuttled—to the dismay of many of Cortés's men—Cortés, still in Cempoala, took Juan de Escalante by the hand in front of all Indians there assembled, as well as the sixty or so old or sick men he was leaving to garrison the settlement at Villa Rica, and announced that he was leaving Escalante in command, and that he was to be obeyed as Cortés himself.

But just as the army was about to set out, yet another brushfire had to be extinguished. A Spanish ship had been sighted sailing along the coast; it had even landed a small scouting party. This happened to be one of the ships of Alonso Álvarez de Pineda, who had been sent earlier that year by Francisco de Garay, governor of Jamaica, to explore the coastline to the north and west of Cuba. Stung by this intrusion into what he already regarded as his private fiefdom, Cortés hurried to meet the interlopers, capturing six men and causing the ship to flee.[1]

His attention then returned to the matter at hand, the march into the Valley of Mexico.

---

[1] Cortés had attempted to seize the ship as well. Garay had Crown authority not only for such a voyage of exploration but even for establishment of a settlement. He would in fact soon attempt to establish a town on the Pánuco River, some two hundred miles north of Villa Rica, near present-day Tampico—a settlement that would become a thorn in Cortés's side.

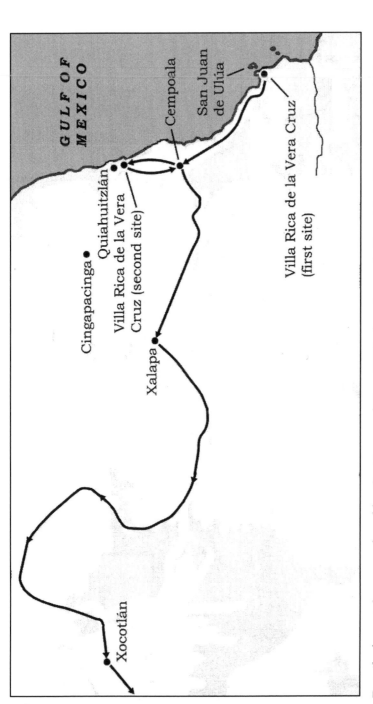

Detail of coastal area explored by Cortés expedition, 1519, showing early Spanish settlements, selected Indian towns, and first stages of march to Tenochtitlan.

5

THE ROAD TO TENOCHTITLAN

One day in August 1519, accompanied by forty Indian chiefs and two hundred porters to assist with artillery, the expedition set out: the small Spanish army began its climb into the chilly mountains towards Xalapa, which they reached in two days.[1] Since the strangers' intent to free this region from service to Mexico was known, their reception in villages along the way was uniformly good. Yet the Spaniards had other problems—accustomed to hot, humid coastal weather, they were totally unprepared for the mountain cold.

> We now entered an unpopulated country where it was very cold, with hail and rain. We were short of food that night, and a sharp wind blowing from the snowy heights off to one side made us shiver all night. We had, after all, come from Cuba, and then from a very hot coast at Villa Rica, and we had brought nothing to cover ourselves with but our armor. We felt the cold intensely.
>
> From there we came to another pass, where we found a collection of houses with great cues. We noted large piles of firewood there for the service of the idols. At that time we had nothing to eat, and the cold was piercing. We soon came to the lands of a town called Xocotlán,[2] where we sent in two Cempoalan Indians to tell the cacique that we were arriving, in

---

[1] As Cortés was setting out on his mission to Tenochtitlan, the Portuguese Fernão de Magalhães, or Ferdinand Magellan, sailing for Spain, was leaving on a westward voyage—sailing around continents as necessary—whose goal in part was to see where in fact the Indies lay and to ascertain whether the Portuguese, who were by now trading there, were poaching in Spain's half of the globe. (Lacking the capacity to determine longitude with accuracy, it would have been impossible for any mariner to prove such a case.) Magellan's fleet was the first Spanish expedition actually to reach the Indies, some three decades after Columbus's announcement that he had reached them.
[2] Thought to be today's Santiago Zautla, in the state of Puebla, about sixty miles from Xalapa, altitude approximately seven thousand feet above sea level.

hopes that they might take us into their houses. This town was subject to Mexico. **– Díaz**

While in Xocotlán, Cortés took every opportunity to preach against idol worship, since what the Spaniards were seeing throughout the region shocked them deeply. Díaz particularly remembered Xocotlán.

> I remember that in a plaza where their cues stood we saw piles of human skulls arranged in such a way that they could be counted, which we did. We counted more than a hundred thousand skulls—again I say, more than one hundred thousand! In another corner of the plaza we saw stacks of human thigh bones, too numerous to count. They had skulls strung between wooden posts all over. Three papas appeared to be in charge of these bones and skulls.
>
> The deeper we penetrated into this country the more of such things we saw. **– Díaz**

On the advice of local Indians regarding the best path to take to the interior, the small force then proceeded to move southwest toward Tlaxcala,[1] adding small numbers of Indian warriors to the army from virtually every village through which they passed. The Tlaxcalans, as the Spaniards would soon learn, would not be so easily conscripted to their cause.

Always preferring diplomacy or flattery to force, Cortés—despite the unnerving reports he was receiving about the Tlaxcalans' preparations for battle—sent Indian messengers on ahead with assurances that he and his men wanted no more than to pass through Tlaxcalan lands unhindered, that they were here to free all peoples from the rule of the despot Montezuma, and that they would be happy to be assisted in this endeavor by the Tlaxcalans. To demonstrate his benign intent, he sent a gift of a red Flemish hat to the Tlaxcalan elders.

His answer arrived in the form of a well-planned and orchestrated Indian attack by what Díaz claims were more than three thousand disciplined warriors wielding long-handled wooden paddles with razor-sharp obsidian chips embedded in both edges—[2]devastating weapons up close. Artillery, muskets, and crossbows, however,

---

[1] Well over seven thousand feet above sea level. The Tlaxcalans, in frequent conflict with the Aztecs, had yet to be subdued by them.

[2] Díaz's numbers will be used without qualification, although they are not necessarily reliable. The weapons were the formidable *macuahuitls*, capable of cutting off a man's head with a single blow.

carried the day. To the Spaniards' detriment, the Tlaxcalans found out in this skirmish that these strangers and their large animals could be wounded.

The following day, September 2, the Spaniards cowered under a hail of arrows from six thousand warriors. Cortés attempted to parley, but was unsuccessful, so he ordered his army to attack. The warriors fell back in good order, drawing Cortés's men into an ambush by an estimated forty thousand Indians—all in red and white livery—under a young Tlaxcalan chief named Xicotenga.

And while we were at grips with these great warriors and their appalling broadswords, a few of their strongest determined to seize a horse. They rushed at a mare—[1]a fast mare, well trained to battle—and got their hands on her. She was being ridden that day by Pedro de Morón, an expert horseman, who with three other riders had charged into the enemy ranks, supporting one another as they had been ordered to do. The Indians got hold of Morón's lance, rendering him helpless, and hacked at him with their broadswords, wounding him badly. They then went for the mare, slashing her neck so deeply that it was left dangling by only a fold of skin, and she fell dead. If the other horsemen had not hurried to Morón's side, he would have been killed there too.

We might possibly have rescued him with our company of infantry, but we feared that if we moved at all we would have been routed. We were in great danger. We finally moved over there and succeeded in extracting Morón, who was being dragged away by the enemy, half-dead. We then cut the girths and pulled the saddle off the mare so as not to leave it there. Ten of us were wounded in this effort, but, as I recall, we killed four of their captains. Walking in close formation, we inflicted terrible damage with our swords.

At this point the enemy began to retreat, taking the mare with them. They soon sent pieces of her around to all the towns of Tlaxcala. We later heard that they had offered up to their gods her shoes and the Flemish hat, . . .

---

[1] This was the same mare that Cortés had used in his ruse in Tabasco in March.

The mare they killed had belonged to Juan Sedeño, who, incapacitated by three wounds he'd received the previous day, had lent her to Morón, a great rider. I don't remember ever seeing Morón again. He died of his wounds—either that day or a couple of days later. – **Díaz**

Following an hour-long battle in which the Spaniards suffered fifteen men and four horses wounded, the Indians retreated, both sides regrouping and looking to their weapons for the next engagement. On September 4 Cortés sent a messenger to Xicotenga, begging to be allowed to pass unmolested. Xicotenga, ignoring the request, replied that he had augmented his already-large force by fifty thousand warriors, a message that struck fear into many Spanish hearts. The two priests with the expedition were kept busy hearing the confessions of those who had become convinced that death awaited them on the morrow.

Next morning, September 5, 1519, we formed up our horsemen. Even the wounded men had to ride, and contribute whatever they could. The crossbowmen were ordered to be very careful with their supply of bolts—some men were to shoot while others loaded. The musketeers were told to do the same. Those with sword and shield were advised to aim their cuts and thrusts at the enemy's bowels to keep them from getting as close as they had the day before. The artillery was ready for action, and the horsemen had already been instructed to back up one another. But they were to shorten their holds on their lances today, to sally forth and return at a trot without stopping to fully spear an enemy, but to strike only at face and eyes, so as not to get separated from the squadron.

We set out from our camp with battle-flag flying and four men to protect the standard-bearer. We hadn't gone even a quarter of a league when we saw the fields absolutely filled with warriors, with their plumes and insignia, and making a great din with trumpets and horns. – **Díaz**

As Cortés's four hundred men, many of whom were sick and wounded, assembled on the field for battle, what they did not know was that a large number of Tlaxcalan warriors were reconsidering their resistance to these strangers. This led to confusion in the Indian ranks, since many even refused to fight. When the battle was joined on

September 5 the Spanish artillery and muskets were able to wreak havoc on the Tlaxcalans' closely massed and confused forces.

Even as the Tlaxcalans were having second thoughts about their strategy, a number of Cortés's own men were becoming battle-weary and pessimistic. They had lost forty-five men already to battle or disease, and another dozen were down with fever, including Cortés himself.

If the Tlaxcalans are a peaceful people, as we've been told, a delegation of these men told the prostrate Cortés, and we can't even handle them, how will we deal with Montezuma's thousands? And why have we received no news from our base camp at Villa Rica? Cortés was entreated to make another peace overture, to make it clear that all was forgiven, even the death of the mare. He assented. Captives were freed to carry a conciliatory message, and Marina was told to instruct the messengers on what had to be said. But Marina's instructions were framed in her own way, with little regard to conciliation.

> Let me say that Doña Marina, although a native woman, was as tough as a man. She heard every day how the Tlaxcalans were going to murder us all and eat our flesh with *chillis*. She had seen us surrounded on the battlefield, and now wounded and sick. Yet we never detected the slightest weakness in her, but rather a strength far beyond what most women have. Doña Marina and Aguilar instructed our messengers to say to the Tlaxcalans that they must make peace with us at once, and if they did not come within two days, we would kill them all, lay waste to their lands, and hunt the rest of them down in their city. **– Díaz**

While the Tlaxcalan elders were unsuccessfully pressuring Xicotenga to relent, Cortés, although still feeling the effects of his fever, had started testing the peace on his own by leading an expedition into a Tlaxcalan settlement peacefully, dealing kindly with all. In return, the men were happily offered both food and women by the relieved populace, who seemed finally to realize that the strangers wanted no more than to pass through their lands unmolested.

With survival now a real possibility, many of Cortés's men began a concerted effort to convince him to return to Cuba. They had been fortunate to get this far, they said, but they could go no farther with such a small force, and with enormous numbers of potentially hostile Indians on all sides. They took him to task for having scuttled the ships, but declared themselves ready to build a new one to send for help from Cuba—anything to get out of this hellish land. If they were attacked again, this delegation argued, they would have no chance.

Cortés listened patiently, but in the end would have none of it. He stated that in his opinion they were the bravest Spaniards in history, and that for them to have gotten this far was absolute proof that they also enjoyed divine protection. Our enemies are bringing us food now, he argued, so why should we turn back? And what would Montezuma think or do if he heard that these "gods" had run away from a few Tlaxcalans? No one ever said this would be easy, he told them. Put Cuba out of your head. We're not going back.

As Cortés was beginning to contemplate the real possibility of peace with Tlaxcala, Xicotenga was readying a night attack against the Spanish camp. Unfortunately for Xicotenga, and more unfortunately for the spies he sent to reconnoiter the camp, the latter were caught. Cortés ordered the thumbs or hands of several of them to be cut off, and sent the mutilated men back with a message that Xicotenga might attack his camp any time he wished. The Spaniards would be ready. When the attack came, it was easily repulsed.

By mid-September it was clear that with or without the participation of the now-renegade Xicotenga, there would be peace with Tlaxcala. Cortés now dared to consider the possibility of adding these excellent Tlaxcalan fighters to his army.

When word reached Montezuma that the small force of strangers had defeated the armed might of Tlaxcala he shuddered, but immediately dispatched emissaries with his congratulations and gifts. Spread out on the ground before Cortés now were richly worked gold and jeweled ornaments and numerous bundles of fine cotton from the Aztec capital. Amazingly, the envoys were empowered to ask what Cortés might require in the way of annual tribute to his king—a tribute Montezuma would gladly pay on condition that Cortés would cease his advance upon Mexico. The land was difficult, warned the emissaries, and the teules were likely to suffer great hardship there.

Astonishingly, into the midst of this scene with Montezuma's men now strolled a young and virile Xicotenga, his large retinue arrayed in red and white, come finally to talk peace.[1] He begged Cortés's pardon

---

[1] Cortés's relationship with the young Xicotenga would never be easy. On evidence of Xicotenga's later treachery—and despite having a cordial

for having opposed the Spaniards, and importuned him to visit Tlaxcala's capital, promising a most hospitable welcome. Cortés was as kind to him as he had been to the Mexicans, but neither of his two groups of suitors trusted one another, each trying to dissuade Cortés from dealing with the other. Even as the still feverish commander was putting off the Tlaxcalans' earnest supplication that he visit their capital city at once and rest there, new ambassadors arrived from Tenochtitlan bearing even more gifts—jewels, and richly worked cloth with feathers and other embellishments—and begging that he turn back. Then a delegation of Tlaxcalan chiefs arrived, some on litters or in hammocks, others being carried on the backs of underlings, all begging him to visit their city and be finished with Montezuma's men. Cortés, still too unwell to travel, kept putting them all off, but by September's third week he had recovered, and the Spaniards, accompanied by more than five hundred Tlaxcalan porters hauling their artillery, now moved into the Tlaxcalan capital, to remain there till mid-October. Montezuma's messengers, wary of being caught among the Tlaxcalans but wishing to observe the course of events, also moved to the capital, sticking very close to the Spaniards.

The reception in Tlaxcala was stirring.

When the caciques saw that we were headed to their city with our baggage train, they ran ahead to make sure that everything was ready for our arrival, including having our quarters adorned with flowers. When we got to within a quarter league of the city, the same caciques who had hurried on ahead came out to meet us, along with their children, their nieces and nephews, and many of the leading people, each clan, party, or faction forming its own group.

There were in fact four factions in Tlaxcala, not counting that of Tecapaneca, lord of Topeyanco, which made a fifth. Their subjects from all over the province appeared, each group in its own particular livery, which, although they were of sisal (cotton still being unavailable to them), were of excellent quality and beautifully embroidered and decorated. Following them were the papas from all over the province. There were many of them because of the many great cues that they have here. These papas carried braziers with glowing coals, and

relationship with the young man's father, Xicotenga the Elder—Cortés would have him murdered.

burned incense in them over us. Some of them wore very long white garments like surplices, with hoods, similar, as I have said, to what our canons wear. Their hair was long and tangled, matted with blood, impossible to untangle unless they cut it first. The blood issues from their ears, which they had sliced up that very day in sacrifice. In a show of humility the papas bowed down in our presence. Their fingernails are extraordinarily long. We were told that these papas were pious men who led good lives.

Many of the city's principal men hurried to Cortés's side to walk with him. From the moment we entered the city, the streets and rooftops were overflowing with Indians, men and women, welcoming us with great smiles on their faces. – **Díaz**

Against the wishes of his hosts, Cortés insisted that the Spaniards would share their lodgings with Montezuma's men. Lodgings were also found for the warriors from Cempoala and from the other towns, who were swelling Cortés's force. On the side, he warned his men to be on their guard, but, so sincere were the Tlaxcalans that this turned out to be a needless precaution. Wine and communion wafers recently requisitioned from over the mountains in Villa Rica had arrived, and the priest Juan Díaz celebrated Mass in Tlaxcala. But the men found it hard to be civil to a people whose customs they found revolting.

In this city of Tlaxcala we found wooden cages full of Indians, both male and female, being fattened up until they were ready to be sacrificed and eaten. We broke open and destroyed these cages and let the prisoners go. These sad creatures at first refused to leave, but clung to us, and thus escaped with their lives. From then on, in whatever town we entered, the first thing our captain did was to order the cages broken open and the prisoners, who were found everywhere, released.

Seeing this enormous cruelty, Cortés expressed his great displeasure with the caciques of Tlaxcala, reproaching them angrily. They in turn promised from then on neither to kill nor to eat any more Indians. It seemed to me, however, that their promises had little value, since they returned to their old ways as soon as we turned our heads. – **Díaz**

The Tlaxcalan elders now offered their gifts, including gold, but with apologies for their inadequacy. Montezuma had systematically robbed them of everything, they said, and this was the best they could do. But we do have one valuable gift for you, they added, gesturing—possibly with a smile—toward five young women, handsome and bejeweled, all daughters of Tlaxcalan chiefs, standing in a group nearby with their attendants. Cortés offered his profuse thanks, but—as he had done in Cempoala—said that the women could not be accepted unless some steps were first taken by the Tlaxcalans to abandon their foul religious practices. Counseled, however, by Fray Bartolomé and others to go slowly here, Cortés soon relented, but did succeed in having the girls receive minimal instruction in the faith, and to be baptized at Mass—all receiving Spanish names—before being distributed to his senior commanders. One of these young women, the warrior Xicotenga's sister, was given to Cortés, but he passed her on to Pedro de Alvarado.

Cortés was now free to give more careful consideration to his objective. He began questioning the Tlaxcalans, likely within earshot of Montezuma's ambassadors, about the Mexicans and their capital, Tenochtitlan, which was, he knew, situated on a built-up island in the middle of a lake.[1] He was told, first off, that Montezuma was capable of putting 150,000 men in the field against him.

The Tlaxcalans then spoke of the great fortifications of the Mexicans' city. They described the lake and the depth of the water; the causeways by which one entered the city; the wooden bridges across gaps on every causeway, and how one

---

[1] This was Lake Texcoco, one of a system of five interconnected lakes that became separate from one another at times of low precipitation, and that flooded into one another to form a single lake when runoff was high. The lake system measured approximately forty-five miles north to south and twenty miles east to west. Since the lakes were subject to water influx but had no outflow, they had become saline. Lake Texcoco being the lowest-lying of the five, salinity was highest there. To improve the quality of the water a former Aztec regime had constructed a north-south dike from shore to shore, isolating the island capital (to the west of the dike) from the remainder of the lake. Since there was a dependable influx of overland runoff to this western basin, and controlled outflow was possible through the dike, water quality on the island side of the dike had gradually improved. Lakes Xochimilco and Chalco, to the south, also benefited from this control. The saline water was not without benefit: Cortés would later note that in Tenochtitlan there was a brisk trade in salt extracted from the lake water.

could pass through these gaps by water. If the bridges were removed, they pointed out, one could be caught on a causeway between two of these gaps and never reach the city. They described how most of the city was built upon the lake, and how it was impossible even to get from house to house except by drawbridge. Canoes were in abundance. The rooftops, they said, were flat, and equipped with a sort of screen from behind which the inhabitants could fight. They told how the city was provided with fresh water from a spring in a place called Chapultepec, a half-league away. This water was brought in via aqueduct, they said, and then loaded into canoes by vendors who sold it throughout the city.[1]

The conversation turned to their weapons. The Mexicans had two-pronged javelins, Cortés was told, that they hurled from spear-throwers, weapons capable of piercing any armor. They had excellent archers, and flint-tipped lances five or six feet long, sharper than knives, as well as shields and cotton armor. They had many slingers, said the Indians, who hurled rounded stones, and they had other types of good, long lances as well. They used swords with two cutting edges.

The Tlaxcalans then brought out large pictures painted on sisal cloths depicting the battles they had fought with the Mexicans, and the Mexicans' manner of fighting. – **Díaz**

In the course of his sessions with the Tlaxcalan chiefs, Cortés was told that most of the Tlaxcalans' troubles had emanated from Cholula, a large town inhabited by a treacherous people a day's march to the south, on one of two roads leading to Tenochtitlan. He was advised strongly to avoid this town, and to approach Tenochtitlan—if indeed he was foolhardy enough to approach it at all—by the slightly more direct route through Huexotzinco, a town friendly to the Tlaxcalans. Much to the dismay of his hosts, however, Cortés announced that he liked the look of Cholula, actually visible in the far distance, and he wanted to see it up close. After once again tamping down the objections of the Cuban landholder clique within his army, he ordered the men to ready themselves for the short (less than twenty-mile)

---

[1] Chapultepec was on the mainland west of the city. The aqueduct ran from there across the lake to the western (Tacuba) causeway, from which point it followed the causeway into the city.

march to Cholula—today adjoining the Spanish-founded city of Puebla.

Prior to his departure, however, Cortés began his usual psychological assault on this putative enemy, in this case known to be a strong Montezuma ally. He sent on ahead to inquire why no one from Cholula had been sent out to meet him, to pay their respects to the victorious strangers, and to offer obedience to their king. If you don't come soon, he had instructed his messenger to say, we'll have to consider that you are ill-disposed toward us. Yet even as he was dispatching the envoy, four important Cholulans arrived bearing rich gifts, and warning against the treachery of the Tlaxcalans. Cortés greeted them warmly, graciously accepted their offerings, and encouraged them to spend a couple of days with him, promising to be in their town with them very soon.

By mid-October, Cortés, his force now strengthened by a thousand Tlaxcalan warriors, was on the road to Cholula, which lay less than seventy miles from Tenochtitlan. He was met by emissaries from Cholula who, bowing to the inevitable entrance of the strangers into their town, nonetheless insisted that their enemies, the Tlaxcalans, remain outside. Cortés acquiesced, asking the Tlaxcalans to camp outside the town, but informing his hosts that those carrying his tepuzques, or cannon, would be entering with him. The Tlaxcalans were uneasy. Alonso de Aguilar (not the interpreter),[1] one of Cortés's soldiers, remembered the moment.

> As we were entering the city, some priests, dressed in their fashion, came out to meet us. They burned incense before us, but said nothing. The Tlaxcalan chiefs, when they saw this, told Cortés, "This kind of reception is a bad omen. They mean war, and plan either to sacrifice us or just plain murder us. You and your Spaniards be ready, and we'll help you." – **Alonso de Aguilar**

The Spaniards marched into a town filled with men and women gawping at them, and especially at their horses. Perhaps uneasily, they scanned the multitudes chattering and pointing, many from the rooftops. At length they were led to their spacious quarters, with the Cempoalans and Tlaxcalan cannon-porters lodged nearby. Before long

---

[1] Nine years after the conquest of Tenochtitlan, this Aguilar would give up his possessions to enter the Dominican order. He would thereafter be known as Francisco de Aguilar.

Cortés launched into his standard address, saying that he had come to teach them the right way, to give up their foul religious practices and to embrace the one true God. The Cholulans smiled at such naïveté, but in view of the strangers' record of accomplishment, saw fit at least to offer their loyalty to the strangers' king. Then a signal was given and enormous amounts of food arrived for Castilian and Indian alike. But Cortés was not to be bribed so easily. He and his men found abomination at every turn.

> I can't omit mentioning the cages with thick wooden bars that we found there, all filled with Indian men and boys being fattened for sacrifice and consumption. We broke these cages open and Cortés told the prisoners to return to their own lands. He then threatened the caciques and captains and papas, warning them that they must never keep anyone in this way again, nor consume any more human flesh. They promised to comply but never did. **– Díaz**

On Day 3 of the Spaniards' stay in Cholula, the food service mysteriously stopped. The Cholulan chiefs, moreover, seemed edgy, uneasy, even afraid.

> Through our interpreters Cortés asked them what it was they were afraid of and why they would bring us nothing to eat. He added that if our stay in their city was causing an inconvenience to them, we would in any case be leaving tomorrow for Mexico, to visit and speak with the great prince Montezuma. He asked them to supply *tamemes* to carry our baggage and tepuzques,[1] or lombards, and to give us some food. The principal cacique became so flustered he could hardly speak. He promised to look for some food, but, he said, the great Montezuma had ordered them not to feed the Spaniards, and he wanted us to proceed no farther.
>
> While Cortés was talking with the caciques, three Cempoalan Indians, our friends, arrived. They quietly told Cortés that, very close to our quarters, they had discovered pits in the streets, all covered with wood and earth, very cleverly concealed. They had uncovered one and found it filled with sharpened stakes, capable of killing any horse that fell into it. They also, said the Cempoalans, had seen stockpiles of stones, with adobe breastworks, on roofs. It certainly did not seem

---

[1] A *tameme* was a porter.

innocent, they said, because in another street they had also found heavy log barricades.

At that moment eight Tlaxcalan Indians arrived, those whom we had left in the fields outside Cholula, and they said to Cortés, "Be careful, Malinche, this city is unfriendly. We know that last night they sacrificed seven people to their war god, five of them children, to gain the victory over you. And we've just seen them sending their women and children out of the city with their baggage."

After hearing this, Cortés sent the Tlaxcalans back to their captains with instructions that they should be ready to move as soon as they were summoned. **– Díaz**

To demonstrate his total trust, Cortés requested the services of two thousand Cholulan warriors to accompany him to Tenochtitlan. The request came as a great relief to the caciques, who doubtless saw that this force could be used as a hammer to crush the strangers on the anvil of a Mexican force that they knew was being rushed to prepare an ambush outside Cholula. Two papas, who had been persuaded by Doña Marina to tell what they knew, now told the captain-general that ten thousand Mexican warriors were lying in ambush in the ravines beyond the town and ten thousand more had already infiltrated the town. All but twenty of the Spaniards, said the papas, were to be slaughtered, the twenty being saved for the sacrificial knife. Cortés kept all this information to himself, focusing on reassuring his hosts of his innocent intent.

On discussing the matter with his captains, Cortés found the predictable division of advice. Some were for changing the route, proceeding to Tenochtitlan through the safer Huexotzinco, others for returning to Tlaxcala, and likely others who counseled a retreat to the coast and ultimately to Cuba. But the bulk of the advice came down on the side of fighting right where they were. Call in the Tlaxcalans, these men said, and let's have it out right now. It was a version of this plan that carried the day.

Since Cortés had told his hosts that they planned to leave on the following day, he had the men make a show of tying up their baggage and getting ready to move out. He, moreover, told Montezuma's men, still with them, that he had discovered a plot among the Cholulans, and that they had indicated that Montezuma was behind it. Since such treachery on the part of a friend would be impossible, said Cortés, the Mexican emissaries should stay out of sight until the matter had been cleared up. To make sure they communicated with no one, they were put under guard. Cortés ordered that all horses be left saddled and bridled all night.

If there had been a shred of doubt about the planned attack it was now blown away by an old Indian woman who had taken a liking to Marina, and who warned her to get out of the way. Upon being informed by Marina of this conversation, Cortés questioned the woman himself, then had her put under guard.

At dawn the warriors arrived — many more than the requested two thousand. They were friendly, ebullient, apparently secure in the knowledge that the trap was well laid. They poured into the high-walled courtyard where Cortés and his men were lodged. Cortés quietly ordered that the two papas who had served as his informants be told to go home.

> When dawn broke what a marvelous thing it was to see the caciques and papas hurrying into the courtyards with their warriors, all laughing and smiling, happy, as if they already had us in their snares and nets! They even brought more warriors than we had asked for. As large as these courtyards are — for they're still standing as a memorial of the past — the warriors hardly fit into them. Despite the early hour, we were ready for what we had to do. As the Cholulans and their warriors filtered into the space, soldiers with swords and shields took up positions at the gate to see that not a single armed Indian left there alive. **– Díaz**

The moment had arrived. Cortés began to address his victims, whose faces no doubt gradually lost their confident smiles as they came to understand what he intended to do.

> Sitting astride his horse, with Doña Marina, also mounted, at his side, Cortés asked the caciques why, when we had done them no harm, they had decided last night to kill us. To merit such betrayal, had we said or done anything beyond what we had said or done in any town we had passed through? Was it because we had admonished them not to be evil, not to sacrifice human beings or bow down to idols? Was it because we had told them not to eat their neighbors' flesh or engage in sodomy? Was it because we had tried to show them a better way to live, he asked, or tell them things about our holy faith, without any sort of compulsion?

Why do we now see you, he asked, preparing long, stout sticks with collars and ropes, and storing them in a house near the great cue? Why have you been making barricades in the streets for the last three days, and digging pits there, and building breastworks on your rooftops? Why have you sent your women and children and their possessions out of the city? Your real intentions are so apparent, you can't hide them. You haven't even given us food. To mock us you bring us water and wood and tell us there is no maize. And we all know that just outside town a large body of troops is waiting in ambush, with a great number of others who joined them last night, believing we must pass that way on our path to Mexico.

Is this how you repay us who have come to treat you as brothers, he asked, to tell you what Our Lord God and our king command? You wish to kill us and eat our flesh — in fact you've already got the pots on the fire with salt, chillis, and tomatoes! If this is what you had in mind, would it not have been better to fight us like real warriors, in the field, as your neighbors the Tlaxcalans did? We know for certain what you've been planning in this city, he said, and what you've promised to your god of war, namely, that you'll sacrifice twenty of us to him. We know that three nights ago you already sacrificed seven Indians in hopes that he would grant you victory over us. But he is evil and false, and has not now, nor has ever had, any power over us, and the fruits of all this evildoing and betrayal are about to fall upon you men here. **– Díaz**

The assembled warriors, seeing themselves hopelessly trapped, attempted to talk their way out of their plight. They had no chance of success.

Doña Marina translated Cortés's speech, and made sure his hearers understood it. The papas and caciques and captains now spoke up. What the captain said was true, they admitted, but they were not responsible for this. Montezuma's men had come with the order from the great prince himself. Cortés replied that such egregious treachery could not, by royal law, go unpunished, and for this transgression they would all have to die. He then ordered a musket fired. This was the agreed-upon signal, and we dealt them a blow that they would never forget.

We slaughtered them, the false promises of their gods availing them nothing.

Less than two hours later our Tlaxcalan allies, whom we had left in the fields, arrived. They had been fighting fiercely in the streets, and had soon routed the many companies of Cholulans deployed there to prevent their entry into the city. The Tlaxcalans then ran amok, plundering and taking prisoners, and we could not stop them.[1] – **Díaz**

The Aztec account of this moment:

An assembly was held in the courtyard of the god, but when they had all gathered together, the entrances were closed, so that there was no way of escaping.

Then the sudden slaughter began: knife strokes, and sword strokes, and death. The people of Cholula had not foreseen it, had not suspected it. They faced the Spaniards without weapons, without their swords or their shields. The cause of the slaughter was treachery. They died blindly, without knowing why, because of the lies of the Tlaxcaltecas.

And when this had taken place, word of it was brought to Motecuhzoma. The messengers came and departed, journeying back and forth between Tenochtitlan and Cholula. The common people were terrified by the news; they could do nothing but tremble with fright. It was as if the earth trembled beneath them, or as if the world were spinning before their eyes, as it spins during a fit of vertigo. – **Aztec account**

The massacre at Cholula, whatever the truth of its causes or the number slaughtered, became emblematic of the conquest of Mexico. It struck a deep nerve in Las Casas, who, it must be stated, was not present at the event, and may have had a naïve appreciation of Indian intentions.

All the lords of the land . . . came out to receive the Christians in procession, and with great respect and reverence conducted them to their quarters in the city and in the houses of the principal lords. But the Spaniards made up their minds to carry out a butchery there, or a punishment (as they call it), in order to sow fear of them and of their ferocity in every corner of that land. One should know that this has in fact

---

[1] It is thought that five thousand to ten thousand Indians were slaughtered at Cholula.

always been the aim of the Spaniards when they enter a new land—to carry out a cruel and conspicuous slaughter to make these meekest of lambs tremble before them. . . . When the lords and nobles arrived and came to speak with the Spanish captain, they were taken prisoner without anyone being aware of it so that the news could not be spread.

The Spaniards had requested the services of five or six thousand Indians to carry the army's baggage, and on their arrival they sent them into the courtyard at their quarters. Whoever has seen these Indians as their bodies are loaded with the Spaniards' burdens cannot avoid feeling compassion and pity. They come naked but for a covering over their private parts, with a small mesh bag thrown over their shoulder, containing their meager meal.

[In Cholula] they all squatted down like lambs alongside their comrades gathered in the courtyard. The Spaniards had stationed armed guards at the gates. Then all the rest took their weapons in hand and thrust their swords and lances into the bodies of these lambs so that none might escape. After two or three days many Indians who had hidden and taken refuge beneath the corpses (of which there were many) began to stir and raise themselves up, and, covered with blood, they went weeping and begging mercy of the Spaniards, pleading that they might not be slain. But neither mercy nor compassion could be found in the Spaniards. As quickly as these unfortunates came forward, they were hacked to pieces. As for all the lords, of which there were more than one hundred, every one of them in bonds, the captain ordered them to be taken out and burned alive on stakes driven into the earth. But one lord, . . . proved able to free himself and assembled twenty or thirty or forty men at their great fortress-like temple, which they call a cue, and there he defended himself for the rest of the day. But the Spaniards, from whom there is no refuge, especially for these unarmed people, set fire to the temple and burned them all. **– Las Casas**

On firmer ground now, Las Casas continued:

It is noteworthy that the title under which [the Spaniards] made their *entradas*, through which they commenced the destruction of all those innocent people and the depopulation of their lands—whose large populations should have been the cause of great joy and pleasure to a true Christian—was to say that they had come to make them subject and obedient to the king of Spain, and if they refused, they would be killed or enslaved. . . . I beg all those Christians who know something of God and of reason and even of human laws to consider this: For any people that had lived secure in its lands, owing no debt to any, and governed by its own lords, how would it not paralyze the heart to hear the words suddenly pronounced, "Give obedience to a foreign monarch whom you have never seen nor ever heard, and if you refuse, rest assured that we will chop you into pieces"—especially when history has shown that they actually do it? **– Las Casas**

To which Díaz the soldier, generally an apologist for Cortés, replied:

These were the great cruelties about which the bishop of Chiapas, Fray Bartolomé de las Casas wrote, and about which he has never ceased to speak.[1] He maintains that with no fault on the part of the Cholulans, simply for our amusement and because we felt like it, we committed this act. He writes so well that he could persuade anyone who did not witness the event, or who knows nothing about it, that it happened as he says. But it actually occurred in a manner totally opposite to the way he describes it. The Dominicans should be careful of this book because it does not reflect reality.[2]

I'd like to point out further that the good Franciscan friars, the first religious order to be sent by His Majesty to New Spain after its conquest,[3] went to Cholula to learn how and why this event took place. In the course of their investigation they interviewed the very papas and older people who were there. On finishing their inquiry they concluded that events unfolded in the way that I have described, not in the manner described by the bishop.

---

[1] In 1544, subsequent to these events but prior to the writing of Díaz's account, Las Casas was named bishop of Chiapas, Mexico. The writing referred to is likely the bishop's *An Account Much Abbreviated of the Destruction of the Indies.*

[2] In 1522 Las Casas would join the Dominican order in Santo Domingo.

[3] Nueva España, or New Spain would become the official name of the conquered Mexican land.

If we had not acted in this manner our lives would surely have been in great danger from the companies of Mexican and Cholulan warriors waiting with all their earthworks and barricades. If, to our great misfortune, they had murdered us there, we could never have conquered New Spain so quickly, nor would any other fleet have dared to set out for this land, nor once arrived could they have landed, for the ports would surely have been defended. And the people here would have remained in their idolatrous state. – **Díaz**

The remaining Cholulans, aghast at the bloodbath, pleaded with Cortés for peace. In the presence of Montezuma's equally aghast envoys Cortés feigned anger, shouting that the city deserved to be destroyed, but that he would spare it—not for the sake of the Cholulans, but for the sake of his friend Montezuma. He spent the next few days seeing that city markets were reopened and encouraging horrified survivors to return to normal life. Since most of the city leaders were dead, however, he himself had to appoint new caciques to oversee this process.

The warriors who had been lying in ambush, meanwhile, having heard of the vicious reversal of their plans, headed back to Tenochtitlan as quickly as possible.

Let's turn now to the squadrons sent by Montezuma— those positioned in the ravines just outside Cholula, with their breastworks and their blind alleys to prevent our horses from charging. Once they learned of the events in the city these forces scurried back to Mexico as quickly as possible to tell the great prince Montezuma what had happened. Montezuma, however, had already heard the news from two principal men who had been in the city. We later learned that when Montezuma received this news he became deeply angered, and—in an effort to learn what the outcome of our journey to Mexico might be, and whether he should permit us to enter the city—immediately sacrificed several Indians to his god Huichilobos.[1] We were told he had locked himself up for two days with ten of his highest-ranking papas, continuing with his sacrifices and devotions as he awaited his god's response.

The reply eventually received was that he should send messengers to us begging pardon for the people's actions in

[1] Díaz's rendering of Huitzilopochtli, the Aztec's sun god.

Cholula, and extending a friendly invitation to enter his city. Once we were inside, said the god, our food and water could be withheld or the bridges removed, and we could be slaughtered. In a single day we would be wiped out, and the prince could then make his sacrifices to Huichilobos, who had given this counsel, and to Tezcatlipoca, the god of hell. The victors would eat their fill of our arms and thighs, while our bowels and the rest of our bodies could be gorged upon by the serpents and tigers they kept in wooden cages for this purpose.[1] **– Díaz**

Within two weeks, the city was more or less back to normal. The ever-wily Cortés during this time sent messengers to Montezuma, reporting on what had happened as if Montezuma could have known nothing about it. He offered protestations of friendship again, promising that he would soon arrive to meet the great prince of the Mexica. The Tlaxcalan caciques urged him not to go, or, if he must go, to take all of them as protection. Cortés again said he needed only a thousand Tlaxcalan warriors for his cannon and baggage. It wouldn't be right, he said, to bring a horde of Montezuma's enemies into his city. The Cempoalans wanted no part of whatever awaited Cortés at Tenochtitlan. They requested leave to go home, and Cortés, after attempting unsuccessfully to convince them to stay, allowed them to go. The Spaniards and Tlaxcalans then set out westward over the 12,000-foot-high Eagle Pass between the nearly 18,000-foot,[2] snow-covered volcano Popocatépetl and its companion to the north, the 17,000-foot Iztaccíhuatl. They would soon be in Tenochtitlan.

When the massacre at Cholula was complete, the strangers set out again toward the city of Mexico. They came in battle array, as conquerors, and the dust rose in whirlwinds on the roads. Their spears glinted in the sun, and their pennons fluttered like bats. They made a loud clamor as they marched, for their coats of mail and their weapons clashed and rattled. Some of them were dressed in glistening iron from head to foot; they terrified everyone who saw them.

---

[1] There were, of course, no tigers in Mexico. Díaz may have been referring to pumas or jaguars. The word occurs in Cortés's accounts as well.

[2] Known to the Aztecs as the Eagle Pass, it is known today as the Paso de Cortés.

Their dogs came with them, running ahead of the column. They raised their muzzles high; they lifted their muzzles to the wind. They raced on before with saliva dripping from their jaws. **– Aztec account**

The Spaniards, laboring up into the November cold of the Eagle Pass, were now on the shoulder of the giant volcano Popocatépetl, which, even from many miles away, could be seen throwing off smoke and fire.

We were all—including Cortés—astonished at this, since we had never seen a volcano. One of our captains, Diego de Ordaz by name,[1] asked permission of Cortés to climb up there and see what it was. Cortés not only gave his permission, but actually ordered him to go. He took two soldiers with him, and a few prominent Indians from Huexotzinco. When they had gotten halfway up Popocatépetl—the Indian name for this mountain—the Indians, frightened, tried to dissuade Ordaz from climbing any higher. No one, they said, could withstand the earth tremors, and the flames, stone, and ashes that would be thrown from the volcano's mouth. There were some cues farther up, they said, established for the idols called the teules of Popocatépetl, and they would go no farther than that.

Ordaz and his companions therefore left them and climbed higher. While they were climbing, as we were told later, the volcano began to shoot out great tongues of fire, ejecting half-burnt, porous rock, along with a great deal of ash. To them, the whole sierra seemed to be in motion. They stayed rooted to the spot for an hour until the flames died down and the ash and smoke was diminished. They then continued their climb up to the crater, which, they said, was round and a quarter-league wide. From there they could see the great city of Mexico with its lake and surrounding towns. **– Díaz**

Montezuma's god Huitzilopochtli was meanwhile still counseling the prince to let the strangers into the city—advice that would ultimately have a bad result for him. The god told him that it would be easy to kill them there. In any case the Spaniards were on their way, and Montezuma decided that more gifts were called for, gifts to be

---

[1] Although Ordaz had come to Mexico a Velázquez partisan, having served as a steward in the governor's household, he appears to have served Cortés well.

borne by his highest-level chieftains. The strangers seemed to appreciate gold.

Then Motecuhzoma dispatched various chiefs. Tzihuacpopocatzin was at their head, and he took with him a great many of his representatives. They went out to meet the Spaniards in the vicinity of Popocatépetl and Iztactépetl, there in the Eagle Pass.

They gave the "gods" ensigns of gold, and ensigns of quetzal feathers, and golden necklaces. And when they were given these presents, the Spaniards burst into smiles; their eyes shone with pleasure; they were delighted by them. They picked up the gold and fingered it like monkeys; they seemed to be transported by joy, as if their hearts were illumined and made new.

The truth is that they longed and lusted for gold. Their bodies swelled with greed, and their hunger was ravenous; they hungered like pigs for that gold. They snatched at the golden ensigns, waved them from side to side and examined every inch of them. They were like one who speaks a barbarous tongue: everything they said was in a barbarous tongue.

– Aztec account

The lightly clad men spent a night shivering in a snowy camp atop the pass and, after avoiding another ambush, at length reached the south shore of the small, southernmost lake, at Ayotzingo. Local Indians must have sensed change in the wind, because they approached the strangers, complaining bitterly of their treatment by Montezuma's men—heavy taxation and frequent rape of their women being their principal complaints. Cortés counseled patience. Things would soon be different, he told them.

At this point Montezuma had another change of heart: the strangers would not be permitted to enter his city. He sent more gold and jewels to the approaching force, promising to send even greater treasures to the coast if only the strangers would not come to his city. It was a feeble last-ditch effort by an already beaten foe, and Cortés knew it. He expressed amazement to Montezuma's ambassadors that such a great friend could be sending such contradictory messages: "Come, don't come; come, don't come." If we've come this far to meet him, he told the men, why would we turn back now? What would our king think of us, what would Montezuma himself think of us? We expect to be welcomed as friends, he said, and if your prince does not like our message, we'll quietly return home. The emissaries departed.

Perhaps sensing inevitable defeat, Montezuma now sent one of his nephews, Cacamatzin, lord of Texcoco, to welcome Cortés into the city. The young prince arrived borne on a litter that was richly worked with green feathers, silver, and precious stones. As he was helped out of the litter, the ground was swept before him and pieces of straw were removed from his path. The Spaniards were hugely impressed. If this prince deserves such pomp and display, they wondered, what must Montezuma receive? Cortés embraced the young man who would lead him into the city, and thanked him profusely for honoring him with his presence.

On the following day the Spaniards mounted their first causeway, crossing little Lake Chalco to arrive at Iztapalapa, on the south shore of the larger lake. They could not believe their eyes.

> When we entered this city of Iztapalapa, we were overwhelmed at the palaces where we were to stay. They were enormous and very well constructed, with magnificent stone, filled with cedar and other fragrant woods, with great rooms and courtyards, and with woven cotton awnings, all a marvel to behold.
>
> After a thorough tour of the interior we were taken into the orchard and gardens, so pleasant to wander through. I never tired of looking at the various kinds of trees, each with its own distinct odor, or the walkways filled with roses and other flowers, or the many fruit trees and rose bushes, or the fresh-water pond, indeed everything. Large canoes could even come into these gardens from the lake, without their crews needing to land, through a channel they had made. Everything was whitewashed and mortared, with all sorts of stonework and artwork that one never tired of looking at. The pond attracted birds of all types and breeds.
>
> I believed there could be nothing in the world like this, Peru at that time being neither known nor thought of. But now it's all been thrown down, lost, and nothing of it remains.
> – **Díaz**

Cortés himself took up the narrative:

> This city of Iztapalapa, which lies on the shore of a large salt lake, has twelve or fifteen thousand inhabitants. Half the city is on the water and half on land. The city's chief is building

a few new houses, as yet unfinished, which are as good as the best houses in Spain. They're large, and the workmanship in masonry, floors, and woodwork is excellent. Except for an absence of stone relief work and a few other refinements seen in Spanish houses, they have everything we have in the way of furnishings. Upper and lower rooms look out upon cool gardens, with many trees and sweet-smelling flowers. There are well-made fresh-water pools or tanks, complete with steps leading down into the water. The main house has a gallery, with lovely corridors and rooms, which overlooks a large garden. In the middle of the garden is a rectangular fresh-water pool with fine stonework, and around it a tiled walk — four hundred paces on a side, 1,600 paces around the entire edge, and wide enough for four to walk abreast. Beyond this walk lies the garden wall, which is a latticework of canes, and beyond that, shady groves and fragrant herbs. The pool is frequented by all manner of fish and birds, including wild duck and garganey and many other species of waterfowl — so many that they frequently cover the entire surface of the pool.
– Cortés

The strangers, Montezuma was told by his returned envoys, were on the doorstep.

When the envoys arrived in the city, they told Motecuhzoma what had happened and what they had seen. Motecuhzoma listened to their report and then bowed his head without speaking a word. For a long time he remained thus, with his head bent down. And when he spoke at last, it was only to say: "What help is there now, my friends? Is there a mountain for us to climb? Should we run away? We are Mexicanos: would this bring any glory to the Mexican nation?

"Pity the old men, and the old women, and the innocent little children. How can they save themselves? But there is no help. What can we do? Is there nothing left us?

"We will be judged and punished. And however it may be, and whenever it may be, we can do nothing but wait." **– Aztec account**

6

INTO THE AZTEC CAPITAL

On November 8, 1519, after nearly seven months of primitive living punctuated by hard fighting, about four hundred dirty and hungry Spaniards, with snorting warhorses and slavering hounds, and accompanied now by a thousand grim Tlaxcalan warriors, stepped onto the broad southern causeway, five miles long, that led to Tenochtitlan.

> We left Iztapalapa next morning, our escort of high-ranking caciques still with us. We advanced on the eight-paces-wide causeway that leads straight to the city of Mexico, and with hardly a turn. Despite its great width it was filled to overflowing with people, some heading into the city, some coming out. Many were stopping to stare at us, so many in fact that we could hardly move. The towers and cues were full of people, and the lake thick with canoes. It was little wonder that they stared, since they had never before seen horses, or men like us.

> We were struck speechless by the things we saw. It was hard to accept that it was real—on the one hand great cities filling the land, and on the lake, even more. Canoes were everywhere. We noticed the drawbridges at intervals on the causeway, but before us was the great city of Mexico. And we were fewer than four hundred soldiers! We couldn't help but remember the warnings we'd received from the Indians of Huexotzinco and Tlaxcala and Tlalmanalco and all the others who had told us not to go to Mexico, that once they had us inside, they would kill us all. – **Díaz**

In the distance, the Spaniards could see a welcoming party awaiting them—more chiefs and nobles, all dressed richly.

> Many high-ranking men and caciques, all arrayed in rich cloaks and resplendent liveries, came out to greet us. The causeways were filled with them. The great Montezuma had sent them on ahead to meet us, and when they reached Cortés, they told him in their language that we were most welcome to their city, and as a sign of peace they touched the ground with their hand and, bending down, then kissed that hand. – **Díaz**

Cacamatzin, borne on his rich litter, had led the group to the welcoming party. He and other great chiefs who had accompanied the procession now moved ahead to join Montezuma himself, who could be discerned approaching on his own litter.

We stopped here for some time while Cacamatzin, lord of Texcoco, as well as the lords of Iztapalapa, Tacuba, and Coyoacán, went forward to meet the great Montezuma, who was now approaching in an opulent litter, in company with other great lords and caciques who owned vassals.

When we had arrived close to the city, at a place where we saw other small towers, the great Montezuma came down from his litter. The four lords then took him by the arm under a canopy that was the color of green feathers, and was richly decorated with gold, silver, pearls, and chalchihuites, which were suspended from a sort of border. We gaped with wonder.

The great Montezuma now came forward, magnificently clad according to their fashion. He wore sandals of a type they called *cotaras*, with soles of gold and straps studded with precious stones. The four lords who supported him were also very richly dressed in their manner. It seemed as if these clothes had been set aside for them out here, since, when they had come out to receive us, they had not been dressed like this. Four other great caciques bore the canopy, and still others were occupied in sweeping the area where the great prince would have to walk, then spreading out cloaks to keep his feet from touching the ground. Except for the four lords—his nephews— who supported him, none of these caciques looked in his face, but rather kept their eyes reverently downcast. – **Díaz**

The meeting, much anticipated by the Spaniards, and much dreaded by the Aztec king, was about to take place.

When Cortés was made to understand that the great Montezuma was approaching, he dismounted, and as Montezuma drew near to him, they bowed deeply to one another. Montezuma said some words of welcome, and our Cortés responded, through Doña Marina, that he hoped he saw him well. It seems to me that Cortés, with the assistance of Doña Marina, who stood next to him, then offered his right hand, but Montezuma, instead of grasping it, held out his own to Cortés. Cortés then took out a necklace that he had ready, a necklace of colored, intricately worked glass beads called *margaritas*. They had been strung on a gold cord impregnated with musk to give the whole a pleasant odor. He placed this necklace around the neck of Montezuma. When he went to embrace the prince, however, the lords who accompanied Montezuma stopped him, for they considered such behavior an indignity.

With the assistance of Doña Marina, Cortés then told Montezuma how it rejoiced his heart to have seen such a great prince, one who had done so many favors for him, and how overwhelmed he was to have such a prince come out to greet him. Montezuma addressed some courteous words to Cortés, then ordered two of his nephews, the lords of Texcoco and Coyoacán, to go with us and show us to our lodgings. **– Díaz**

The same moment recalled from the Indian perspective:

The Spaniards arrived in Xoloco, near the entrance to Tenochtitlan. That was the end of the march, for they had reached their goal. Motecuhzoma now arrayed himself in his finery, preparing to go out to meet them. The other great princes also adorned their persons, as did the nobles and their chieftains and knights. They all went out together to meet the strangers. . . .

Thus Motecuhzoma went out to meet them, there in Huitzillán. He presented many gifts to the captain and his commanders, those who had come to make war. He showered gifts upon them and hung flowers around their necks; he gave them necklaces of flowers and bands of flowers to adorn their breasts; he set garlands of flowers upon their heads. Then he hung the gold necklaces around their necks and gave them presents of every sort as gifts of welcome.

When Motecuhzoma had given necklaces to each one, Cortés asked him: "Are you Motecuhzoma? Are you the king? Is it true that you are the king Motecuhzoma?"

And the king said: "Yes, I am Motecuhzoma." Then he stood up to welcome Cortés; he came forward, bowed his head low and addressed him in these words: "Our lord, you are weary. The journey has tired you, but now you have arrived on the earth. You have come to your city, Mexico. You have come here to sit on your throne, to sit under its canopy."

– Aztec account

The prince then addressed Cortés at some length.

When Motecuhzoma had finished, La Malinche translated his address into Spanish so that the captain could understand it. Cortés replied in his strange and savage tongue, speaking first to Malinche: "Tell Motecuhzoma that we are his friends. There is nothing to fear. We have wanted to see him for a long time, and now we have seen his face and heard his words. Tell him that we love him well and that our hearts are contented."

Then he said to Motecuhzoma: "We have come to your house in Mexico as friends. There is nothing to fear."

La Malinche translated this speech and the Spaniards grasped Motecuhzoma's hands and patted his back to show their affection for him. – **Aztec account**

At this watershed moment the Aztecs noted not only the actions of Cortés, but also those of his men.

The Spaniards examined everything they saw. They dismounted from their horses, and mounted them again, and dismounted again, so as not to miss anything of interest.
– Aztec account

Montezuma, whose thousands could have easily annihilated the strangers at this point, not only conducted them into the city but showed himself ready to serve their king.

We entered Tenochtitlan by crossing a causeway wide enough for three or four horses to ride abreast comfortably. . . . The water swarmed with canoes overflowing with people, all staring at us. It was quite frightening. . . .

Little by little we were taken to an enormous courtyard with enough halls and royal palaces to house more than two thousand men, really large beautiful buildings. A portion of one of them was assigned to us. They brought us food — fowl, bread, maize — more than enough to take care of us all. In the presence of a recording secretary, Montezuma pledged his fealty to the emperor, and vowed to serve him in everything as to his lord and master. He made it clear that we were most welcome. He told us that his ancestors had predicted that a bearded and armed race would one day arrive from the east, and that they were not to be opposed, for they would be the lords of the land. He took us for immortals, and called us teules, which in their language means gods. With these words and many more that I must omit, this great man left for his palaces and halls, of which he had many all over this vast, water-enclosed area. – **Alonso de Aguilar**

The men, who had spent months sleeping on hard ground, were now put up in fine palaces, replete with comfortable beds. They greedily drank in the details of what they saw in those first hours.

These palaces were, as I say, large, and a real sight to see. Within them were many rooms—bedrooms, dressing-rooms, large and beautiful halls. There were canopied four-poster beds with mattresses made of great pieces of cloth. There were pillows covered with leather and filled with soft tree-fiber. We found excellent quilts as well as fine white fur robes, really splendid wooden seats, and good matting. – **Alonso de Aguilar**

Shortly after their arrival in this apparent paradise, however, the Spaniards broke the enchantment with a demonstration of their power. It had the desired effect.

The Spaniards fired one of their cannons, and this caused great confusion in the city. The people scattered in every direction; they fled without rhyme or reason; they ran off as if they were being pursued. It was as if they had eaten the mushrooms that confuse the mind, or had seen some dreadful apparition. They were all overcome by terror, as if their hearts had fainted. And when night fell, the panic spread through the city and their fears would not let them sleep. – **Aztec account**

Montezuma's advisors were beginning to doubt their ruler's wisdom in his handling of these intruders. They had been shocked at the honor shown to Cortés by their lord's draping of a necklace around this barbarous captain's neck. And now they had been ordered to see to the strangers' provisions.

In the morning the Spaniards told Motecuhzoma what they needed in the way of supplies: tortillas, fried chickens, hens' eggs, pure water, firewood and charcoal. Also: large, clean cooking pots, water jars, pitchers, dishes and other pottery. Motecuhzoma ordered that it be sent to them. The chiefs who received this order were angry with the king and no longer revered or respected him. But they furnished the Spaniards with all the provisions they needed—food, beverages and water, and fodder for the horses. – **Aztec account**

Perhaps one of the reasons for their growing anger was Montezuma's housing of the strangers in the very palace in which he kept the treasure of his late father, Axayacatl.[1]

> They conducted us to our quarters, which turned out to be in some large houses with room for us all. This had once been the palace of Montezuma's father, Axayacatl, and Montezuma now kept his great shrines here. He also had here a secret chamber filled with gold and jewels, the treasure that he had inherited from his father, and which he never touched. We thought they may have brought us to stay in this particular place because they considered us teules, and here we were among their own teules. Whatever the reason, this is where they brought us.
>
> The houses had enormous halls. For our captain, there were rooms hung with tapestries of the country, and, for each of us soldiers, rush-matted, canopied beds. . . . We divided up our lodgings by company and stored our artillery in a convenient place. Then we all — horse and foot — were given clear orders to stay extremely alert. Following this, our hosts served us a sumptuous meal in their native style. **– Díaz**

As Cortés and his men settled in for their first night in Tenochtitlan,[2] they had little idea what tomorrow would bring, let alone the day after, or the day after that. They were here — four hundred Spaniards with their Indian allies — to conquer this people, who numbered in the many tens of thousands. How would this be accomplished? How long could they mask their intentions? Cortés would very shortly take bold steps to achieve his objectives, but no one could foresee the ultimate outcome.

Once the Spaniards had been installed in their quarters and fed, Montezuma and his retinue reappeared. In a brief conversation, Cortés told the Indian prince that he had been sent by his king — from the direction of the sunrise (fitting into Montezuma's expectations of a god from the east) to beg that he and his people become Christians.

---

[1] One of the greatest of the Aztec kings, he had ruled from 1469 to 1481. The men would not discover this treasure immediately.

[2] They were lodged in a complex of palaces and cues near the great cue, or Templo Mayor, an enormous truncated pyramid with two ninety-foot towers set atop its platform. Human sacrifices were carried out on this platform daily.

Probably still puzzled and dubious, Montezuma signaled a servant to bring forth yet more gifts for Cortés and all his men. The conversation was brief, yet, before leaving, Montezuma reinforced his order to see that his guests lacked for nothing. The Spaniards accompanied the great king to the street, Cortés later cautioning his men once again to be on their guard.

On the following day Cortés took four of his captains and five soldiers (including Díaz) and walked the short distance to his host's palace.

> Since Montezuma knew we were coming, he met us in the midst of his great hall, surrounded by his nephews, because no one but they were allowed access to Montezuma unless it was a matter of great urgency. He made a deep bow to Cortés and Cortés to him. They took one another by the hand, and Montezuma led Cortés to his dais, where he was made to sit at the prince's right hand. Other seats were brought in, and the rest of us were also invited to sit. – **Díaz**

Cortés declared to the Aztec prince that now that they had had a chance to rest, he would fulfill the purpose of his coming. He then launched into a speech. After some remarks about the evils of their idol worship — again through the tortuous language-conduit of Aguilar and Marina — he began to hit his stride.

> Cortés now begged the favor of the prince's attention to what he had to say. He then, very clearly, began to expound on the history of the world since creation, explaining how we were all brothers, children of one father and one mother — Adam and Eve — and how one of those brothers, our great emperor, had been suffering because of the souls being lost to idol worship, a practice that leads only to the living fires of hell. He had sent us to save these people, he said, to beg them to adore idols no more, to sacrifice their people no more, and to practice sodomy and robbery no more, since all of us are brothers. He went on: Soon our great emperor will send men who live very holy lives, he said, better men than us, in order to teach you. Our present task is only to make this known to you, and to beg the favor of your compliance.
>
> Since Montezuma seemed on the point of saying something, Cortés ceased speaking, only saying to the rest of us. "Let's go. We've opened the conversation, and that's all we need do right now." – **Díaz**

Cortés motioned his men toward the door and rose to take his leave, but as he did so, Montezuma rose from his seat. He too had something to say. Like his guest, he, too, concealed his real intentions in a layering of flattering words and false humility.

Montezuma then said that ever since the Spaniards' first expeditions, [those of Francisco Hernández de Córdoba and Grijalva], our first voyages of discovery, he had wished to invite these new visitors into the cities of his kingdom in order to do them honor, and now his gods had granted his wish. Here we were in his house, which, he said, we should consider as our own. We should take our ease and rest, he said, and enjoy the service of his people. If he had at times sent them messages asking them not to come to his city, it was not his doing, but it was because his people were frightened of them. It was said that we could produce fire and lightning, and that our horses were killing many people, and that we were brave teules, and other such childish nonsense. Now that we were here he could see that we were made of flesh and bone, intelligent, and brave, and he no longer believed what had been said about us. He was even ready to share with us, he said, everything he had. Cortés and all the rest of us then told him how much we appreciated his great kindness and abundant good will.

Montezuma now said with a laugh—because, like a great prince, he always spoke cheerfully—"Malinche, I know very well what your great friends the Tlaxcalans have told you about me, that I'm like a god, or teule, and how everything in my house is gold and silver and precious stones. But you're an intelligent man—you should treat all this as a joke. As you can see, Señor Malinche, I'm flesh and bone like you, my houses and palaces are made of stone and wood and mortar. I am a great prince, it's true, and I surely have the wealth of my ancestors, but you should not take too seriously the lunacies you've heard about me—just as I do not take seriously the stories of your thunder and lightning."

Cortés, also laughing, replied that enemies always say the worst things about each other, but that in these parts he could not hope to have found a more noble prince than he, and it was not without reason that the prince had come to the notice of our emperor. **– Díaz**

Montezuma then ordered further gifts—gold and fine cloaks—to be distributed among his Spanish guests, who now returned to their quarters.

Thanks to several chroniclers of these stirring events, we are not lacking in knowledge of Montezuma, his people, or his city. Both Díaz and Cortés recorded their impressions of the Aztec king.

The great Montezuma looked to be about forty. He was fairly tall, well-proportioned but slender, not very dark, about the same shade as most Indians. His hair was not long, coming to just over his ears. He had a short, well-shaped, but sparse beard. His face was somewhat long and cheerful, and his eyes quite pleasant. In his look or in his whole demeanor he could show geniality or gravity as the occasion demanded. He was neat and clean, bathing every afternoon. He kept many women, daughters of his principal men, around him, but had two women of noble birth as his legitimate wives. When he was enjoying intimacy with any of his women, it was done so secretly that only a few of his servants knew about it. He was not a sodomite. Clothing worn one day, he would not wear again for three or four days. More than two hundred principal men served as his guard in the great halls near his quarters. Only some of these were allowed to speak to him . . . .

At mealtime his cooks prepared more than thirty dishes for him, in their native manner. These would be kept hot for him over small adobe braziers. More than three hundred plates of this food would be made available to him, and more than a thousand for his guard. . . . I've heard that he frequently ate the flesh of young boys. Since he had such a variety of dishes in front of him, though, we couldn't tell whether some of them might have been human flesh or if they were something else. Every day he was offered fowls, turkey, pheasant, partridge, quail, wild and domestic duck, venison, wild boar, marsh birds, doves, rabbits, hares, and a large variety of other birds and animals that roam this land—of which there are so many that I can't name them very quickly. So we tried not to look at what he was eating. I do know that once our captain had reproached him for making human sacrifices and eating human flesh, he ordered that this fare no longer be served to him. **– Díaz**

All the lords who came into his house entered barefoot, and when those few who were summoned by him came before him, they came with lowered head, downcast eyes, and in an attitude of humility. When they spoke to him they did not look at him, but exhibited great reverence. I know they did this out of respect because some of them reproved Spaniards for shamelessly looking in my face when they spoke to me. It seemed irreverent and brazen to them.

When Montezuma went out — an infrequent occurrence — all those who accompanied him and all whom he came upon in the streets turned their faces aside, so that in no way might they look at him. All others prostrated themselves until he had passed. One of his lords always preceded him bearing three long thin rods, an action whose purpose was, I think, to warn people that he was coming. When he descended from his litter, he would take one of these rods in his hand and carry it wherever he was going. **– Cortés**

Cortés was deeply impressed by the opulence of the city, beginning with Montezuma's residences, some of which boasted zoological gardens and collections of human oddities. Like a tourist writing home, he described it all in his next letter to the king.[1]

Both inside and outside the city, Montezuma had many residences, each for a different pastime. These houses were as beautiful as can be imagined, obviously built for a very great lord. The magnificence and grandeur of his palace in the city can hardly be described, and for this reason I won't attempt it. Suffice it to say that in all Spain nothing would compare.

He had one house, somewhat less magnificent, with a lovely garden overlooked by balconies with wall facings and flagstones of beautifully worked jasper. There were rooms in this house large enough to lodge two great lords with their entire retinues. Outside the house were ten pools, frequented by every type of water bird found in these parts, all quite tame. Saltwater pools had been provided for seabirds, and fresh-water pools for riverine birds. These pools were all drained from time to time for cleaning, then refilled from aqueducts. Each species of bird was fed according to its habits in the wild. To those that required fish, fish was given, to those that

---

[1] He wrote no letters to Diego Velázquez.

preferred worms, they gave worms, and to those that required maize or smaller grains, the appropriate grains were given. I can attest to Your Highness that the fish-eating birds were given 250 pounds of fish per day, all fish taken from the brackish lake. Three hundred men had no other duty but to look after these birds, with other men assigned to healing any that fell ill. At every tank or pool were very nicely ornamented galleries or overlooks where Montezuma might come to amuse himself by gazing on the birds.

In this house there was a special room for men, women, and children who had been born with white faces and bodies, with white hair, eyebrows, and eyelashes. . . . In another house he kept deformed men and women—dwarfs, hunchbacks, and people with other deformities. These various monstrosities were segregated into rooms by type, and all had people to care for them. **– Cortés**

The men could not get their fill of these rich novelties and sights.

Let's look now at the large number of performers that Montezuma kept for his amusement—dancers and stilt-walkers and people who seemed to fly through the air and others like clowns to make him laugh. He had set off an entire part of the city for them alone. And of craftsmen to keep his houses in repair—stonecutters, masons, carpenters—and of the houses themselves, he had as many as he wanted.

Let's not forget his flower gardens and groves of sweet-smelling trees, and the countless varieties he had of all these plants, and their wonderful arrangement. Then there were his fresh-water tanks and ponds, with water flowing in on one side and out on the other. And the baths that he had there, and the little birds that nested in the trees, and the medicinal and useful herbs—it was all a sight to see. To maintain all this he had an army of gardeners. Everything was plastered or whitewashed stonework, whether it was the baths or walkways, or the more private spaces beneath arbors, or the areas set aside for dance and song. There was so much to see in these gardens—as there was everywhere—that we couldn't help but marvel at his seemingly limitless power, at how many people it took to keep all this up, and at the number of Indians who were masters of their trades. **– Díaz**

The great cue near which they were lodged made a deep impression on the men, not least upon Cortés himself.

> Among these temples is one, the principal temple, that the human tongue can barely describe, so large and unique is it. This temple is so large that a village of five hundred inhabitants could easily fit within its very high walls. Elegant homes, with great halls and corridors, are found around its edge. These are the homes of the religious men who keep the temple. There are easily forty towers here, all high and well constructed. Fifty steps must be climbed to reach the main part of the most important of these towers, which is taller than the bell-tower of Seville's cathedral. The towers' stonework and woodwork is as fine as one could find anywhere. All the stonework in their chapels, where they keep their idols, is adorned with images in relief. Surrounding woodwork, too, is carved with images of assorted monsters and other figures and designs. These towers are the burial places of lords, and the chapels within them are each dedicated to the idol venerated by that particular lord. **– Cortés**

Young Andrés de Tapia, one of Cortés's captains, added further detail.

> Facing this tower, and about a crossbow's shot away from it, were sixty or seventy very tall posts set upon a broad rock-and-mortar platform. On steps surrounding this platform were a large number of human skulls set in mortar, with the teeth facing outward. Flanking this display were two towers completely made of mortared-in skulls, with no admixture of stone. Here the teeth also faced outward. The distance between the posts seemed to be about two feet. As many short poles as would fit were set between these posts, and on each pole were skewered five skulls, all pierced through the temples. I myself and one Gonzalo de Umbría counted the poles, and multiplied by five heads per pole. We came up with 136,000 heads, not counting those built into the towers. **– Tapia**

The Spaniards spent the next three days like simple tourists, rubbernecking, observing the people, the architecture, and the manner of life in the vicinity of their quarters, not yet daring to venture farther. The soldier Díaz and the captain-general Cortés took note of everything.

This great city of Tenochtitlan sits in the middle of a brackish lake.[1] On any side, the distance to shore is about two leagues.[2] The city, which is about the size of Seville or Córdoba, has four entry points, each serviced by a manmade causeway as wide as two cavalry lances. Its main streets are quite broad and straight, although many streets are partly on land and partly on water, in which place they paddle their canoes. All streets are broken into sections by water-filled gaps, which are in some cases quite wide. To cross these openings they have bridges made of long and wide wooden beams, all very stout and skillfully made. Some of these bridges can easily support ten horsemen crossing together. – **Cortés**

The future destroyer of all this continued:

There are many fine houses in this city, the reason for this being that all the lords of the lands subject to Montezuma have homes here, and reside here for part of the year. And besides these lords there are many wealthy citizens, with equally grand houses. All of these people, in addition to having imposing homes, cultivate pleasant flower gardens both on their upper and lower floors.

Along one of the causeways to this city run two mortared aqueducts,[3] each two paces wide and five feet deep. One of these is used to convey a stream as thick as a man's body of very good fresh water to the heart of the city, and all drink from this. The second channel, normally empty, is used when the first is being cleaned. Where these aqueducts pass over one of the breaks in the causeway, along a bridge, the water runs through channels as wide as an ox's body, and it is from here that the city is served. Men atop the bridges load canoes waiting below with water from the aqueduct, and the men in

[1] The more saline water had been confined by a dike to the east of the island. The area of the island, including the northern zone of Tlatelolco, was about fifteen square miles. The island population may have been as high as three hundred thousand, although some scholars think it was lower.

[2] About five miles.

[3] These aqueducts ran from freshwater sources in the hills of Chapultepec, on the lake's western shore.

216 ~ Conquistador Voices/Cortés

the canoes then sell it through the streets of the city. The loaders are paid for their work.

At all entry-points to the city, and wherever the canoes are unloaded — points where most provisions would be brought in — are huts with officials who take a percentage of everything that comes into the city. I don't know if this tax then goes to the prince or to the city, but I believe it's most likely for the prince, because in markets I've seen in other provinces of this land, it goes to the lord.

Every day, in all the markets and public places in this city, many laborers and artisans of all kinds wait to be hired for a day's wages.

The people here are better-mannered and take more care with their dress than in other provinces and cities. The reason for this is that Montezuma and his lords are always here, and the people behave accordingly. . . . Considering that these people are so barbarous and far from the knowledge of God, and from commerce with civilized nations, it's remarkable to see how much they've accomplished in all things. **– Cortés**

An anonymous Spanish soldier commented on the appearance of the people.

The men's clothing is made of a soft cotton cloth, like a bedsheet, but not as large, very beautifully worked in a variety of ways, with fringes and borders. Each man wears two or three fastened across his chest. In winter they wear a kind of cloak made of very tiny feathers — it looks like *cremesino*,[1] and is similar to our fur caps. It might be red, black, white, purple, or yellow. They cover their privates, front and rear, with a kind of flashy cloth like the large kerchiefs they tie around their heads when traveling. These are colorful, with equally colorful edging and embroidery, and have tassels that hang front and back. The men wear shoes with soles and decorated heels, but without vamps. Laces run from between their toes to the instep, where they're wrapped and fastened with buttons. They wear nothing on their heads except in combat, or in their festivals and dances. Their hair they wear long, and bound up in various ways.

---

[1] Possibly like a red silk or wool.

The women wear a kind of soft cotton blouse, sleeveless, that resembles those we call *sobrepelliz* in Spain. They're ample and long, embroidered in marvelous ways throughout. With their intricate fringes and borders, they're absolutely charming. The women wear two, three, or four of them of different lengths and arranged in various ways so that they look like skirts. From the waist down they wear a garment of pure cotton that reaches their feet. It too is highly adorned. They wear nothing on their heads, especially in cooler regions. Their lovely hair, which may be black or chestnut, they grow long. With their colorful clothing, and the long hair flowing down their backs, they are indeed a beautiful sight.

– Anonymous

After four days in this intriguing city, but having seen only a small portion of it, Cortés sent word to Montezuma that he wished now to visit the city's northern part,[1] where, he had learned, the large market and another great cue were located. Montezuma acquiesced, but, perhaps sensing trouble, said he would accompany the Spaniards there himself.

The men were astounded at what they saw.

A number of caciques, sent on ahead by Montezuma, accompanied us. And once we arrived in the great plaza, called Tlatelolco, never having seen such a thing, we were awestruck at the number of people around us, by the variety of merchandise available, and by how well arranged and ordered everything was. The caciques who were with us continued to point things out for us. Every possible type of merchandise was for sale, and everything well marked and in its place.

– Díaz

Men who had served in Constantinople, Rome, and all over Italy said they had never seen anything like this Mexican marketplace.

Let's begin with the dealers in gold and silver and precious stones, feathers, blankets, embroidered goods, and male and female slaves. They bring as many slaves to sell here as the Portuguese bring blacks from Guinea. To keep them from escaping, most are locked into collars fixed around their necks at the end of a long pole, but some they bring unrestrained. . .
.

---

[1] Tlatelolco.

We saw sellers of black beans and sage, and of a variety of other vegetables and herbs. In one part of the plaza they were selling fowl and turkey, rabbits, hares, deer, young ducks, little dogs, and food of that nature. There was a section for fruit-sellers, and for women who sold cooked food, cakes, and tripe. There were a thousand kinds of pottery, from large water jars to small jugs, all displayed in a particular area. They had honey-sellers and taffy-sellers, and sellers of other sweets like nougats. There was a section where wood was sold—boards, cradles, beams, chopping blocks, benches. Then there were people selling pitch-pine for torches, and related items.

I can't fail to mention, although with apologies, that they sold many canoe-loads of human excrement that was stored in the inlets near the plaza. This is used not only in the manufacture of salt, but also in curing hides, and they insist on its necessity for both these processes. Finally, I know many will laugh at this, but what I'm about to say is true: in order to conserve their excrement, along all their roads they have provided shelters made of cane or straw or grass into which people can enter without being seen from the road and purge their bowels. **– Díaz**

Cortés recorded his own impressions of this great market square.

One square is twice as big as Salamanca's, with stalls all around, where every day upwards of sixty thousand souls are engaged in buying and selling. Whatever can be found in this land is for sale here, from food to ornaments of silver and gold, as well as of lead, brass, copper, tin, stone, bone, shell, and feather. They sell lime, both rough and hewn stone, adobe bricks, raw wood, and wood that's been worked in various ways. In one street they sell game and any kind of bird found in the region—chickens, partridges and quails, wild ducks, flycatchers, garganey, turtledoves, doves, marsh birds, parrots, eagle-owls and eagles, falcons, sparrow-hawks, and kestrels. Of some of the raptors they sell the skin complete with plumage, head, beak, and claws. They also sell rabbits, hares, deer, and small gelded dogs, which have been raised for food. **– Cortés**

The Spaniards, accompanied now by Montezuma in his litter, were then escorted to the cue, a truncated pyramid with 114 steps to the top, where human sacrifices were carried out. Ever solicitous of the welfare of his enigmatic and frightening guests, Montezuma ordered several papas to assist Cortés in ascending the pyramid, but the captain-general pushed them away, and the Spaniards climbed the very steep stairway unassisted. What they saw from the top took their breath away—the city, lake, causeways, and lakeside towns lay spread out at their feet to the very horizon.

The gawping young Díaz took in every detail, but found himself distracted by the cue itself.

> Let me now describe the large and splendid courts in front of the temple of Huichilobos—an area as large as the plaza of Salamanca, and the spot where the church called Santiago de Tlatelolco now stands.[1] Two masonry walls stood before the temple entrance, and the court was paved with large, flat stones, burnished, whitewashed, immaculately clean. . . . At a short distance from the cue stood another small tower that housed idols. To me it was pure hell, since on one door was painted a frightful mouth, such as they paint to represent Hades, and the mouth, open, displayed great fangs ready to swallow souls. Images of devils and bodies of serpents surrounded the door.
>
> A little apart from there stood a place of sacrifice, all black with smoke and encrusted blood. Inside the house we saw many great pots, pitchers, and jars, all filled with water, for it was here that they cooked the poor Indians who had been sacrificed and were to be eaten by the papas. Next to the place of sacrifice we saw numerous knives and chopping blocks like you'd see in a butcher's shop. Behind that accursed house, at some distance from it, were great piles of firewood, and not far from this a large water jar that was filled from a covered aqueduct that brings water from Chapultepec.
>
> I always thought of that house as Hell. – **Díaz**

The anonymous soldier described the manner in which the victims were sacrificed.

> They take the one to be sacrificed and first lead him, finely dressed, through the streets and plazas with great pomp and celebration. People tell him of their needs and wants, begging him—who is soon to be with their god—to present these

---

[1] The convent of Santiago de Tlatelolco was established on this site in the 1530s, and later a church of the same name was built nearby.

petitions to the god. They give him food and anything else he may want, and in this way all kinds of things are collected . . . but it all goes to the priests.

They then take him to the temple, where they have a great party in which he also takes part. After this, the priest who will conduct the sacrifice undresses him and leads him to the side of the temple stairs, where a stone idol stands. He is laid on his back, and his hands and feet are bound on either side. At this point the people begin again to dance and sing around him, and remind him of the representation he must make to their idol. Then the sacrificing priest, an important official among them, returns. He takes a stone blade as sharp as steel and as long as a large knife, and in the time it would take to make the sign of the cross he plunges the blade into the victim's chest, opens it, and digs out the warm and beating heart. The heart is immediately taken by the high priest, who anoints the mouth of the principal idol with its blood. Blood is then cast toward the sun or toward some star (if it is nighttime), and the mouths of the temple's other stone or wooden idols are anointed. The cornice of the chapel door where the principal idol stands is anointed, and finally the heart is burnt, with the ashes kept as a relic. – **Anonymous**

Cortés asked Montezuma to show him the idols. Probably knowing that no good could come of this, Montezuma granted his wish, leading him into a small room with altars, upon each of which was a great stone idol. Cortés, thoroughly revolted, asked his host how a man of his sophistication could believe in such nonsense. Then he suddenly told the king that he wanted to erect an altar to the Virgin Mary in this very room, to reveal the fear that would overtake his idols in the presence of her image. Montezuma flared up at him and Cortés backed off, turning on his heel and leading his men briskly down the precipitous stairway, back to their quarters.[1] Montezuma and his chiefs were left behind.

On arrival at his apartments, Cortés — abruptly claiming to be tired of setting up an altar every day for Mass — decided to ask Montezuma for masons to build an altar to the Virgin in their living area, an altar

---

[1] Díaz noted that some of the soldiers, due to having "pustules or running sores," found the descent to cause pain in their thighs,

on which Mass could be celebrated. On receiving this request, Montezuma duly sent masons, and the altar was built in two days.

Spanish adventurers, thoroughly secure in a brand of Catholicism that permitted great excesses of violence and cruelty, nonetheless tended to take divine worship and evangelization very seriously.

> We had Mass in our quarters every day until the wine ran out. For when Cortés and some of the other captains and friars had been ill during the Tlaxcalan campaign, there was a run on the wine that we had reserved for Mass. Although we were now without wine, we nonetheless went to our chapel every day and prayed on our knees before the altar and sacred images. We did this in the first place because we were obliged to do so and in the habit of doing so as Christians, and in the second place because we hoped that Montezuma and his captains, seeing us on our knees before the cross — especially when we prayed the Ave Maria — might be inclined to imitate us. **– Díaz**

Prior to the arrival of the Aztec masons, some of Cortés's men, trying to decide where best to put the altar, had stumbled upon a secret door, discovering behind it a room filled with gold and jewels — the treasure of which they had heard rumors, the treasure of Montezuma's father Axayacatl. It was agreed that the door would immediately be resealed, and the discovery left unmentioned.

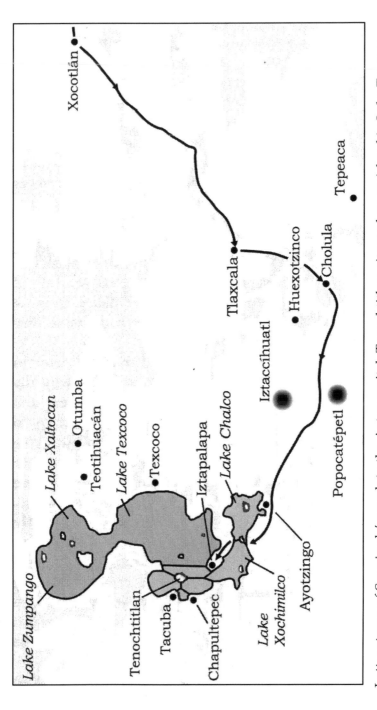

Latter stages of Spaniards' march to the Aztec capital, Tenochtitlan, situated on an island in Lake Texcoco, one of five interconnected lakes. A major battle was fought at Tlaxcala. Two large volcanoes are shown.

7

THE SEIZURE OF MONTEZUMA

Cortés's captains now took the opportunity to have a heart-to-heart with their commander. Paraphrasing: "Have you looked around us?" they asked. "Don't you see that we are in deep trouble here? They can shut off our food and water at any time, they can raise the bridges on the causeways and trap us. We're surrounded by thousands upon thousands of people—on land and water—who would turn against us in a moment at a word from their chief. We're getting news from our Tlaxcalan friends that bad things are in the wind already. We ourselves have noticed that the people who bring us our food are growing insolent. What are we going to do? The only thing left for us, if we want to remain here, is to take Montezuma prisoner, for our own protection."

"Don't you think I haven't been thinking about the same thing?" answered Cortés. "We'll have to take him prisoner, it's true, but I'm not yet sure how to do it."

News brought from the coast on the following day made quick action imperative. Montezuma's commander in the area, Qualpopoca, had begun again to demand the tribute formerly paid by coastal towns, the tribute that had been stopped by Cortés. The Totonacs' refusal to pay had led to threats against them. Escalante and his small force at Villa Rica had stepped in, and a battle had ensued during which a number of Spaniards, including Escalante himself, had been killed. To make matters worse, the once-friendly Cempoalans and other Totonacs, seeing the inability of the Spaniards to protect them, were now in revolt against the Spaniards as well.

Cortés's small force, which had been in the island capital—potentially the jaws of death—for less than a week, was even more vulnerable than the coastal garrison had been. They would have to take immediate, possibly violent, action if they hoped to seize the reins of this great city, or, at a minimum, escape with their lives. Montezuma must be taken prisoner at once.

In his second letter to the emperor Charles, Cortés wrote of his decision.

> With six days having passed, Most Invincible Lord, since my entry into Tenochtitlan, and having seen a little of the

city — although admittedly not much of what should be seen — it appeared to me that it might benefit your royal service, not to mention our own safety, if Montezuma were no longer left at liberty, but were to be in my power. This would, I thought, keep him from abandoning his stated intention of serving Your Royal Highness. There was, however, an even more urgent consideration, and it was this: since we Spaniards can be somewhat unbearable and troublesome, a man who wields his great power might — if we annoyed him — not only cause us grave injury, but even obliterate all memory of us. . . . For these reasons, therefore, I determined to take him prisoner and move him into my own quarters, which were very strong. – **Cortés**

The pretext under which Cortés would arrest Montezuma would be the recent killing of the Spaniards on the coast. He would make a show of attempting to understand how Montezuma had allowed this to take place.

Thinking on all the ways I might seize him without provoking a riot, I remembered what the captain I'd left in Vera Cruz had written to me. It concerned what had happened in Almería,[1] and how he had learned that all of it had been done at Montezuma's command. So leaving a strong guard in the streets, I went to Montezuma's houses — as I had frequently done before — to see him. We engaged in some banter, after which he presented me with some gold jewelry. He also presented me with one of his daughters, and, some of the men accompanying me, with the daughters of other chiefs. But I said to him that I already knew what had happened in Nautecal,[2] or Almería, and about the Spaniards that had been killed there. I added that Qualpopoca had laid the blame on him, even to protesting that, he being a vassal of the great prince, it could not have been otherwise. But I told him that I didn't believe Qualpopoca, that I thought he had said this just to escape blame. It seemed to me, I told him, that he should send for Qualpopoca and the other lords who had been responsible for the deaths of the Spaniards, so that the truth might be known. – **Cortés**

---

[1] The Spaniards' name for the Totonac town of Nauhtla, where the recent battle had taken place, about fifty miles north of Villa Rica de la Vera Cruz.
[2] Nauhtla.

When Montezuma heard this he was so astonished that he nearly fainted. He insisted that he had never commanded any of his people to bear arms against us. He would, he said, without delay, send to his captains to ascertain what had happened, and punish them. He immediately removed the royal sign and seal of Huichilobos from his wrist, which he never did except when issuing an order of supreme importance that had to be carried out at once. – **Díaz**

He immediately sent for a few of his men, to whom he gave a small stone figure, like a seal, that he wore on his arm, and he ordered them to go to Almería, sixty or seventy leagues distant, and to bring Qualpopoca back with them. He also told them to find out who else had been involved in the death of those Spaniards, and to bring them as well. If they refused to come voluntarily, he said, they should be brought as prisoners. And if they resisted, aid should be sought from certain nearby towns — which he named — to send forces to arrest them. In no case were they to return without them.

Once these deputies had left, I told Montezuma that I appreciated the zeal he had shown in apprehending those men, since I had to render an accounting of my Spaniards to Your Highness. I then told him that I thought he should stay with me in my own quarters until this matter could be clarified and he could be shown to be blameless. – **Cortés**

Montezuma no doubt went speechless at this suggestion. He then attempted to reassert his authority, which all knew had already been lost. The scene turned pathetic.

As to becoming their prisoner and being removed from his palace against his will, Montezuma said that he was not a person to whom such an order could be given, and that he had no wish to leave the palace. Cortés then presented various reasons why this should be done, and Montezuma responded with his own reasons why it should not be done. More than a half-hour was spent in this manner. Finally Juan Velázquez de León and the other captains said that this was taking too long, that he should already have been taken prisoner. Becoming increasingly agitated, they said to Cortés, "Why are we wasting so many words on this? We either take him prisoner or we stab him to death right now. Think again — if he cries out or makes a disturbance, we have to kill him, and if we do kill him we have a better chance of saving our lives."

Since Juan Velázquez was shouting loudly and angrily — his habitual way of speaking — and Montezuma could see that the other captains were also getting agitated, he asked Doña Marina what was going on. Doña Marina, being very quick, said, "Señor Montezuma, what I would advise you to do is go with these men to their apartments without making a fuss, and I'm certain that you will be cared for in a manner befitting the great prince that you are. Otherwise, you will die here. In their quarters, you'll be told the truth."

Montezuma then said to Cortés, "Señor Malinche, I understand what you're doing, but I have a legitimate son and two legitimate daughters. Take them hostage, and don't disgrace me in this way. What will my chiefs say if they see me taken prisoner?" – **Díaz**

Cortés, fully capable of dispensing vinegar, nonetheless preferred honey.

I begged him not to take this amiss, exhorting him not to think of himself as a prisoner, since he would enjoy complete liberty and no obstacle would be placed on his service and command of his domains. I told him he could choose a room in my quarters, whichever he preferred, assuring him that he could take his ease there as he wished. He would certainly be faced, I said, with no annoyance or unpleasantness. In addition to the service of his own household, I told him, my own men would serve him in any way he wished. We went back and forth on this for a very long time — so long that it would be tedious to write it down for Your Highness, and little pertinent anyway — until at last he agreed to go with me. – **Cortés**

Montezuma had descended step by step to this moment, and his fate was now sealed. He would, moreover, become a perfect model of what would later be called the Stockholm syndrome, where an absence of abuse on the part of a hostage-taker is interpreted as kindness.

He then commanded that the apartment where he was to stay be prepared, and this was immediately done. Then many of his lords appeared, barefoot, and bearing their garments under their arms. They brought in a simple litter, and, all weeping, transported him on it in silence. Thus we went to his new apartments without any but the slightest agitation in the city, which, when Montezuma heard of it, he ordered to cease. The city then became as calm as ever, as it remained for the entire time that I held Montezuma prisoner. This was because he was perfectly at his ease, and with the complete domestic service he had enjoyed at home, which was quite grand. I and all my men, moreover, did everything within our power to meet his needs. **– Cortés**

Thus was the great Montezuma made prisoner. He was allowed to take with him all his servants and women and baths. He was permitted to retain the twenty lords who had always accompanied him, as well as his counselors and captains. And he showed no resentment at any of it. **– Díaz**

The guest had become the host, and the host the guest. But Cortés was only beginning. Potentially trapped among many thousands of increasingly restive Indians, he nonetheless fully intended to avenge the deaths of the Spaniards on the coast—even though they had been killed not by treachery, but in open combat—and to do so in a public manner.

By the fifteenth or twentieth day of Montezuma's captivity, the men whom the prince had sent to bring back Qualpopoca and the others responsible for the deaths of the Spaniards arrived. They had brought not only Qualpopoca, but one of his sons and fifteen other men, affirming that all were chiefs and all were involved in the Spaniards' deaths. Qualpopoca, borne in on a litter, acted the part of a lord, which indeed he was. When these men were turned over to me I ordered them confined under heavy guard, and once they had confessed to having killed the Spaniards, I had them questioned about their being subjects of Montezuma. Qualpopoca responded that if he was vassal of some other prince, who would it be? To me this seemed equivalent to an affirmative response. **– Cortés**

When Cortés was shown [Qualpopoca's] confession, he sent to inform Montezuma that the facts of the case had incriminated him. Montezuma protested his innocence. Our captain then sent to tell him that he believed in the prince's guilt, and that the crime merited punishment in conformity with the mandates of our king, namely, that the person who orders the murder of another, whether they be guilty or innocent, deserves to be killed by them. But, he said, his esteem for the prince was so high, and his love for him so strong, that even if he was guilty of this crime, Cortés would sooner pay with his own life than see the great prince forfeit his. Montezuma received this message in great trepidation.

Without further ado, Cortés sentenced Montezuma's captains to be burned to death in front of the royal palace, and the sentence was duly carried out. And so that no disturbance might erupt, he ordered Montezuma to be put in chains during the burnings. The prince roared with anger at the indignity, but soon became even more frightened than before.

After the burnings, Cortés came to Montezuma's quarters with five captains and removed the chains himself. He then spoke to him in such a kindly way that all trace of the prince's anger vanished. Cortés told him that not only did he consider him a brother, but as much more. And if he was now lord of many cities and provinces, Cortés would, if time allowed, do all in his power to make him lord of lands and peoples that he had not yet been able to subdue. – **Díaz**

Cortés and his men showed the greatest solicitude for their captive prince.

Montezuma was quite pleased with the flattery and attention he received from us, and the daily conversation that he enjoyed with us all. And whenever we—including Cortés—came into his presence, we always removed our mailed hats or helmets (for we always went armed), and he responded with great civility and respect. – **Díaz**

Because our captain was a detail-oriented man, he worried that Montezuma might suffer distress at being confined. He therefore made an effort every day after prayers (for, not having wine, we said prayers instead of attending Mass) to pay him court as if he were still free. Cortés was customarily accompanied in this exercise by four captains, with Pedro de Alvarado, Juan Velázquez de León, and Diego de Ordaz normally among them. They always asked the prince very solicitously how he was getting along, begged him to issue orders to them that would be complied with at once, and all the while encouraged him not to be troubled by his present condition. He replied that he actually was happy as a captive, either because our gods had given us power over him, or because his Huichilobos had permitted his captivity. We spoke frequently to him about our holy faith and the great power of our lord the emperor.

Sometimes Montezuma would play a game of theirs with Cortés called *totoloque*. It's played with some smooth little pellets, which for this game were made of gold. You toss the pellets for some distance, as well as some little disks, also made of gold, and after five throws you win or lose some gold pieces or precious stones that the players have staked. I remember one day that Pedro de Alvarado was keeping score for Cortés and one of Montezuma's nephews, a great lord, was keeping score for his uncle. Pedro de Alvarado always added an extra point to Cortés's score, and Montezuma noticed it. Laughingly he said that he didn't want *Tonatio* (for that's what they called Alvarado) keeping score any more because he made so much *ixoxol* with the score,[1] which meant in their language that he cheated, always adding an extra point. Cortés and all of us who were standing guard that day couldn't help but laugh at the great Montezuma's remark. – **Díaz**

It was never necessary to tell most of us whose duty it was to guard him of the great courtesy we were required to show this great prince. For his part, he knew each one of us by name. He even knew the kind of person we were, and he was very kind to us, giving us all precious stones, and, to some of us, cloaks and beautiful girls.

I was a young man then. Whenever I stood guard or came into his presence, I always removed my helmet with great deference. The page we had assigned to him, Orteguilla, had told him that I had been to this land twice before, on voyages of discovery. One day I asked Orteguilla if he would present a request for me to Montezuma — "Ask him," I said, "if he might give me a pretty girl." Montezuma was told of my request, and he summoned me. "Bernal Díaz del Castillo," he said, "they tell me you are poor in clothing and gold. But today I'm going to give you a fine girl. Treat her well because she's the daughter of an important man, and they'll give you cloaks and gold as well."

---

[1] *Tonatio* meant "The Sun" in Nahuatl, after Alvarado's blond hair and beard.

> I responded with great humility that I kissed his hands for such great kindness, and that I prayed God Our Lord to prosper him. **– Díaz**

At this time Montezuma took advantage of what he believed was the friendship of his captors to request leave to visit the temple of Huitzilopochtli, to pray and make sacrifices. With warnings that he must not make human sacrifices and—under pain of instant death—not stir up his people, Cortés reluctantly agreed, and Montezuma, accompanied by Spanish officers, Fray Bartolomé de Olmedo, and 150 soldiers (including Díaz), was borne off on his litter to the cue. He was assisted in climbing the steps, and, once at the top, quickly succeeded in contravening one of Cortés's commands.

> Four Indians had already been sacrificed there the night before, and although our captain and the Mercedarian friar remonstrated with him, it availed them nothing. Montezuma considered it necessary to sacrifice more men and boys and we could do nothing but gloss over it, for Mexico and other large cities were by now on the point of rebellion, fomented by Montezuma's nephews.

> After he had made his sacrifices, which didn't take long, we went back with him to our quarters. He was very cheerful, and thanked us soldiers who had escorted him to the cue by giving us jewels. **– Díaz**

Unknown to Montezuma, the Spaniards had put into motion a plan for escaping from this island city if the need arose. Orders had been sent to the coast to carry some of the scuttled ships' sails and tackle the nearly two hundred miles to the lake shore, accompanied by a blacksmith and forge and all available iron and tools. If raised bridges and blocked causeways denied them escape, the Spaniards would escape across the water. They would construct brigantines,[1] large enough to transport all men and horses. When the requested equipment arrived, Cortés explained his shipbuilding plan to Montezuma, told him that the vessels would be for pleasure sailing

---

[1] Large, flat, open sloops, each of which could carry light cannon and more than three dozen men, and which could also be rowed. Not to be confused with the later and larger two-masted sailing ship of the same name, the sixteenth-century brigantine was used principally for shallow-water and coastal navigation. With the assistance of luck, some were capable of ocean-crossing.

only, and asked him to send skilled men to cut oaks and to assist the Spanish carpenters in constructing them. The Aztec prince again acquiesced, sending enough skilled Indians that two brigantines were built very quickly.[1]

Montezuma, on seeing the finished product, hinted that he might like a ride.

Once the brigantines had been built and put into the water—fully rigged, with masts stepped, royal and imperial banners run up, and seamen appointed to handle the vessels—they were tested under both sail and oar, and found to be very satisfactory. When Montezuma heard of this, he told Cortés that he'd like to go hunting in a game preserve he had on a rocky island in the lake—a place where not even the greatest caciques were allowed to hunt under penalty of death. Cortés told him he'd be happy to let him go, but that he must remember what was said to him when he visited his idols, that if he caused any disturbance he would pay with his life. He could go there in a brigantine, said Cortés, since it would be much faster than a canoe.

Montezuma, pleased to have been invited aboard the faster of the two sloops, brought with him many lords and principal men. The other brigantine was also filled with caciques, including one of his sons. Montezuma's beaters were told to follow in canoes and other craft. Cortés ordered Juan Velázquez de León, who was captain of the guard, as well as Pedro de Alvarado, Cristóbal de Olid, and Alonso de Ávila with two hundred soldiers to go aboard with him and to watch him closely.

The captains I've named, all scrupulous men, not only brought the soldiers aboard, but also four brass cannon with all the powder we had. They also brought Mesa and Arbenga, our gunners. Because of the weather they set up an ornate awning on deck for Montezuma and his chiefs. Since the breezes during that season are quite fresh, and because the mariners delighted in driving the vessel hard to please Montezuma, they flew across the water, leaving the beaters and dignitaries in the canoes far behind in spite of their many paddlers. Montezuma was thrilled, remarking on how great it

---

[1] According to Cortés, four were built in all.

was to combine sails and oars. He went ashore on the island, which was not far away, killed all the game he wanted — deer, hare, rabbit — and returned very content. As we were approaching the city, Pedro de Alvarado, Juan Velázquez de León, and the other captains ordered the cannon fired, delighting the prince even more.

Since he was such a frank and pleasant person, we treated him with all the respect accorded princes in these parts, and he treated us in the same way. **– Díaz**

This idyllic interlude could not last. As December moved along to year's end, The Spaniards knew that they were ultimately the prisoners. In spite of this awareness, as they lived out each day their discussions frequently turned to the enormous quantities of gold at hand, and Cortés eventually asked Montezuma for the location of his mines. He then demanded Indians to guide his men to these, in some cases, distant places, sent the parties out, and sat back to await their reports.

The resultant news was good — plenty of gold seemed available in the countryside. Cortés then informed Montezuma of his decision to demand tribute for the emperor Charles in the form of gold and jewels to be collected from village chiefs in all corners of the prince's realm. Montezuma himself would be required to pay this tribute as well. The captive prince, still apparently believing that cooperation was the key to survival, immediately dispatched messengers throughout his lands to order payment of the tribute. With regard to the donation expected from himself, Montezuma quietly mentioned that he knew the Spaniards had discovered the treasure-room in their apartments. He astonished them by declaring that they could have it all.

Cortés immediately ordered the removal and examination of this treasure, and his men, assisted by goldsmiths and silversmiths supplied by Montezuma, began to remove jewel incrustations and other embellishments to get at the pure gold, a process that took three days. They now proceeded to turn this unique, intricately worked Aztec treasure into small, plain, vulgar, but highly portable, ingots.

The Aztec nobles were struck dumb by the strangers' arrogant theft of their royal treasure and by the evident collusion of their prince. They refused to continue feeding the Spaniards. La Malinche, however, would have none of it. Her Spaniards, she said — exhausted from their exertions in melting down Aztec gold — must be fed.

La Malinche called the nobles together. She climbed up to the palace roof and cried: "Mexicanos, come forward! The Spaniards need your help! Bring them food and pure water. They are tired and hungry; they are almost fainting from exhaustion! Why do you not come forward? Are you angry with them?"

The Mexicans were too frightened to approach. They were crushed by terror and would not risk coming forward. They shied away as if the Spaniards were wild beasts, as if the hour were midnight on the blackest night of the year. Yet they did not abandon the Spaniards to hunger and thirst. They brought them whatever they needed, but shook with fear as they did so. They delivered the supplies to the Spaniards with trembling hands, then turned and hurried away. – **Aztec account**

Although the gold was to be divided among the men, it was itself divisive. Following deduction of the royal fifth, then of Cortés's fifth as captain-general, then the amount due him to cover expenses he had undertaken, plus shares for the men at Villa Rica, and double shares for the two priests, little seemed to be left for the several hundred fighters who had borne the hardship. The men noted, moreover, that a few recognizable pieces had disappeared from the pile.[1] The lowly soldier seemed destined to receive little or nothing. This caused murmuring, then even the outbreak of a quarrel among two officers, who drew swords on one another. In an attempt to regain control, especially since the violence might soon be directed toward himself, Cortés ordered the men arrested until tempers cooled, and proceeded to soothe his army with honeyed words about the much greater treasure that awaited them upon the fall of this city, even offering to lend money to any of his men who needed it.

Still bent on securing the emperor's approval for his bold outlaw action in Mexico, Cortés wrote a glowing description of the treasure, with special attention to the portion soon to be remitted to the Crown (without mention of what was being reserved to himself). If the

---

[1] Some of these pieces had been quietly removed by men needing a stake for continued gambling. Gambling was rife among the troops (who had even manufactured a deck of cards out of an old drum-skin), as they whiled away the hours awaiting their captain-general's orders.

emperor actually read this account, it must have caused him to think carefully about how to treat this lawbreaker.[1]

When whatever could be melted had in fact been melted down, Your Majesty's fifth was seen to amount to some 32,400 gold pesos. This was without counting any gold or silver jewelry, or featherwork or precious stones or anything else of value, all of which I set aside for Your Holy Majesty. This portion might amount to a hundred thousand ducats or more. These treasures, in addition to their basic value, are marvels of originality and uniqueness, and for this reason, priceless. It is difficult to imagine any prince of whom we know in this world possessing such precious items.

And lest Your Highness think I am fantasizing in this, may I say that everything that one can find here, on land or sea, or anything of which Montezuma has ever heard, he has had modeled very realistically in gold or silver or jewels or feathers. These have been done so perfectly that they appear almost real. He has in fact given me many of these things for Your Highness. I have also sketched objects for him to have modeled in gold—things like sacred images, crucifixes, medallions, various ornaments, necklaces, and many other of our things. Your Highness's share of the silver amounts to something like a hundred marks, which I had the natives make into large and small plates, as well as bowls, cups, and spoons. They made them as perfectly as we were able to make them understand.

In addition to this, Montezuma gave me many garments of his own, which—even though they are of cotton, not silk— have no parallel in the world for color or workmanship. Some of this clothing was for men, some for women, all of it quite striking. He gave me bedspreads better than our silk ones. He gave me tapestries suitable for a great hall or church, and quilts of feathers or cotton, all very colorful and marvelous to see. He gave me so much more that I find it hard to describe it all to Your Majesty. He also gave me a dozen blowpipes of the type

---

[1] Since the emperor was frequently absent from his Castilian realm, and since, in any case, his first language was not Castilian, it is easy to believe that he either did not receive or did not read all of Cortés's laboriously crafted letters. Possibly he was given summaries by his counselors.

he uses. I cannot adequately describe their beauty — all painted with the finest paints and subtle colors, picturing all manner of little birds, animals, trees, flowers, and other things from nature. Mouthpiece and muzzle were each wrapped in a band of gold eight inches wide, and around the middle was another, beautifully worked. To accompany these blowpipes he gave me a gold-mesh pouch for pellets, promising to have some pellets made for me, of gold. **– Cortés**

As winter turned to spring, and Montezuma's captains and relatives watched their once-esteemed prince sink slowly into the sepulcher of Spanish influence, their resolve to do something about these brazen foreigners was nearly crystallized into action. They had much to be angry about. Montezuma had had his own nephew and second highest-ranking leader in the kingdom, Cacamatzin, arrested for plotting against the Spaniards. He and those still loyal to him had actually sworn fealty to the far-off and unknown Charles. He had given away his father's gold and jewels, and stripped the entire empire of irreplaceable treasure for these Spanish pigs. Worst of all, he had lately permitted them actually to construct an altar to their Virgin Mary atop the great cue, and to celebrate their religious functions there. It was clear that their leader had been thoroughly cowed, and no longer thought of much beyond saving his life.

Anger among the Aztec chiefs and papas was by now powerful and deep. Meetings were being held without Montezuma's knowledge. The gods were telling the Mexicans of their displeasure over the altar and the stolen treasure. It was time to make all-out war on these impudent interlopers. Montezuma, finally apprised of what was afoot, warned Cortés that he and his men must get out while there was still time. Again Cortés, at first taken aback by this new intelligence, proved to be master of the moment.

Cortés and our captains were distressed and even somewhat alarmed, and little wonder, having received such sudden news that our lives were in great and immediate danger. Cortés thanked him for the warning, but said that two things troubled him — one, they had no ships in which to depart this land, since those in which they arrived had been destroyed by his order, and two, Montezuma would have to come with us to be presented to our great emperor. He begged him therefore to restrain his papas and captains until the Spaniards had been able to build three ships in the coastal dunes. It would be to their advantage not to start a war, he added, because, if they did, they would all be killed. To make Montezuma believe he had every intention of building ships and leaving, Cortés asked him to send carpenters with two of our expert shipbuilders to begin cutting trees near the coast.

On hearing that he would have to accompany Cortés to see the emperor, Montezuma became even sadder than before, but he agreed to send carpenters, encouraging Cortés to set them to work immediately and waste no more time in talk. In the meantime he would order the papas and captains not to stir up the city, and to keep Huichilobos pacified with sacrifices, although not human sacrifices.

Following this dramatic conversation Cortés and his captains took their leave of Montezuma, and we were all left in an anxious state, wondering when the war would begin.

– Díaz

8

SETBACK AND CALAMITY

T hrough March and April, 1520, the men, more than usually anxious at their likely fate, kept a more than usually sharp lookout. They slept in their armor, sandals on their feet, weapons near at hand. Horses were kept saddled and bridled.

In late April or early May, however, they were jarred by a thoroughly unexpected piece of news — eighteen Spanish ships had just anchored off the coast, disgorging some nine hundred armed men. Unbeknownst to them at first, these troops were led by Pánfilo de Narváez, Velázquez's captain in the trampling of Cuba. Narváez's mission was to defeat Cortés's army and return to Cuba with its off-the-tracks captain-general in chains. It had taken Velázquez nearly a year to assemble this force,[1] and it was clear that he wished it to be overwhelming.

Montezuma, who received news of this event a full three days before Cortés, was delighted. He secretly sent gifts, welcoming the newcomers to his domains. Perhaps, he thought, he and his kingdom could be saved after all. When Cortés was informed of the men's arrival and shared the news with Montezuma, the Aztec king feigned surprise, yet could not mask his pleasure. Now you have ships, he said, now you can go home.

But again, both Montezuma and Narváez had underestimated Cortés, who would boldly represent himself to the arriving captain as the king's representative in Mexico, even though Narváez's claim to this title was more legitimate. He would even suggest that the newcomers might be considered invaders of the king's domains. Yet in true Cortés fashion he would first feign ignorance of the Spanish captain's identity and purpose in coming to Mexico, then offer his full cooperation in achieving any benign purpose. He was careful to balance this offer, however, with a plain threat.

> When I heard this news I determined to send a friar whom I had brought in my company with a letter from myself, as well as another from the alcaldes and regidores of the town of Vera

---

[1] The governor was said to have emptied Cuba of able-bodied men to raise this army.

Cruz, who were with me in the city. These letters were addressed to the captain and his people who had arrived in that port, explaining to them very thoroughly what had happened to me in this land, and how I had taken many cities, towns, and fortresses, pacifying them, and bringing them into Your Majesty's royal service. I mentioned that I now held the land's principal ruler prisoner, going on to describe the character of this great city, and how it abounded in gold and jewels for Your Highness. I explained how I had sent a report on this land to Your Majesty, and now asked them to do me the favor of explaining who they were.

Were they subjects of the kingdoms and dominions ruled by Your Highness? If so, I said, would they please write to tell me if they came to this land by your royal mandate to colonize the land? Or were they perhaps passing on, or perhaps just returning? I said that if they lacked any necessity, I would do all in my power to see it supplied, even if they had come from outside Your Majesty's realms. But, I said, if they refused to answer these questions, I would require them on the part of Your Majesty not to disembark in Your Majesty's lands, but to leave them. I warned them that if they did not comply, I would march against them with all the force at my disposal, including both Spaniards and Indians, and I would take them prisoner or kill them as if they were foreigners attempting to invade the lands and dominions of my king and lord. **– Cortés**

Shortly after his arrival Narváez had demanded the surrender of the garrison at Villa Rica. When his envoys entered the town to make this demand, however, Cortés's capable young captain, Gonzalo de Sandoval, having been dispatched there by Cortés, had them arrested and conducted to Tenochtitlan to speak with the captain-general personally.

Five days after the friar departed with this dispatch, twenty of my men from Vera Cruz arrived in the city of Tenochtitlan with a cleric and two laymen they had seized in that town. From them I learned that the fleet and the people who had arrived in that port were sent by Diego Velázquez, and that they were led by one Pánfilo de Narváez, an inhabitant of the island of Fernandina.[1] I also learned that they

---

[1] A name applied to Cuba at this time.

had eighty horse, a great deal of ball and powder, and eight hundred foot, among whom were said to be eighty harquebusiers and 120 crossbowmen. I was told that their leader was calling himself captain-general and lieutenant-governor of these parts, and that he had documentation from Your Majesty to prove this. – **Cortés**

Cortés treated the Narváez men cordially and sent them back with gold to be distributed among their companions. Narváez responded by confiscating all the treasure that Cortés had left at Cempoala and making preparations to march on Mexico.

Cortés now knew that he had to leave the city and act at once against this new threat—a threat not only to the delicate situation of the Spaniards in the capital but also to his control of the coastal Indians.

When I saw the great damage that was beginning to occur, and how the arrival of Narváez was stirring things up in the land, it seemed to me that my going to where he was might calm the situation considerably, because once the Indians of that area saw me, they would think twice about any uprising. I also hoped to come to an agreement with Narváez that might cause this incipient revolt to disappear. I therefore departed that same day, leaving the fortress well supplied with maize and water, and garrisoned by five hundred men with some powder and ball.[1] Then with the rest of the men—about seventy—and some of Montezuma's chiefs, I headed for the coast. – **Cortés**

Prior to departing, he took care to warn Montezuma against committing any treachery in his absence.

Before leaving, however, I had a long talk with Montezuma, telling him to bear in mind that he was now a vassal of Your Majesty and that he was on the point of being rewarded for the services he had rendered. I told him that I was leaving the Spaniards, with all the gold and jewels that he had given me for Your Majesty, in his care. I was setting out, I said, to learn who these new arrivals were, for I still did not

---

[1] Díaz indicates that a smaller force of largely useless men was left in Tenochtitlan. Tapia also says this garrison force numbered only fifty, in which case a larger, more capable force would have been sent against Narváez's nine hundred. Cortés's numbers seem erroneous.

know. I believed they were hostile, I said, and not subjects of Your Majesty.

He promised to see that my men were well provided for, and to guard closely everything I had left there belonging to Your Majesty. As for the men of his who were to accompany me, he said they would lead me by a road that never left his domain, and would see that I was provided with everything I needed. He begged me to inform him if these men on the coast should prove to be hostile, for he would then send many warriors to do battle with them and drive them from the land. For all this I thanked him, and promised that Your Highness would amply reward him. **– Cortés**

Leaving the garrison in Mexico under the short-fused but normally dependable Alvarado, Cortés covered as quickly as possible the two hundred miles to the coast and, on a rainy night, with his relatively small force attacked the large Spanish camp.

So a little past midnight on the Feast of Pentecost I entered the enemy camp. Just prior to that, however, our vanguard had stumbled across two of Narváez's sentries, of whom one was captured and the other got away. Our prisoner told us how the force was disposed. To keep the other sentry from alerting the camp prior to our arrival, I hurried forward as quickly as possible, but was not fast enough—the sentry reached the camp almost a half-hour before me.

On my arrival I noticed that the entire force—four sections of two hundred men each—was armed, horses saddled, ready to fight. We arrived so quietly, however, that by the time they did discover us and sound the alarm, I had already reached the courtyard of the place where everyone had their quarters and all were now gathered. They had occupied three or four towers there as well as all the other strong positions roundabout. On the steps of the tower where Narváez was, they had positioned some nineteen artillery pieces. We ran up these steps so quickly, however, that they had no time to fire more than one, and it misfired, thank God, doing no damage. **– Cortés**

Andrés de Tapia was part of the attacking force, as was Alonso de Aguilar.

When we arrived near the enemy camp it was raining, and had been raining for quite some time. Because of this, the enemy's artillery officer had covered the touchholes of his field pieces with wax. We got near their sentinels without being detected, but they soon fled, crying, "To arms, to arms," our own men behind them, beating our own call to arms on the drum. The *marqués* sent eighty of us to attack the enemy captain's quarters while he stayed in our rear disarming men and taking them prisoner.[1]

The enemy troops were easily captured because the two calls to arms had sounded at the same time, causing the enemy—who believed our men to be their own—to mix in with us and inquire what the disturbance was. Since they were on the point of setting out from the camp, their horses were already saddled. The marqués had had the foresight to have the cinch straps on these saddles cut, and when their men tried to mount, they fell off.

We eighty men moved forward to the captain's quarters,[2] where he had about thirty soldiers with him, and in front of his quarters were ten or twelve field-pieces. Their gunner and others, all in a dither, were removing stones or tiles from the touchholes and trying to prime the pieces on top of the wax, thinking to fire them, but nothing happened. We overcame these men, then went after their captain and the men with him. From behind, more of his soldiers broke through us, rushing to their captain's aid. We succeeded in hemming them all inside the building, but couldn't enter ourselves, so we set fire to it and they gave up. We took the captain and some of the others prisoner. – **Tapia**

The thing was so neatly done that by sunrise nearly all of them had given up. Captain Narváez, however, being a fighting man, continued to defend himself strenuously with a broadsword. He was advised by our soldiers to surrender, but he refused. One of our men then knocked him down and took his eye out with a pike. At this point Cortés arrived, and the captain surrendered to him. – **Alonso de Aguilar**

Except for two men who were killed by a single shot, the whole thing was accomplished without loss of life. In one hour

---

[1] The *marqués*, or marquis, was Cortés. Although he did not in fact hold the title at this time, in later years he would be awarded the title of Marquis of the Valley of Oaxaca.

[2] Narváez's quarters.

we captured all those we wished to capture, and relieved the entire force of its arms. **– Cortés**

Cortés insisted that nothing be taken from Narváez's men, and that anything already taken be returned. They were Spaniards, and what he wanted from them above all was their pledge of loyalty and assistance at Tenochtitlan. Handing out gold to Narváez's men liberally, dangling the promise of great riches for all, he won over many of them, even if some came over reluctantly.[1] In any case the number of Spaniards now available for an attack on the city was much more than doubled.

Unfortunately for the Spaniards, however, Cortés had left the wrong man—Pedro de Alvarado—in charge at Tenochtitlan. Word was brought to him in the midst of his triumph that Alvarado's men had slaughtered a large number of Indians during a celebration. Details were sketchy, but it appeared that six Spaniards had been killed in the action, and that the city was seething. Cortés, suddenly feeling control of events slipping from his grasp, rushed with his now greatly-expanded army on a forced march over the mountains back to Tenochtitlan, sending word ahead that in no case must Montezuma— his trump card—be allowed to escape.[2]

The Indian festival in question was the most important celebration of the Aztec year—Toxcatl, in honor of the god Tezcatlipoca. Alvarado's permission had actually been sought to hold the gathering, and he had granted it. Yet he seems to have soon developed an uneasy feeling about such an enormous mob of celebratory Indians outside his door. Worse than this, he had received intelligence of a plot being hatched against his small force.[3] As preparations for the festival

[1] W.H. Prescott, in his *History of the Conquest of Mexico*, says that Cortés fought the battle for Mexico "quite as much with gold as with steel."

[2] Among the Narváez people returning with Cortés to Tenochtitlan were several women who had accompanied their men here. Narváez himself was left imprisoned at Villa Rica for approximately two years as Cortés conquered and solidified his hold over Mexico. On his release Narváez made his way to Spain, where he petitioned the Crown for redress of grievances. He would soon be rewarded with an important commission, featured in Volume II.

[3] Some scholars suspect that the idea of a plot was planted by the Tlaxcalans.

proceeded, the Spaniards—apprehensive, hard-faced—made a tour of the plaza.

The Spaniards came out of the palace together, dressed in armor and carrying their weapons with them. They stalked among the women and looked at them one by one; they stared into the faces of the women who were grinding seeds. After this cold inspection, they went back into the palace. **– Aztec account**

The next day the assembly began. The Indians, apparently eager to impress the Spaniards with their music and song, had no inkling of what Alvarado had decided to do.

Early the next morning . . . they gathered in front of the idol in single file and offered it gifts of food, such as round seedcakes or perhaps human flesh. But they did not carry it up to its temple on top of the pyramid.

All the young warriors were eager for the fiesta to begin. They had sworn to dance and sing with all their hearts, so that the Spaniards would marvel at the beauty of the rituals.

The procession began, and the celebrants filed into the temple patio to dance the Dance of the Serpent. When they were all together in the patio, the songs and the dance began. . . .

The great captains, the bravest warriors, danced at the head of the files to guide the others. The youths followed at a slight distance. Some of the youths wore their hair gathered into large locks, a sign that they had never taken any captives. Others carried their headdresses on their shoulders; they had taken captives, but only with help.

Then came the recruits, who were called "the young warriors." They had each captured an enemy or two. The others called to them: "Come, comrades, show us how brave you are! Dance with all your hearts!"

At this moment in the fiesta, when the dance was loveliest and when song was linked to song, the Spaniards were seized with an urge to kill the celebrants. They all ran forward, armed as if for battle. They closed the entrances and passageways, all the gates of the patio: the Eagle Gate in the lesser palace, the Gate of the Canestalk and the Gate of the Serpent of Mirrors. They posted guards so that no one could escape, and then rushed into the Sacred Patio to slaughter the celebrants. They came on foot, carrying their swords and their wooden or metal shields.

They ran in among the dancers, forcing their way to the place where the drums were played. They attacked the man who was drumming and cut off his arms. Then they cut off his head, and it rolled across the floor.

They attacked all the celebrants, stabbing them, spearing them, striking them with their swords. They attacked some of them from behind, and these fell instantly to the ground with their entrails hanging out. Others they beheaded: they cut off their heads, or split their heads to pieces.

They struck others in the shoulders, and their arms were torn from their bodies. They wounded some in the thigh and some in the calf. They slashed others in the abdomen, and their entrails all spilled to the ground. Some attempted to run away, but their intestines dragged as they ran; they seemed to tangle their feet in their own entrails. No matter how they tried to save themselves, they could find no escape.

Some attempted to force their way out, but the Spaniards murdered them at the gates. Others climbed the walls, but they could not save themselves. Those who ran into the communal houses were safe there for a while; so were those who lay down among the victims and pretended to be dead. But if they stood up again, the Spaniards saw them and killed them.

The blood of the warriors flowed like water and gathered into pools. The pools widened, and the stench of blood and entrails filled the air. The Spaniards ran into the communal houses to kill those who were hiding. They ran everywhere and searched everywhere; they invaded every room, hunting and killing. – **Aztec account**

Montezuma was doubtless appalled, but he had no control over the Spaniards, and he had lost any power he may have once had to abate his own people's wrath. The entire city rose up against them.

When the news of this massacre was heard outside the Sacred Patio, a great cry went up: "Mexicanos, come running! Bring your spears and shields! The strangers have murdered our warriors!"

This cry was answered with a roar of grief and anger: the people shouted and wailed and beat their palms against their mouths. The captains assembled at once, as if the hour had been determined in advance. They all carried their spears and shields. Then the battle began. The Aztecs attacked with javelins and arrows, even with the light spears that are used for hunting birds. They hurled their javelins with all their strength, and the cloud of missiles spread out over the Spaniards like a yellow cloak. **– Aztec account**

Alvarado's men barricaded themselves in their palace, doubtless praying fervently for the early arrival of the army from the coast.

On June 24, 1520, Cortés arrived on the lake shore at the head of an exhausted force of over one thousand foot, ninety horse (his own army augmented now by most of the Narváez men), and two thousand Tlaxcalan warriors. It quickly became obvious that the brigantines had been burned. Alvarado's men—and they themselves—would now have no escape except over a causeway. The easier solution—namely, not to enter the city again—was rejected by an angry and determined Cortés. They entered the city without incident, hastening to join Alvarado and his men in their fortress-like palace. Cortés took Alvarado aside and exploded at him for what he regarded as a monumental error on his part. And the error was compounded, he shouted, by the effect it would have on the Narváez men—men to whom he had boasted that the Spaniards were held in great esteem by the Indians of Tenochtitlan. Because of Alvarado's folly he had now been made to look like a fool.

The city appeared to be quiet but the Spaniards' skin prickled with dread. There was good reason.

> Next morning after Mass I sent a messenger to the town of Vera Cruz to give them the good news of the Christians' survival, and of how I had entered the city, and all was secure. But in less than half an hour the messenger returned, beaten up and wounded, crying out that all the Indians of the city were on a war footing, and had raised all the bridges. Immediately following this a multitude of Indians fell upon us so thickly that neither streets nor houses could be seen for the throng. They came with the most blood-curdling whoops and cries imaginable. A shower of stones from their slings fell on us inside our fortress—it seemed to be raining stones, and the arrows and spears fell so heavily that all the walls and courtyards were stuck with them, to the point where it was difficult for us to move around. I went out to meet them head-on in two or three places, and they fought with a vengeance.

In one place, a captain of ours went out with two hundred men, but before he could withdraw, they killed four of his men and wounded him and many others. In the place where I was fighting, they wounded me and a number of other Spaniards. We were able to kill only a few of them, for they took refuge on the other side of bridges. From the rooftops and terraces they continued to pelt us with stones, although we succeeded in seizing and setting fire to some of these places. **– Cortés**

When dawn broke, the enemy began to fight us much more savagely than on the day before. The warrior throng was so dense that we had no need to aim our artillery pieces, but only to direct them toward the massed Indians. Although the artillery did great damage—we also had thirteen harquebuses, not to mention the guns and crossbows—it made a very small dent in their ranks. They seemed hardly to notice it, since if ten or twelve men were cut down, the ranks immediately closed with no apparent damage. Leaving behind in the fortress whatever men I could spare, I went out again and captured a few houses, killing many of their defenders. But so many were they that no matter what injury we caused, it seemed but a nick to their forces. We had to fight all day, but they fought in shifts, replacing one another, and still they had men to spare. That day they wounded another sixty or seventy Spaniards, although none died. We fought till dark, returning to our fortress completely exhausted. **– Cortés**

Young Bernal Díaz had seen no warfare on this scale before, nor had many of the veterans.

I can hardly describe the tenacity of their fighting. Nothing bothered them—not cannon fire, not muskets, not crossbows, not hand-to-hand combat, not the slaughter of thirty or forty of them every time we charged. They only fought harder than before. If we gained a little ground, or a part of a street, they pretended to fall back, hoping we would follow so as to separate us from our base. They would then hit us with less risk, and do their best to keep us from reaching our quarters alive, for they did us most damage when we were retreating. To get out and burn their houses proved impossible for us because the houses were separated from one another by deep-water channels, and they removed the bridges. From the rooftops they hurled boulders and stones and shafts so thickly that we couldn't stay there. They did great damage to us, wounding a large number.

I don't know why I'm describing these things so calmly, because three or four soldiers we had with us who had served in Italy swore to God many times that they had never seen such fierce fighting among Christians or against the French king's artillery, nor even against the Great Turk. Nor had they ever faced anyone like these Indians, with their courageous closed-rank charges. **– Díaz**

For protection from the rain of deadly missiles, Cortés ordered the construction of a piece of equipment adapted from the ancient Roman *testudo* formation, referred to by Cortés as an "engine."[1]

Seeing the great damage the enemy were doing to us, how they were wounding and killing us at will, and how, although we were doing great harm to them ourselves, there were so many of them that it didn't seem so, we spent that entire night and all the next day in constructing three wooden engines. Twenty men would be assigned to each — among these, a few crossbowmen and harquebusiers. The rest would carry pikes and pickaxes and iron bars to break into the houses and knock down the adobe barricades that had been built in the streets. The wooden boards of the engines would serve as protection from the stones being hurled at them from the rooftops. But even while these devices were being constructed, the enemy's attacks did not cease. They were so fierce that if we attempted to leave our own fortress, they immediately tried to force an entry. Repulsing these attacks was very heavy work. **– Cortés**

The Indian attack proved to be too much for the testudos.

Next day, after having finished the engines, I placed them at the front of our column with four artillery pieces behind them, along with men bearing shields and more than three thousand Tlaxcalans who had come to assist us. I then moved out to capture some rooftops and bridges. Arriving near a particular bridge, we put the engines up against the walls of some houses, and then raised ladders we had made for getting up there. But we encountered such an overwhelming force

---

[1] The Spaniards' *testudo*, or tortoise shell, consisted of a layer of boards over a wood framework, under which a number of men could advance with some protection from falling missiles.

defending this bridge and these rooftops, men who rained such a torrent of heavy stones upon us, that the engines were knocked out of action, a Spaniard killed, and many of us wounded without our advancing even a step, although we fought hard against them from early morning till noon.

At that hour, with heavy hearts we pulled back to our fortress, and the enemy was so encouraged by our failure that they nearly succeeded in gaining our gates. **– Cortés**

In this close-quarters urban fighting, with all streets laced with canals, the Spaniards' horses were of little use.

When the horses charged at the Indian squadrons, they were hit with so many arrows and darts and stones that they couldn't stand up to it, no matter how well protected they were. If they succeeded in actually getting close to the enemy, the Indians saved themselves by jumping into the canals or lake, and others would sally from behind newly constructed adobe walls with long lances to finish off the horsemen. Nothing we could do worked against them.

Nor did we succeed in burning or destroying their houses. As I've said, these houses were all separated by canals, with bridges across them, bridges that had been removed. It would have been extremely difficult to cross these channels by swimming because from the fortified rooftops they could rain rocks and stones down on us. We would have had no chance. In addition to this, whenever we did succeed in setting fire to a house it took a long time to burn. Moreover, the flames did not easily jump from one house to another because, . . . they were too far apart, separated by water. **– Díaz**

At this point the Indians ran for the highest ground they could command — the lofty cue next to the Spanish fortress. They could now rain their missiles upon the Spaniards from above.

They took over the great temple, and nearly five hundred Indians, most of whom seemed like persons of rank, climbed up to the top of the main tower. They brought with them plenty of bread, water, and other provisions, and a large supply of stones. All the rest were brandishing very long lances with flint heads, broader than ours, and no less sharp. Since our fortress and the temple were close to one another, the Indians on the tower were able to do a great deal of damage to our people in the fortress. Two or three times the Spaniards

tried to climb the tower, but it was very high, with a hundred and some steps, the ascent was difficult, and its defenders were well provided with stones and other weapons. We had, moreover, failed to take the surrounding rooftops, which gave them an advantage. For all these reasons, every time the Spaniards tried to climb up they were driven back down. Many were wounded in this attempt. The warriors who witnessed this from a distance took such encouragement from it that they fearlessly came right up to the walls of our fortress.
– Cortés

Suddenly more than four thousand warriors ran to the top of the cue, reinforcing other detachments already there with long lances and stones and darts. Taking up a strong defensive position, they resisted for some time our attempts at scaling the cue. Neither our towers nor our cannon or crossbows or muskets or even our horses were of any avail.[1] Every time the horsemen tried to charge across the great, slippery flagstones of the courtyard, the horses lost their footing and fell. And since the steps to the top were being defended so staunchly, and because we were being pressed so closely on both flanks, even though our cannon were taking out ten or fifteen of them at a time, and our sword thrusts and cavalry were killing many more, we found it impossible to ascend the cue despite our best efforts to do so. **– Díaz**

It became clear to all that the cue must be taken, and Cortés moved out to lead the bloody advance up the temple's steep side.

Seeing that if they continued to hold that tower, in addition to doing us a great deal of injury, they would become even more encouraged to fight us, I left the fortress, with my left hand disabled from a wound I had received on the first day. Strapping a shield to my arm, I headed for the tower with a few Spaniards, and had some of them surround it—an action that could be managed, although not without danger to these men, who, every step of the way, had to battle an enemy who was being continually reinforced. With a few Spaniards following, I commenced climbing the tower steps. Defending the stairway very strenuously, they knocked three or four

---

[1] "Towers" is Díaz's word for the testudos, not to be confused with his references to the cue's towers.

Spaniards down the steps, but with the help of God and his Blessed Mother, for whose house this tower had been set aside and whose image had been placed here, we reached the top of the tower and took the fight to them there. Some of the enemy were forced to jump down from the tower onto some ledges, of which there were three or four around the tower, separated vertically from one another by about fifteen feet. Others fell all the way to the ground. Injured by the fall, they were easily dispatched by the Spaniards at the base of the tower. Those who were on the ledges and rooftops fought from there so fiercely that it took us more than three hours to finish killing them all. No one escaped. **– Cortés**

What a battle this was! We were all streaming with blood, covered with wounds, with many dead. . . . We set fire to the idols and burned a good part of the hall that had housed Huichilobos and Tezcatlipoca. In all this the Tlaxcalans were of invaluable assistance. **– Diaz**

The Indians nonetheless succeeded in winning the day.

As we were descending the steps of the cue, three or four thousand Indians, all leading warriors, succeeded in rolling us down the steps, six or ten steps at a time. Other squadrons, stationed on battlements or within embrasures of the great cue, were firing so many darts and arrows at us that we couldn't face any one of them. We soon determined that, in spite of the difficulty and risk, we had to retreat to our quarters. Our towers were broken, all of us were wounded, and we had lost sixteen men. The Indians never ceased to press us, including new companies that began to assail us from the rear. In this melee we captured two papas, whom Cortés told us to bring with us and guard very carefully. **– Díaz**

On reaching their fortress, they found Indians in the process of breaking down its walls.

Cortés, in the face of near-certain annihilation of his forces, desperately groped for some advantage. He mounted a rooftop and tried to reason with the shouting Mexican warriors below, doubtless dodging missiles as he did.[1]

---

[1] The dauntless Marina must have been the one actually addressing the warriors.

I addressed the Mexican captains, who . . . were fairly dismayed at what they had witnessed. I told them there was no refuge for them. I pointed out that we were causing them grave injury every day, that we were killing many, that we were burning and destroying their city, and that we had no reason to stop until they and the city had been obliterated. They responded that they could clearly see the injury and death we caused, but they were determined to give their lives to see the end of us. They told me to look at all the streets and plazas and rooftops of the city, to see how they were overflowing with people. They had already calculated, they said, that they could afford to lose twenty-five thousand Mexicans for every one of us they killed. They would ultimately triumph because we were few and they were many. They informed me that all causeways leading into the city had been torn up — which was nearly true, since all but one had been torn up. We therefore had no escape, they concluded, except across the water. They knew well, they added, that we had little food or water, and that we would soon perish of hunger if they didn't kill us first.

In this they were quite right. If we had had no other war to fight except the war against hunger and thirst, we would have been dead very soon. This conversation went on for quite some time, each side marshaling its best arguments against the other. **– Cortés**

His frightened army on the verge of obliteration, Cortés took pains to demonstrate that it still had bite.

When night fell I went out with a few Spaniards, and, catching the enemy unawares, we reached a street where we were able to burn more than three hundred houses. I returned by another route, since all had rushed to the site of the fires, and burnt many more houses, paying special attention to those near our fortress, from whose rooftops they had been doing us great harm. The enemy were very frightened by what we did that night. On my return, I ordered the engines that had been damaged the day before to be repaired and made ready.
– Cortés

Montezuma, no doubt sick to his heart at these events, and understanding that, despite his people's advantage in numbers, Cortés would prevail as he had in the past, made an effort to stop the violence.

He mounted a rooftop to stand with the Spaniards and with Itzcuauhtzin, Tlatelolco's ruler, who shared his view that it was pointless to oppose the Spaniards, and who would plead with the people to lay down their arms.

At sunset, Itzcuauhtzin climbed onto the roof of the palace and shouted this proclamation: "Mexicanos! Tlatelolcas! Your king, the lord Motecuhzoma, has sent me to speak for him. Mexicanos, hear me, for these are his words to you: 'We must not fight them. We are not their equals in battle. Put down your shields and arrows.

"He tells you this because it is the aged who will suffer most, and they deserve your pity. The humblest classes will also suffer, and so will the innocent children who still crawl on all fours, who still sleep in their cradles.

"Therefore your king says: 'We are not strong enough to defeat them. Stop fighting, and return to your homes.' Mexicanos, they have put your king in chains; his feet are bound with chains."

When Itzcuauhtzin had finished speaking, there was a great uproar among the people. They shouted insults at him in their fury, and cried: "Who is Motecuhzoma to give us orders? We are no longer his slaves!" They shouted war cries and fired arrows at the rooftop. The Spaniards quickly hid Motecuhzoma and Itzcuauhtzin behind their shields so that the arrows would not find them.

The Mexicans were enraged. . . . Now they refused to go away or to put down their arms. – **Aztec account**

The Spaniards at this point moved—with Montezuma—into the royal palace, which was quickly placed under siege, with every point of entrance or egress closely guarded.

The Mexicans kept a close watch to prevent anyone from stealing in with food for the Spaniards. They also stopped delivering supplies: they brought them absolutely nothing, and waited for them to die of hunger.

A few people attempted to communicate with the Spaniards. They hoped to win their favor by giving them advice and information or by secretly bringing them food. But the guards found them and killed them on the spot: they broke their necks or stoned them to death. . . .

They seized anyone who was dressed like a porter or any other servant. "Here is another traitor," they would say. "He is bringing news to Motecuhzoma." The prisoner would try to save his life by pleading with them: "What are you doing, Mexicanos? I am not a traitor!" But they would answer: "Yes, you are. We know you are one of his servants." And they would immediately put him to death.

They stopped and examined everyone in the same way, studying each man's face and questioning him about his work. No one could walk out of doors without being arrested and accused. They sentenced a great many people for imaginary crimes; the victims were executed for acts they had never committed. The other servants, therefore, went home and hid themselves. They were afraid to be seen in public: they knew what would happen to them if they fell into the hands of the guards or the other warriors. **– Aztec account**

Spanish power, however, was unraveling. There seemed no way out. The Narváez men were abusing Cortés openly. Seemingly endless reserves of enemy troops came at them in waves. He strove desperately to come up with a plan.

We spent that night dressing our wounds and burying the dead. We also prepared for another day of fighting—strengthening and rebuilding parapets that they had knocked down and filling breaches they had made, and talking about how we could continue this war without taking such heavy casualties. The conversation went nowhere. We could think of no remedy. Narváez's men cursed Cortés, announcing to all their detestation of him and this entire land, and even of Diego Velázquez, who had sent them here, raving about how peaceful life had been in Cuba. They got carried away, making less and less sense. . . .

At the crack of dawn we discerned many more warrior bands moving to surround our quarters. If we thought we had seen a hail of rocks and arrows the day before, it promised to be thicker today, along with louder whooping and whistling. New companies attempted to force their way through our defenses, and neither our cannon nor muskets seemed capable of stopping them, although we certainly did them plenty of damage. **– Díaz**

To Cortés it seemed that Montezuma offered the last wisp of hope. He would have to speak personally to his people in the Spaniards' behalf.

> In view of this situation, Cortés decided that Montezuma should get up on a rooftop and tell his people to cease making war upon us, that all we wanted to do was to leave their city. When he was told of Cortés's wish it was said that he responded with great anguish, "What more can Malinche want of me? I have no desire to live or to hear his voice again. It's because of him that I've been reduced to this low state!" He refused to come, and he was reported to have said that he no longer wished to see Cortés or hear his voice or his false speeches or promises or lies. The Mercedarian friar then went with Cristóbal de Olid, and spoke to him very respectfully and in a kindly way. Montezuma said to them, "I believe that I can do nothing to end this war, because they've already chosen my replacement and have decided that none of you will leave this city alive. I believe that all of you are about to die." – **Díaz**

Montezuma, however, again acquiesced, and soon appeared above the chaotic scene. It was clear that he wished to speak gently to his people. The clamor and missiles subsided. Spanish hearts strongly urged his success. As he began to speak, four attentive chiefs stepped forward from the crowd below to inform him, not unkindly, that he was no longer king, that his younger brother Cuitláhuac, lord of Iztapalapa, had been chosen to rule in his place.

> Scarcely had he finished speaking when a shower of stones and darts was launched toward him. Those of our men who were standing near him, since they had seen that while he was speaking the crowd demonstrated no hostility, had momentarily let their guard down and failed to shield him quickly as they had planned. Three stones struck him, one in the head, another on the arm, and a third in the leg. And although they begged him to have his wounds treated and to eat something, and although everyone spoke very kindly to him, he refused. And before we knew it they came to say that he was dead. – **Díaz**

Not surprisingly, the Indian account of Montezuma's death differs.

> On the third day, Motecuhzoma climbed onto the rooftop and tried to admonish his people, but they cursed him and

shouted that he was a coward and a traitor to his country. They even threatened him with their weapons. It is said that an Indian killed him with a stone from his sling, but the palace servants declared that the Spaniards put him to death by stabbing him in the abdomen with their swords. **– Aztec account**

Whatever the truth about the prince's death, Cortés now entered upon an orgy of killing, causing the streets of Tenochtitlan to run with blood.

It was late afternoon when Montezuma, who had been struck in the head, gave up his soul. In the quarters where he had been kept, others of his lords were still being held. Cortés, after conferring with his captains, ordered them all killed, no one to be left alive. After killing them, they dragged the bodies out and threw them out of the doorways . . . .

A few Indians who had escaped the killing removed some of the bodies. Then at about ten o'clock that night there appeared a terrifying mob of women bearing fiery brands and braziers. They had come looking for their husbands and kinsmen, who had already been killed and thrown out into the street. They had come seeking Montezuma as well. As they recognized their family members — which we, who were keeping watch on the rooftop, could see very clearly by the light of the torches — they threw themselves down on the bodies with a loud outburst of grief and lamentation, shrieking and wailing in a manner that struck terror into us. I who write this was standing guard on the rooftop. I said to my companion, "Look at that vision of hell down there." As for me, in the course of this entire war, no matter what else I had to go through, I was never as frightened as I was that night by the lamentations of those women. **– Alonso de Aguilar**

The Spanish captain-general now released Montezuma's body to his people.

To convince them that Montezuma was indeed dead, Cortés ordered six principal Mexicans and the rest of the papas whom we held prisoner to carry him on their shoulders and hand his body over to the Mexican captains. They were also to convey Montezuma's orders at the time of his death, for those who were bearing his body had been present at his deathbed.

They told the complete truth to Cuitláhuac, how he had been killed by three stones thrown from the crowd.

When they saw him dead, the Mexicans began a lamentation that soon turned into an enormous outcry and wailing. Throughout this display, however, their attack upon us never flagged, with a blizzard of darts, stones, and arrows falling upon us. They then increased the intensity of their attack, shouting at us, "Now you'll pay for the death of our king and lord and the dishonor you've brought to our gods. And as for the peace you seek from us, come out here and we'll see what kind of peace it will be." – **Díaz**

9

LA NOCHE TRISTE AND ESCAPE

With howling, shrieking mobs filling the streets, the Spanish position was clearly untenable for even another day. On June 30, the date of Montezuma's death, and only six days after Cortés's return from the coast, it was decided that, no matter what the difficulty or the consequences, an escape from the city must be immediately attempted. It would have to be via the Tacuba causeway, to the west, the only path left open. Casualties would necessarily be high. The Spaniards then prepared to enter upon a night that would ever after be burned into the survivors' memories as the *noche triste*, the night of sorrows.

> By now we had come to see that every day our strength was diminishing and that of the Mexicans increasing, that many of our men had died and all of us were wounded, and that even though we might fight bravely we could never drive back or escape the bands of Indians that attacked us around the clock. First we had run short on powder, now on food and water, and with the great Montezuma dead, they had rejected all our demands for a truce and peace. Moreover, the bridges had been taken up. In a word, we were staring death in the face.
>
> Cortés with all his captains and soldiers agreed that we had to get out of there by night, at a moment when the warrior squadrons seemed to be off their guard. To delude them a little more, that afternoon we sent a papa whom we had held prisoner — a principal man among them — together with a few other prisoners, to beg them to let us leave the city peacefully eight days from today. We would then give them all the gold we had. This was to put them off their stride, since we intended to escape that very night. **– Díaz**
>
> The plan was to make a portable bridge out of a wide beam, and very quietly to use it for crossing over the water-filled gaps in the causeway. It seemed as difficult as climbing to heaven without a ladder, because the city was overflowing with people just waiting for a chance to feast on the flesh of the poor Spaniards. But because we were so surrounded and

bottled up, like men already beaten and lost, they paid little attention to us except for preventing our escape. They did this by setting torches and braziers on top of the flat rooftops of their houses in order to see us if we tried to flee. Escape therefore seemed impossible to us — the light made by these fires was as bright as midday. **– Alonso de Aguilar**

The little army made final preparations now, as 550 men — mostly Tlaxcalans — hefted the vital bridge, their only path to survival.

Four hundred Tlaxcalans and 150 soldiers were assigned to carry the bridge that we had made, to place it in position, and to guard it until the army and baggage had crossed. Two hundred Tlaxcalans and fifty soldiers were appointed to carry the cannon. To lead the fighting force at the head of this column Cortés appointed Gonzalo de Sandoval and Diego de Ordaz. Francisco de Saucedo and Francisco de Lugo were to lead a company of a hundred young men in two equal companies who were expected to move quickly to wherever they were needed. Cortés himself, along with Alonso de Ávila and Cristóbal de Olid would march in the column's center with several other captains. The rearguard would be led by Pedro de Alvarado and Juan Velázquez de León. Interspersed among Narváez's captains and soldiers would be three hundred Tlaxcalans and thirty of our soldiers, who were to guard the prisoners and protect Doña Marina and Doña Luisa.[1]

By the time these arrangements had been made, it was already night, and time to take out the gold, which would be either loaded up or doled out. Cortés commanded his steward, Gonzalo de Guzmán, and other soldiers who were also his servants, to have the Tlaxcalans take out the gold, jewelry, and silver, and pile it in one of the halls. He then told the royal officials, Alonso de Ávila and Gonzalo Mejía, to take control of the royal portion. For this purpose he gave them seven horses that were wounded and lame, a mare, and more than eighty of our Tlaxcalan allies, telling the men to load up the animals and Indians with whatever they could. The gold had been melted into broad ingots, and much of it was still piled high in the hall.

---

[1] Doña Luisa was the daughter of the Tlaxcalan chief, Xicotenga the Elder, and sister of young Xicotenga, who had led the ferocious Tlaxcalan resistance against the Spaniards.

Cortés then summoned his secretary and the king's notaries and said, "Bear witness for me that I can do no more with this gold. In this apartment and hall we have more than seven hundred thousand pesos' worth, and, as you can see, it can neither be weighed nor taken control of. I therefore give what is left here to any soldiers who wish to take it, for otherwise it will only fall to these dogs." And on hearing this, many of Narváez's soldiers and some of our own men loaded themselves down with it. **– Díaz**

Had they foreseen the consequences of falling into the water with pockets and baggage heavy with ingots, these doomed fortune-seekers would easily have overcome their greed. But not all were so foolhardy as to weight themselves with gold.

I had no desire, I assure you, but to save my life, but I didn't pass up the chance to gather from some dishes that I found four chalchihuites, stones that the Indians consider very valuable, which I tucked into my tunic under my armor and whose value later served me well in curing my wounds and buying me food. **– Díaz**

The time now came for the actual escape. Rain soon began to fall.

Once this was done and night had fallen, Captain Hernando Cortés, along with his captains, ordered us to slip out very quietly. Silence, however, would not be good enough. Indeed the bright moonlight as well as the light thrown by the torches and braziers on the rooftops and along the streets would make it impossible for us to escape unseen. A number of Christians had been wounded. We put them on horses, two or three to a horse, since we scarcely had enough mounts for all. But as the night advanced the wind came up and it began to drizzle. Then at nine or ten o'clock the heavens fairly exploded with thunder and hail. We took this to be less a natural event than a divine intervention to help us escape, for God could not possibly leave us all there to die that night. **– Alonso de Aguilar**

Darkness soon fell and with it came mist and drizzle. Sometime before midnight, therefore, the bridge was picked up by its bearers and we began to move out. We took our baggage with us, as well as the horses, the mare, and the Tlaxcalans, all laden with gold. The bridge was placed across the first gap in the causeway and Cortés and those who were with him—including many mounted men—crossed first. While this was happening we heard voices raised, and then the trumpets, cries, and whistles of the Mexicans. In their language they were calling to the men of Tlatelolco, "Out, come out right away with your canoes, the teules are fleeing! Cut off their escape—they must not leave here alive!"

We suddenly became aware of innumerable bands of warriors descending upon us, and the lake around us thick with canoes. Many of our soldiers had already gotten across the gap and we couldn't defend ourselves well. But now the Mexicans began to seize control of the bridge. They wounded and killed our men, who could not help one another. And since fortune can be unkind in such circumstances, we suffered one calamity after another. Due to the rain, two horses slipped and fell into the water. Because I and some of the men around Cortés saw this happen, we attempted to secure that part of the bridge, but so many Mexicans converged on the spot that, as hard as we battled, we could make no further use of the bridge. And now the opening began to fill up with dead horses and Indians, both male and female, and servants, and bundles, and boxes. **– Díaz**

Whether the bridge was removed by the Mexicans or whether, as Alonso de Aguilar states, it broke, the Spanish army no longer had a way to cross the wide gaps in the causeway. A method was soon provided.

We carried our portable bridge with us, but it soon broke under the weight it had to bear. This meant that there was no way for us to get over the five or six gaps that were left, each more than ten feet across and filled with deep water. But Our Lord saved us: our Indian porters (of both sexes), who were carrying very large bundles, fell into the first gap and drowned, and their piled-up bodies formed a bridge that could be crossed even on horseback. Once we saw this, we pushed our Indians on ahead and when they drowned we crossed over on their bodies. We succeeded in crossing all the causeway gaps in this manner. The bodies of some Spaniards were mixed in with the bodies of the Indians. **– Alonso de Aguilar**

This horror had been occurring behind Cortés, who had already crossed several gaps.

I crossed quickly with five horsemen and a hundred foot-soldiers, getting across all the open gaps by swimming until we reached the mainland. Leaving these men there, I turned back to where the fighting was still intense, and where we were receiving appalling damage—both Spaniards and the Tlaxcalans who were with us. They were killing us on every side, and we were killing them. Many Spaniards were dead, as well as their horses. All the gold, jewelry, clothing and things that we had taken with us were lost. Our artillery had disappeared.

Collecting the few men who were still alive, I sent them on ahead, while I, with the three or four horse and nearly twenty foot who were brave enough to come with me, served as the rear guard, battling the Indians until we arrived at the city of Tacuba, beyond the end of the causeway, on the mainland. God only knows the labor and danger we sustained in this crossing, because every time I turned toward the enemy, I faced a hail of arrows and bruising stones. And because there was water on both sides of us, they could wound us at will, then jump into the water when we turned to retaliate. Because of this, they suffered little injury, except for those who—because of their great numbers—tripped over one another and fell into the water, where they drowned. Through this immensely heavy toil I succeeded in getting all our survivors to Tacuba with no further injury or loss of life to Spaniard or Indian ally, except for one horseman who rode with me in the rear guard. The fighting continued to be heavy on all sides, but especially in the rear where the enemy was still pouring out of the city in pursuit of us. **– Cortés**

Cortés's army had escaped the city, but it was hardly the army it had been hours before. The price had been extraordinarily high. On reaching the lake shore, rapid estimates of casualties were made, but the full extent of the butcher's bill would become clear only later.

When Cortés and the other captains met Pedro de Alvarado and saw that he brought no more soldiers with him, they were bitterly disappointed. Pedro de Alvarado said that Juan Velázquez de León lay dead at the bridge, along with many horsemen, both ours and Narváez's—more than eighty in all. He also said that he and the four soldiers who were with him, after their horses had been killed, made a perilous crossing over the gap on the backs of human corpses, dead horses, and boxes, since the gap was packed with them. – **Díaz**

Among those who perished at the bridge were the sons and daughters of Montezuma, the prisoners we were taking with us, Cacamatzin,[1] lord of Texcoco, and several other provincial chiefs. But enough about our setbacks. We were thinking of what now lay ahead of us. We were all wounded, and we had managed to save only twenty-three horses. We had lost our cannon and all our powder. The few crossbows we had left we restrung and began making bolts for them. What weighed most heavily on our minds, however, was whether our friends the Tlaxcalans would retain their good will toward us. – **Diaz**

As night fell we found ourselves surrounded by Mexicans, crying out to us, shooting darts and arrows in our direction, launching missiles at us from their slings. We decided to leave that place at midnight. With the Tlaxcalans guiding us, therefore, and keeping good order, we moved out. The wounded were kept in the middle of the column, and the lame were given staffs. Those who were ill or unable to walk were set upon the croups of horses who were themselves lame and unfit for battle. Horsemen who were unwounded were placed at the head of the column and on either flank. Wounded Tlaxcalans were kept within the body of our squadron, while the healthiest faced the Mexicans together with us. Thus were the wounded protected, and the strong placed in a position to confront the enemy. The Mexicans kept harassing us, calling out loudly, shouting and whistling, saying: "Where you're going, no one is going to come out alive." We didn't yet know what they were talking about.

I've forgotten to mention what a thrill it was for us to see our Doña Marina and Doña Luisa, Xicotenga's daughter, alive. The Tlaxcalans had helped them get across the gaps. A Spanish woman named María de Estrada . . . also escaped. The first to get across the gaps were some of Xicotenga's sons, brothers of Doña Luisa. Most of the female servants we had been given in Tlaxcala and Mexico perished. – **Díaz**

---

[1] Among those who also perished this night were five Spanish women who had accompanied the Narváez men.

As one contingent of warriors harassed the retreating Spaniards and Tlaxcalans, those remaining behind took stock of a city overflowing with death.

> As soon as it was daylight, the Aztecs cleared the dead Spaniards and Tlaxcaltecas out of the canals and stripped them of everything they wore. They loaded the bodies of the Tlaxcaltecas into canoes and took them out to where the rushes grow; they threw them among the rushes without burying them, without giving them another glance.
>
> They also threw out the corpses of the women who had been killed in the retreat. The naked bodies of these women were the color of ripe corn, for they had painted themselves with yellow paint.
>
> But they laid out the corpses of the Spaniards apart from the others; they lined them up in rows in a separate place. Their bodies were as white as the new buds of the canestalk, as white as the buds of the maguey. They also removed the dead "stags" that had carried the "gods" on their shoulders.
>
> Then they gathered up everything the Spaniards had abandoned in their terror. When a man saw something he wanted, he took it, and it became his property; he hefted it onto his shoulders and carried it home. They also collected all the weapons that had been left behind or had fallen into the canal—the cannons, harquebuses, swords, spears, bows and arrows—along with all the steel helmets, coats of mail and breastplates, and the shields of metal, wood and hide. They recovered the gold ingots, the gold disks, the tubes of gold dust and the chalchihuite collars with their gold pendants.
>
> They gathered up everything they could find and searched the waters of the canal with the greatest care. Some of them groped with their hands and others felt about with their feet.
>
> **– Aztec account**

Once they had been able to accurately assess their losses, the Spaniards were astounded. The army had been reduced to near its original levels, except that most men were now wounded. The Tlaxcalan allies had also suffered heavy losses. There was as yet no talk of the future, as the exhausted and battered men bent their energies to escaping the relentless Aztec pursuit. Cortés did his best to keep spirits up in an effort that likely fell flat.

Cortés said to us that even though we were so few, numbering no more than 440 men, with twenty horses, twelve crossbowmen, and seven musketeers, and although we were without powder, with all of us either wounded or lame or maimed, we could clearly see that it had been the will of Our Lord Jesus Christ that we escape with our lives, and for this we should forever give him thanks and praise. **– Díaz**

The Spaniards' escape had been along the western causeway, to Tacuba, from which they fled to the north, around the northern end of the lake system. The Mexicans dogged their steps, harassing them day and night, giving them no rest.

I emerged from this fight with a bad head wound, having been struck twice in the head by stones. Once I had bound up my wounds, I moved everyone out of the city because it didn't seem a safe place for us to stay. As we followed the road out, vast numbers of Indians dogged our heels, attacking so tenaciously that they wounded four or five Spaniards and an equal number of horses. They actually killed one of our horses. God alone knows the damage this did and the pain it caused us to see a horse killed, because, after God, we had no security except in our horses. The dead horse's flesh, which we ate, brought us some comfort, and in our deep state of need we left not a scrap of him behind. Since departing Tenochtitlan we had eaten nothing but toasted or boiled maize—although usually in insufficient quantity—and herbs that we picked in the fields.

Seeing that every day more and stronger people were attacking us, while we were wasting away, I ordered that night that crutches be made for the wounded and sick, or some other aid that would enable them to stand up and walk, and that they no longer be carried on horseback. This would free up the horses for use by the healthy Spaniards in fighting. In light of what happened afterwards, it seemed to me that this idea had come from the Holy Spirit.

Having traveled next morning about a league and a half from camp, we were attacked on all sides by a very large body of warriors, so large in fact that the view of the land around was blotted out. They battled us fiercely, engaging us at such close quarters that we could scarcely distinguish between ourselves and them. **– Cortés**

They had reached Otumba, east of the lake system, where an enormous force of Mexicans brought them to pitched battle.[1] Miraculously surviving this encounter and disengaging successfully, the Spaniards limped east and southward toward refuge in Tlaxcala. They had suffered a great disaster. Between their flight from Tenochtitlan and the battle at Otumba, fully two-thirds of their force had been lost.[2]

Their need for rest was overpowering.

> I spent twenty days in this province of Tlaxcala, recovering from my wounds, which my journey and the lack of proper treatment had made considerably worse. The other men of my company who had been wounded had to rest and recover as well. Some of them died, as much from their exertions as from their wounds. Others were left lame or crippled. Some of the wounds were very bad, and we had few means of curing them. I myself lost two fingers from my left hand. **– Cortés**

The Spaniards spent the remainder of July among their allies in Tlaxcala, nursing their wounds, their leader considering what to do next. Montezuma's successor Cuitláhuac was consolidating his forces in Tenochtitlan in preparation for repelling any renewed Spanish assault, and sending out large parties of warriors to keep the Spaniards from any advance toward the lakes. The hope in Tenochtitlan was that the Spaniards, on the heels of such a devastating defeat, would return to the coast and depart. But Cortés, who considered his recent disaster no more than a setback, had no intention of returning to the coast, much less departing. He began instead to ponder a new line of attack.

---

[1] The battle was fought practically within sight of the great pyramids of Teotihuacán, left unmentioned by the chroniclers. The society that had constructed these pyramids had flourished and died many centuries before the coming of the Aztecs.

[2] Many — chiefly the Narváez men, their pockets weighted with gold — had drowned in their escape from the city. An untold number of captured Spaniards had been sacrificed atop the cues.

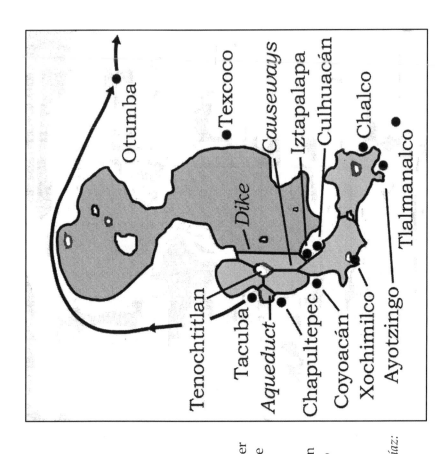

Otumba

Texcoco

Causeways

Iztapalapa

Culhuacán

Chalco

Tlalmanalco

Dike

Tenochtitlan

Tacuba

Aqueduct

Chapultepec

Coyoacán

Xochimilco

Ayotzingo

Detail of region around the lakes. Water to the east of the dike was saline, to the west only brackish. The island was linked to the mainland by several causeways. Potable water was piped in from Chapultepec, on the mainland to the west. Arrowed line indicates the route of the Spaniards' flight from the city on June 30, 1520, the *noche triste*. Based on map in J.M. Cohen, *Bernal Díaz: The Conquest of New Spain.*

10

CORTÉS RESURGENT

With many of his men lying wounded around the Spanish camp, Cortés was in no position for a large-scale offensive. He therefore began to consider problems that had a better chance of solution, such as the need to avenge the recent killings of sixteen Spaniards in Tepeaca, to the southeast. Perhaps this was the time to do it. In early August he announced a punitive expedition to Tepeaca. The Narváez men, poorly trained and wishing only to return to Cuba, put up a show of resistance to participation in further action, but since they received little support from Cortés's veterans, they grudgingly agreed to join in.

Among the rebellious Tepeacans were some who had once pledged fealty to the far-off emperor Charles. On arrival in the town, Cortés now decreed in the presence of a notary that any such backsliders would pay for their action by being made slaves.[1] After easily breaking Tepeacan resistance, Cortés garrisoned their town and renamed it Villa Segura de la Frontera. It would henceforth serve as a center of protection for the road to the coast, as well as a hub for subsequent slave raids.

During the late summer of 1520, as his wounded men in Tlaxcala either died or returned to duty, Cortés—operating now from Tepeaca—collected men, horses, weapons, and supplies from ships anchoring at Villa Rica. He also collected disenchanted settlers from a struggling Spanish colony along the Pánuco River, to the north—a colony that had lately been licensed by the Crown for settlement by the governor of Jamaica, Francisco de Garay. Before long he had added 150 men and twenty horses to his depleted army. He faced continuing hostility, however, over his distribution of gold and newly captured slaves, chiefly the women, for whom there was intense competition. Men who had some awareness of the amount of gold that had been taken from Tenochtitlan were mystified that it seemed to have vanished. Suspicion fell heavily upon the captain-general himself. Regardless of Cortés's attempts to deflect accusations, many men

---

[1] The presence of the notary was intended to give subsequent slave-catching a species of legality.

remained unsatisfied and suspicious. Their distrust of their commander would fester through the remainder of the campaign, to break out strongly at campaign's end.

With regard to the principal objective, the investment and reduction of Tenochtitlan, Cortés saw that it could not be attempted without a naval force to protect the army's flanks from a waterside attack as it advanced along the causeways. Without such protection, the relatively small army at his disposal could not hope to enter the city again. But he had no navy, and for that reason would have to build one. In September he ordered thousands of Tlaxcalans to the mountains to start cutting trees for this purpose. Under direction of his master carpenters, components of thirteen forty-foot brigantines would be shaped. These heavy items would then be carried overland to Texcoco (which lay a mile or so from the lake's eastern shore) for assembly and testing of the finished craft on local waterways. It seemed not to bother him that Texcoco was a staunch ally of Tenochtitlan,[1] and that opposition there was virtually certain. The brigantines would finally be floated down a mile-long canal—still to be excavated—to the lake. To Cortés, with his near-endless supply of Indian warriors and laborers, these problems were mere details. Nothing was undoable.

As the tree-cutting got under way, Cortés received unexpected help from an ally against which his Indian foes had no defense: smallpox. One of Narváez's men had arrived on the coast carrying the smallpox virus. The plague struck Tenochtitlan in September and raged through October and November, even carrying off the new Aztec ruler Cuitláhuac. The coldly calculating Cortés could have hoped for nothing better. For the Indians, who had never experienced this mass death appearing from nowhere, it was hellish.

> While the Spaniards were in Tlaxcala, a great plague broke out here in Tenochtitlan . . . and lasted for seventy days, striking everywhere in the city and killing a vast number of our people. Sores erupted on our faces, our breasts, our bellies; we were covered with agonizing sores from head to foot.
>
> The illness was so dreadful that no one could walk or move. The sick were so utterly helpless that they could only lie on their beds like corpses, unable to move their limbs or even their heads. They could not lie face down or roll from one side

---

[1] It was in fact a Triple Alliance partner.

to the other. If they did move their bodies, they screamed with pain.

A great many died from this plague, and many others died of hunger. They could not get up to search for food, and everyone else was too sick to care for them, so they starved to death in their beds.

Some people came down with a milder form of the disease; they suffered less than the others and made a good recovery. But they could not escape entirely. Their looks were ravaged, for wherever a sore broke out, it gouged an ugly pockmark in the skin. And a few of the survivors were left completely blind.

The first cases were reported in Cautlán. By the time the danger was recognized, the plague was so well established that nothing could halt it, and eventually it spread all the way to Chalco. Then its virulence diminished considerably, though there were isolated cases for many months after. – **Aztec account**

Always in the back of Cortés's mind was a need for more troops and more supplies, but, equally, the need to improve his political position at home. To achieve his military objectives, crews of ships calling at Villa Rica de la Vera Cruz were "encouraged" to join him. Supplies, including weapons and powder, were purchased from their owners—using stolen Indian gold, of course—and messengers were dispatched to Hispaniola, Cuba, and Jamaica to recruit men, arms, and horses. To achieve his political ends, in October he sent envoys to Castile. They were charged with delivering to the emperor the long, carefully considered, and self-serving account he had recently written—his second letter to the Crown—describing his actions since leaving the coast in August 1519.[1]

Toward the middle of December he moved his forces from Tepeaca back to Tlaxcala, where he stayed most of that month, largely to hurry along the work of timber-cutting and sawing. At this time he also sent to the coast for all remaining iron, sails, rigging, nails, and anything useful for getting the new lake vessels afloat and ready for action.

Having received carte blanche from his Tlaxcalan allies on the number of warriors that he might have, just after Christmas 1520, with 550 foot soldiers, forty horsemen, a few field guns, and ten thousand

---

[1] Likely unknown to Cortés, the emperor was not in Castile at this time, having departed for his German states the previous May.

Tlaxcalan warriors, he began to move due west across the mountains to Texcoco, where he planned to construct and launch the brigantines. The move was strenuously opposed by mobile Mexican and Texcocan forces, but the Spaniards and their allies could not be stopped. From the high passes, the city of Tenochtitlan could be seen spread out before them, seemingly beckoning. On the last day of the year 1520, they entered Texcoco, unsure of what their reception might be.

The stay in Texcoco was at first uneasy. The Texcocans were known to have murdered Spaniards, and were suspected of having re-taken gold regarded by the Spaniards as their own. For their own particular reasons, however, both sides showed restraint. It soon became clear to Cortés that factions existed among the Texcocans. Once he had allied himself with the least hostile faction, he was able to assert his will. He requested Texcocan labor in excavating a mile-long canal from Texcoco down to the lake. The Texcocans, likely noting this stranger's cold-eyed determination, agreed to supply a work force of eight thousand for the project.

After spending nearly two weeks in Texcoco, it became obvious to Cortés that his new allies had not the wherewithal to feed such a large army as his. Because of this, and because he had heard that the inhabitants of Iztapalapa, the Venice-like town on the lake's southern shore, were "ill-disposed" toward the Spaniards, he left a garrison at Texcoco and led the rest of his army a dozen or more miles south and west to attack the town. Mexican and local forces, while resisting sharply from both land and water, were at length overwhelmed by Spanish fire and steel. They were punished even further by the Spaniards' vengeful Tlaxcalan allies, who could not be restrained before more than six thousand men, women, and children had been slaughtered.[1] The fighting ended when the town was flooded, an event caused by the Mexicans' breaching a dike. The Spaniards made a parting effort to burn the flooded town, but it was largely unsuccessful. With much of their equipment swept away and their powder soaked, the Spaniards corralled their celebrating Indian allies and marched back to Texcoco.

Over the next three months the army would make several other forays to towns around the lake shore in a bid to soften up this hostile zone before moving against the city itself.

---

[1] In the fighting here, the chronicler Díaz was wounded severely in the throat.

As work on the canal progressed in Texcoco, Mexicans jeered from afar, and made every effort to hinder the work.

By late January or early February 1521, word came to Cortés that all timber had been cut for the thirteen brigantines, and that all materials were ready to be moved the forty miles to Texcoco for assembly. Gonzalo de Sandoval was sent with a large force to protect this complex transport operation as it wended its way out of the Tlaxcalan forests and into a region open to Mexican attack.

Cortés had been attempting to walk a fine line between friendship with his formerly hostile Texcocan allies — deeply guilty of the murder and sacrifice of Spaniards — and grim insistence that the killing of Spaniards was worthy of the severest punishment. Sandoval's errand, however, provided an irresistible opportunity for avenging what the Spaniards considered a heinous crime.

Having heard that the work on the thirteen brigantines was finished, and that the Indians who were to carry the vessels out were ready, I sent the *alguacil mayor*,[1] Gonzalo de Sandoval, with fifteen horse and two hundred foot, to convoy them out of the mountains. I told him that, on the way, he was to obliterate a large town adjoining Tlaxcalan lands, one that was subject to Texcoco. The reason for this was that the people of this town had killed five horsemen and forty-five foot-soldiers who had been en route from Vera Cruz to Tenochtitlan when I was bottled up there, not suspecting that such a treacherous act could be perpetrated against us.

When we had entered Texcoco, we had found in that city's shrines and temples the hides of five horses, as well tanned as anywhere in the world, and into which had been sewn the animals' hooves and shoes. We had also found a quantity of clothing and other things obviously Spanish that had been offered to their idols as if in victorious celebration. Throughout all those towers and temples, we had seen the blood of our comrades and brothers that had been spilled out and sacrificed. This caused us such grief as to revive in us all the pain we had endured. The traitors of that Texcocan town and those nearby had received our men well, a ploy designed to lull them into a state where they could be treated with the greatest cruelty. While descending a steep downhill section of

---

[1] Chief law enforcement officer.

a mountain pass, all on foot, the horsemen leading and therefore unable to use their mounts, they were taken in a crossfire ambush. Those not killed were carried to Texcoco, where they were sacrificed, their hearts ripped out before the idols.

Some corroboration was given to this account when Sandoval and his men, passing through a town between Texcoco and the place where the Spaniards had been ambushed and captured, saw scrawled in charcoal on a whitewashed wall, "Here was held prisoner the unfortunate Juan Yuste." Yuste had been one of the five horsemen. This was surely a sight to break the heart of anyone. **– Cortés**

Sandoval avenged the Spaniards' deaths by killing a number of people in the Texcocan town (Zultepec), and taking slaves, mostly women and children.

In early to mid-February Cortés's beleaguered army was cheered by the sight of the carpenter Martín López, with eight thousand Tlaxcalans, arriving from the forests bearing newly cut timbers and shaped planks for construction of the ships. The Tlaxcalan bearers were accompanied by their own military force of many thousands, by a contingent of Spanish soldiers, and by two thousand food-bearing porters, men who also spelled those carrying the heavy timbers. Sandoval had added the protection of his own force as the entourage — beset by the distant catcalls and shouted threats of Mexican warriors — labored painfully down the mountain paths, the Indians finally setting down their burdens near the waterways where the vessels were to be built and tested. As excavation of the nearby canal proceeded, practiced hands began to construct the brigantines. The Mexicans became bolder in their attacks, three times attempting to set fire to the vessels under construction.

While the building of the brigantines progressed, Cortés took twenty-five horse and three hundred foot, along with fifty crossbowmen and harquebusiers, six small field guns, and thirty thousand Indians, and headed north around the lake system, raiding as he went, eventually reaching Tacuba on Lake Texcoco's western shore.[1] His purpose in entering Tacuba was to learn the enemy's

---

[1] The city at the western terminus of the causeway along which they had escaped on the noche triste. It was a strong ally of Tenochtitlan — in fact a member of the Triple Alliance.

intentions by parleying with Mexican leaders there, and to probe the capital's defenses. Once the men had arrived in Tacuba, it took time to get to the talking stage.

Of the six days we spent in Tacuba, not a day went by that we didn't have to skirmish with the enemy. Our Tlaxcalan captains and their men continued to ridicule and challenge the warriors from Tenochtitlan, both sides sometimes fighting most beautifully, or arguing, or threatening, or insulting one another—it was a sight to behold. During all this time we were killing many of the enemy without endangering any of our own. We frequently went back along the causeway and bridges to attack them, but the causeway was well defended and they fought back viciously. Sometimes they pretended to fall back, shouting at us "Come on over, come over and enjoy yourselves." At other times they would shout, "Do you think you have another Montezuma here, someone who will do whatever you want?"

One day while these shouting-matches were going on I went up to one of the bridges that had been removed. The Mexicans stood on the other side. I signaled to our men to be quiet. They, too, when they saw that I wanted to speak, commanded silence on their side. I asked them why they were behaving like lunatics who wanted to be wiped out. I then told them to bring someone of authority, because I wanted to speak to him. They replied that all the warriors I saw standing there were persons of authority, and so I could say whatever I wished to them. Because I made no answer to this, they began to insult me. Then one of my men—I don't know who— shouted that they would all starve to death, that we would never allow them to come out to get food. They replied that they were not short of food, and if they did run short, they would feast on ours and the Tlaxcalans' flesh. One of them then took a few maize cakes and threw them toward us saying, "Take this and eat it if you're hungry. We don't need it." And they began to shout at us and assault us. **– Cortés**

During the fighting at Tacuba, Cortés's Indian allies could not be restrained. In anger at having been attacked here when they had fled Tenochtitlan on the noche triste, they sacked and burned much of the town. The force was back in Texcoco by mid-March.

Not only did Cortés at this time have the construction of his navy well in hand and many thousands of Indian allies at his disposal, but Indians from all over, perhaps sensing that these strangers would, against all odds, prevail, were now flocking to him. With many of these groups he had to play the peacemaker, since their rivalries and mutual hatreds went back in some cases very far. With his recent securing of the road to the coast, his orders moved smoothly eastward, and news, supplies, and manpower arrived daily from Villa Rica.

The Spaniards, further probing towns south of the lake system in early April, met stiff resistance at today's Cuernavaca and, for several days, at Xochimilco, on the lake of that name at Lake Texcoco's southwest corner.

> Next day, because all those from Tenochtitlan and roundabout knew now we were at Xochimilco, they determined to come with overwhelming force by land and water to surround us, believing there was no escape for us this time. I climbed up one of the towers where they worship their idols to get an idea of where they were coming from and what their likely line of attack might be, so that I could devise a strategy for countering them. Once we had prepared our defenses, a fleet of more than two thousand canoes arrived bearing more than twelve thousand warriors. The warriors coming at us overland were spread thickly across the fields. Their captains, out in front, were brandishing Spanish swords, calling out the names of their provinces: "Mexico, Mexico, Tenochtitlan, Tenochtitlan!" They hurled insults at us, threatening to kill us with our own swords, which they had captured earlier in Tenochtitlan. **– Cortés**

At Xochimilco Cortés's horse collapsed from exhaustion, and its rider, wounded, was nearly taken prisoner.

> Their method of fighting was to wait for our horsemen with their lances, and they succeeded in wounding four of them. Cortés was in the middle of this melee. The horse he was riding was very good, a dark chestnut. . . . For some reason the animal faltered, and the Mexicans, who were in great numbers, laid hands on Cortés and dragged him off the horse. . . . At that moment more Mexican warriors arrived and tried to take him away alive. This action was witnessed by some Tlaxcalans and by a brave soldier named Cristóbal de Olea, of Medina del Campo in Old Castile. Running immediately toward the

Mexicans, swinging his sword left and right to clear a space, he gave Cortés — who had been badly wounded in the head — time to remount. In this action, however, Olea was severely injured himself, suffering three stab-wounds. . . .

The shrieks, shouts, and whistling that we heard told us that something big was happening where Cortés and the cavalry were, so at great peril to ourselves we disengaged from our own fight and rushed to his side. He had been joined by fifteen horsemen, who were battling the Mexicans around some barricades they had erected near a canal. Our arrival set most of the Mexicans to running off. Olea was pouring blood from his wounds. The streets were filled with warriors. We told Cortés that he and Olea should retire behind some barricades and have their wounds tended to, and Cortés's horse as well. So, not without anxiety, we turned back, having to pass through a storm of darts and stones and arrows that were being showered on us from their ramparts and barricades. Since the Mexicans believed we were now in full retreat, they set upon us most furiously.

Andrés de Tapia and Cristóbal de Olid now arrived with the rest of the horsemen, who had been fighting farther away. Olid's face was streaming blood, as was his horse. Every one of the other men was also wounded. – **Díaz**

On the Spaniards' final day in Xochimilco, Cortés ordered the entire city, except for the house in which they were lodged, burnt to the ground. Working at the back of the men's minds as they departed the smoking rubble was the knowledge that four of their companions, too intent on pillaging, had been captured. These unlucky souls would soon be hauled before the new Aztec ruler, young Cuauhtémoc.[1] After questioning them, he would have their arms, feet, and heads cut off and sent around to the towns of the Spaniards' allies.

Moving north, the Spanish-Indian force advanced upon Coyoacán, which they found deserted. They remained for two days reconnoitering the lake shore there and even advanced onto the causeway, where fighting with Mexicans was bloody. They then

---

[1] This approximately 25-year-old man, a cousin of Montezuma, had been elevated to the throne on the death of the former ruler, Cuitláhuac, from smallpox.

retreated, burning houses and cues in Coyoacán before moving further north, again to Tacuba, where more fighting ensued.

It was raining heavily when we arrived in Tacuba, and for nearly two hours we sheltered in some large courtyards. Cortés then took with him a few of his captains, the treasurer Alderete, who was sick, and the friar Melgarejo,[1] as well as a number of us soldiers. We climbed to the top of that city's cue, from which eminence one could enjoy the view of Mexico, which was very near, and the entire lake, with the large cities spread out along the lake's shore. The friar and the treasurer Alderete were astonished at the sight of so many and such large cities on the water. Seeing the great city of Mexico and the lake and the usual multitude of canoes—some loaded down with provisions, others fishing, and still others empty— they expressed even greater amazement, saying that our arrival in New Spain was not the work of men but of the divine mercy of God, who holds and protects us. They also said that they did not remember ever having read anywhere of royal subjects rendering any greater service to their king than we had done, and that now they could say this with even greater assurance, and they would be certain to report it to His Majesty. . . .

A discussion now took place among our captains and soldiers about whether we should have a look at the causeway, which was close to Tacuba, where we were. But because we had no powder and were short of bolts for the crossbows, and since we were all wounded, we began to recall that previous time, a little over a month ago, when Cortés had tried to get onto that causeway with a large number of soldiers. He had found it dangerous, and was afraid of defeat.

We agreed, therefore, to move on, for fear of having to skirmish with the Mexicans today or later that night. **– Díaz**

---

[1] Julián de Alderete and the Franciscan friar Pedro Melgarejo de Urrea had arrived from Spain in February. Fray Pedro, disliked by Díaz, had borne with him a papal bull granting forgiveness of sins committed in the course of the conquest, no doubt a welcome bit of news to most of the men. These recent arrivals also reported that Fonseca appeared to be falling out of favor with the court, and that affairs in Castile might soon be turning in Cortés's direction, a prediction that proved to be true.

CORTÉS RESURGENT ~ 277

Dealing harshly with their pursuers as they left the town—in a cunning ambush they killed more than a hundred—the men made their way around the north shore of the lake again, and back to Texcoco.

> After having completed our tour around the lakes, and having studied carefully how best to lay siege to Tenochtitlan from land and water, I returned to Texcoco, where I made ready our men and arms as best I could, and hurried the brigantine and related excavation project along toward completion.
>
> I had earlier ordered excavation of a trench that was to extend from where the brigantines presently were—near our quarters—half a league to the lake shore. . . . More than ten feet deep and equally wide, this trench would be flooded to allow us to float our vessels right into the lake. Eight thousand Indians from the provinces of Aculuacán and Texcoco labored at this project for fifty days. The trench walls were staked and plated to keep them from losing water, thereby allowing the vessels to be moved out easily and safely. It was a monumental piece of work and an impressive sight. **– Cortés**

Cortés was a severe taskmaster, heartily disliked by many in his army. Since his arrival in Mexico, he had had to deal with a sizeable contingent of near-mutinous grumblers, first the friends of Velázquez and now those of Narváez. Two days after his return to Texcoco, in the last week of April 1521, as he made final preparations for the siege of Tenochtitlan, he learned of a plot to murder him.

> It seems that a great friend of the governor of Cuba, Antonio de Villafaña by name, from Zamora or Toro, plotted with some of Narváez's soldiers . . . to stab Cortés to death. It would be done in this way: since at that time a ship had arrived from Castile, when Cortés was seated at table eating with his captains, one of the conspirators would bring him a sealed letter, as if it had arrived on that ship, and he would be told it was from his father, Martín Cortés. He would then be stabbed while reading it—along with any captains and soldiers who might try to protect him. . . . It seems that a soldier told Cortés about the plot, so that he might put a stop to it before things erupted. This good soldier informed Cortés that many men of rank were part of the conspiracy.

When Cortés heard this, he heaped gifts upon the man who had informed him, and promised him even more. Then quietly and quickly he let all of our captains know, namely, Pedro de Alvarado, Francisco de Lugo, Cristóbal de Olid, Andrés de Tapia, and Gonzalo de Sandoval. He also told me and two men who served as magistrates that year—Luis Marín and Pedro de Ircio. Other soldiers whom he knew to be loyal he told as well. Now informed of the plot, we made ready and without delay went with Cortés to Antonio de Villafaña's quarters, finding many of the conspirators there with him. With the assistance of four constables we seized Villafaña. Cortés ordered us also to seize the other captains and soldiers, who were attempting to flee. On seizing Villafaña, Cortés snatched from his breast the agreement bearing the signatures of all conspirators. Seeing that many of the signatories were high-ranking men, however, and not wishing to disgrace them, he spread the story that Villafaña had consumed the paper before he could see or read it.

Villafaña not only confessed to the crime, but, during the judicial process that followed, a number of credible and trustworthy witnesses testified against him. The magistrates, sitting with Cortés and the *maestre de campo* Cristobal de Olid,[1] passed sentence, and after making his confession to Father Juan Díaz, Villafaña was hanged from the window of his quarters. **– Díaz**

In his third letter to the emperor, Cortés felt constrained to explain his actions.

An alcalde and I condemned Antonio de Villafaña to death, and the sentence was duly carried out. And although I was aware that other men bore a large share of the guilt in this case, I feigned ignorance of this, continuing to deal with them as friends. Because this was a personal matter, although I might more correctly say Your Majesty's matter, I had no wish to treat them harshly. Little good has this done me, however, since some of the Velázquez men later laid many traps for me, secretly fomenting a lot of noise and scandal. I've had to guard myself against them more than against our enemies. . . . If such

---

[1] Camp commander.

things continue, I plan to punish these men as justice demands.
– Cortés

Shortly after Villafaña's execution, it was announced that the brigantines were ready.

When justice had been served on Antonio de Villafaña, and the conspirators had quieted down, Cortés was informed that the brigantines were ready with rigging and sails, that more than enough very good oars had been made, and that the canal down which the vessels would be brought to the lake was broad and deep enough. He then sent word to all the friendly towns around Texcoco that he needed eight thousand good copper arrowheads from each town, made according to a Castilian model we were supplying them. He also ordered that, in each of these towns, they make and smooth eight thousand shafts of very good wood. We again provided an example of what we wanted. This was all to be delivered to our camp in eight days.

What they brought to our camp in the allotted time was more than fifty thousand arrowheads and an equal number of shafts, the arrowheads being better than the Castilian models we had given them. These bolts were then divided among our crossbowmen, who were told to polish and feather them. . . . He also told the horsemen to have their horses shod and their lances sharpened, to ride every day, to gallop, and to give their mounts plenty of practice in skirmishing maneuvers.

Cortés then sent messengers . . . to [various allied Indian leaders], informing them that after the feast of Corpus Christi we would be setting out to blockade Mexico. He asked for twenty thousand fighters from Tlaxcala, Huexotzinco, and Cholula. These men were now all our comrades in arms, and they already knew the plan, since he had informed them via their own men, who were always leaving our camp loaded down with plunder from our expeditions. He also told those of Chalco and Tlalmanalco and their vassals to be ready when we summoned them, explaining how we planned to invest Mexico and when we planned to start. **– Díaz**

During the early days of May 1521 — no doubt to the great pride of all, and not least of the Indian laborers — the thirteen brigantines were floated without incident down the new canal and into the lake, where they were anchored. Then Cortés assembled his Spaniards to give them last-minute instructions.

Cortés now decided to hold a review of Spanish forces in the great courtyards of Texcoco. Eighty-four horsemen and 650 soldiers with sword and shield, many with lances, took their places. There were 194 crossbowmen and musketeers. Twelve crossbowmen and musketeers were allotted to each brigantine, but none were required to row, since twelve oarsmen—to row six to a side—were also selected for each vessel. A captain was chosen, making a crew of twenty-five for each vessel. Thirteen brigantines of twenty-five men each, plus artillerymen, made for a naval force of well over three hundred. Cortés also distributed all the boat-guns and falconets we had,[1] as well as all the powder he thought they would need. With this done, he ordered a public reading of all rules we were to observe.

First, no man must dare blaspheme Our Lord Jesus Christ, nor his blessed mother Our Lady, nor the blessed apostles, nor any other saints, under severe penalties.

Second, no soldier must ill-treat our allies, since they have come to help us, nor is anything to be taken from them, even war booty, nor are any male or female prisoners, gold, silver, or chalchihuites to be taken from them.

Third, no soldier must dare to leave our camp, by day or by night, to go to any friendly town or any other place to fetch food, under severe penalties.

Fourth, all soldiers must wear very well quilted armor, with gorget, helmet, leg protection, and shield. . . .

Fifth, no person must, on any account, wager for horse or arms, under heavy penalties.

Sixth, all soldiers, horsemen, crossbowmen, and musketeers must sleep in full armor and with sandals on their feet, unless they are severely wounded or ill . . . .

In addition to this, it was proclaimed that the penalty for a soldier's falling asleep on duty, leaving his post, moving from one camp to another without his captain's permission, or leaving his captain on the field and fleeing, was death. **– Díaz**

An unexpected problem now cropped up: a shortage of men willing to row.

---

[1] A falconet was a light cannon with about a two-inch bore.

When the review was over, Cortés realized that there were not enough seamen—who of course knew how to row—manning the oars. He knew well who the seamen were from our voyage, as well as those of Narváez and the others who had come from Jamaica. They had in fact been put on a list, and he had already warned them to be prepared to row. But there were still not enough for thirteen brigantines, and when the time came, some of the seamen actually refused to row. Cortés therefore began to look into who actually was a seaman and who was known to have gone out fishing, and who was from Palos, or Moguer, or Triana, or from any other place where one might expect to find seamen.

Once he had found these men, he ordered them, under the severest penalty for refusal, to man the oars. Some protested that they were of high birth. He ordered them to row anyway. In this way he finally succeeded in getting together 150 oarsmen. These were much luckier than we were, who had to bear the brunt of battle on the causeways, and they still got their share of the spoils. . . . Cortés then named his captains and gave them their orders—what each captain was expected to do, what part of the causeway he should go to, and with which captain on land he was to cooperate. **– Díaz**

Cortés then made a last-minute effort to put steel into his soldiers' hearts.

When I had finished my inspection I charged and strongly exhorted all Spaniards to abide by, as far as they were able, all the rules I had given them for the conduct of the war, encouraging them to take heart and fight hard, since they could see that Our Lord was guiding us to victory over our enemies. They knew well, I said, that when we came into Texcoco we had had no more than forty horsemen, but now God had aided us more than we had expected, with ships arriving bearing horses and men and arms, as they had seen. They should remember above all, I told them, that we were fighting for the increase and spread of our faith, and to bring into the service of Your Majesty all these rebellious lands and provinces. This should, I said, fill them with the courage and will to conquer or die.

All responded enthusiastically and we spent that day very pleasantly, all looking forward to the siege, so that we might

bring this war, on which depended either the peace or continuing rebellion of these lands, to a happy conclusion.
– **Cortés**

On May 12, the day planned for the campaign's opening, it was discovered that the commander of the Tlaxcalan troops, Xicotenga the Younger, had not only decided not to participate in the planned siege, but had returned to Tlaxcala with the purpose of taking over the Tlaxcalan nation. Cortés had by this time had enough of Xicotenga and quietly ordered him murdered. A constable and four cavalrymen were sent out, and the deed was done.

11

THE SIEGE OF TENOCHTITLAN

On May 13, a force numbering up to three hundred thousand men—only the tiniest percentage of which was European—began its advance on Tenochtitlan. Unbeknownst to them, they would be in combat for the next three months.

Two Spanish companies, one under Pedro de Alvarado and the other under Cristóbal de Olid, left Texcoco, marching around the north shore and down the western shore to Chapultepec, where, against fierce resistance, they succeeded in breaking the conduits that carried fresh water from the hills there, cutting off the supply to the city. Since the lake's water was unsuitable for drinking, this act alone promised to have a large effect upon the siege's outcome.

As a third company, under Gonzalo de Sandoval, set out southward for Iztapalapa, Cortés—who would himself enter the battle aboard a brigantine—ordered the thirteen brigantines to weigh anchor and move out onto the lake.

Because the inhabitants of Iztapalapa had been sending up smoke signals from one of the towers of their idols, perched atop a very high hill near the city, the warriors in Tenochtitlan and the other towns around the lake knew that I had brought the brigantines into the lake. They quickly gathered a large fleet of canoes together—five hundred, as far as we could judge—and came out to attack us and find out what these vessels were. As soon as I realized they were heading straight for us, I and the men who were with me . . . boarded quickly. But I ordered the brigantine captains to stay right where they were, in hopes that the men in the canoes, believing we were holding back out of fear, might decide to attack us. They then came at us very fast. But at a distance of two crossbow shots from us they suddenly stopped and waited. I very much wanted our first encounter to be a clear victory. I wanted them to be frightened of our brigantines, because they were the very key to this war, the water being the place where they—and, unfortunately we—would be most vulnerable.

By the grace of Our Lord, as our two forces remained watching one another, a land breeze sprang up, very favorable for closing with them. I then ordered the captains to rout the canoe fleet and to drive them back into the city of Tenochtitlan, bottling them up there. Since the wind was perfect for this, even though the enemy warriors fled as fast as they could, we sailed into the middle of them and sank an enormous number of canoes. We killed and drowned many of their men — it was the most perfect thing imaginable. And in this engagement we sailed a good three leagues or more, until we had confined them all among the houses of the city. **– Cortés**

Here is how the Aztecs saw this beginning of the end:

Two of the brigantines, both with cannons mounted in their bows, attacked a flotilla of our shielded canoes. The cannons were fired into the thick of the flotilla, wherever the canoes were crowded closest together. Many of our warriors were killed outright; others drowned because they were too crippled by their wounds to swim away. The water was red with the blood of the dead and dying. Those who were hit by the steel arrows were also doomed; they died instantly and sank to the bottom of the lake. . . .

Then the Spaniards arrived in Huitzillán, where they found another wall blocking the road. A great crowd of our warriors was hiding behind it to escape the gunfire.

The brigantines came up and anchored nearby. They had been pursuing our war canoes in the open lake, but when they had almost run them down, they suddenly turned and sailed toward the causeway. Now they anchored a short distance from the houses. As soon as the cannons in their bows were loaded again, the soldiers aimed and fired them at the new wall.

The first shot cracked it in a dozen places, but it remained standing. They fired again: this time it cracked from one end to the other and crumpled to the ground. A moment later the road was completely empty. The warriors had all fled when they saw the wall collapsing; they ran blindly, this way and that, howling with fear.

Then the Spaniards debarked and filled in the canal. Working hurriedly, they threw in the stones from the shattered wall, the roof beams and adobe bricks from the nearest houses, anything they could find, until the surface of the fill was level with the causeway. Then a squad of about ten horsemen crossed over it. They galloped to and fro, scouting both sides of the road; they raced and wheeled and clattered back and forth. Soon they were joined by another squad that rode up to support them.

A number of Tlatelolcas had rushed into the palace where Motecuhzoma lived before he was slain. When they came out again, they unexpectedly met the Spanish cavalry. The lead horseman stabbed one of the Tlatelolcas, but the wounded man was able to clutch the lance and cling to it. His friends ran to his aid and twisted it from the Spaniard's hands. They knocked the horseman from his saddle, beat and kicked him as he lay on his back on the ground, and then cut off his head.

The Spaniards now joined all their forces into one unit and marched together as far as the Eagle Gate, where they set up the cannons they had brought with them. It was called the Eagle Gate because it was decorated with an enormous eagle carved of stone. The eagle was flanked on one side by a stone jaguar; on the other side there was a large honey bear, also of carved stone.

Two rows of tall columns led into the city from this gate. Some of the Aztecs hid behind the columns when they saw the Spaniards and their guns; others climbed onto the roofs of the communal houses. None of the warriors dared to show his face openly.

The Spaniards wasted no time as they loaded and fired the cannons. The smoke belched out in black clouds that darkened the sky, as if night were falling. The warriors hidden behind the columns broke from cover and fled; those on the rooftops climbed down and ran after them. When the smoke cleared away, the Spaniards could not see a single Aztec. – **Aztec account**

Cortés, at first on a brigantine, soon joined his land forces.

I rode for a while through the city with the horsemen, and in the streets that were on dry land we lanced all the Indians we met, to the point where they pulled back and were afraid to venture onto land. Seeing that the men of the city were rebellious and determined to die in their own defense, I drew two conclusions: one, that we would recover little or none of the treasure they had taken from us, and two, that they were giving us cause, indeed practically forcing us, to destroy them utterly.

This last weighed heavily on my soul and I tried to think how best I could frighten them into realizing their error and how great was the damage we could do to them. I therefore burned and threw down the towers of their idols and their houses. And that they might feel it the more, I had those great houses on the plaza where I and the Spaniards had stayed prior to being cast out of the city burned to the ground. So grand were these buildings that a prince with a household and retinue of more than six hundred persons could have been at home there. Other houses stood near these, smaller but very much prettier and nicer, in which Montezuma had kept every species of bird found in this country. Although it pained me deeply, I knew it would pain them more, so I resolved to burn them. Our enemies, including those from the cities around the lake, were deeply aggrieved by this, because none of them ever believed that our small force could penetrate so deeply into the city. They were absolutely dismayed. **– Cortés**

Despite the superiority of their weapons, the battle for the city did not proceed smoothly for the Spaniards.

The warriors advanced to the sound of flutes. They shouted their war cries and beat their shields like drums. They pursued the Spaniards, harried and terrified them, and at last took fifteen of them prisoners. The rest of the Spaniards retreated to their ships and sailed out into the middle of the lake.

The prisoners were sacrificed in the place called Tlacochcalco [House of the Arsenal]. Their captors quickly plundered them, seizing their weapons, their cotton armor and everything else, until they stood naked. Then they were sacrificed to the god, while their comrades on the lake watched them being put to death. **– Aztec account**

Cortés, in the rear, became concerned that his vanguard—in the exhilaration now of a successful rout of the enemy—may have neglected to provide a path for retreat. His fears proved to be justified.

Some Spaniards sent to inform me that they had gained so much ground that they were now not far from the marketplace. They said that they planned to continue their advance, since they could already hear the alguacil mayor and

Pedro de Alvarado attacking from their position. I sent to tell them that on no account should they consider moving forward without first ensuring that the water gaps in the streets, where the bridges had been, were well filled in, so that if they had to retreat, the water would present no obstacle. They well knew that this is where the greatest danger lay.

They sent a message back to me saying that everything had been very well filled in, and that I might go there and inspect it myself. Suspecting that they had not done a thorough job in filling in these gaps, I went there to see. I found one gap they had crossed over that was ten or twelve paces wide, with water more than ten feet deep. When they crossed it they had thrown into it reed grass and pieces of wood, and, as they had crossed over very carefully on these materials, a few at a time, they did not sink. But now, drunk with the taste of victory, they imagined they had left it quite strong and safe.

At the moment when I arrived at that bridge, which was highly unstable, I saw that both the Spaniards and a number of our allies were in headlong retreat, with the enemy, like hounds, right on their heels. Seeing the impending disaster, I began to shout, "Stop, stop," and when I got to the edge of the water, I found it already filling with Spaniards and Indians as if not even a straw had been thrown into the breach. The enemy was driving the Spaniards back so hard that, in striving to kill them, they even threw themselves into the water after them. Meanwhile in the canals alongside the streets, Indian canoes had appeared, and any of our men who were still alive were being hauled into them. Since this whole thing had happened so quickly, and I saw my men being killed, I resolved to stay there myself and die fighting.

To me and to the men who were with me, it seemed the most important thing we could do was to rescue the unhappy Spaniards who were drowning. Some we pulled out wounded, others half drowned, still others who had lost their weapons. I sent them on ahead, and at that moment we faced such an onslaught by the enemy that I and twelve or fifteen of those who were with me found ourselves suddenly surrounded. Since I had been fully engaged in rescuing the drowning men, I was paying no attention and was completely unaware of my danger. A few of the enemy warriors seized me and would have carried me off if it hadn't been for a captain of fifty men whom I always had with me, and a young man of his company. This young man, after God, saved my life, and for his brave action, gave up his own. – **Cortés**

The Spaniards had been routed. Despite their carefully laid plans, despite their great valor, despite the assistance of thousands of Indian warriors and the recent devastating plague, all seemed suddenly lost.

The Spaniards who had escaped the rout were retreating along that street, or causeway, which was quite narrow and at the same level as the water, which the dogs had labored to make so. Many of our Indian allies were also fleeing, greatly clogging the passage. So slow was the progress of the retreat, therefore, that the enemy was able to come along both sides of our column by water, and capture or kill at their pleasure. The captain who was with me, Antonio Quiñones by name, said to me, "Let's get out of here and save you, for you know that without you all of us are finished." But he couldn't get me to leave. When he realized I wasn't going to budge, he seized me by the arms in an attempt to turn me around, and even though at that moment I found death more attractive than life, nonetheless because of his insistence, and that of the other men who were there, we began to retreat, with our swords and shields holding off an enemy who continued to wound us from all sides.

Into the midst of this arrived one of my servants on horseback, and he cleared a space for us. But he was immediately lanced in the throat from a low rooftop, and forced to turn back. While we were engaged in this rear-guard action to enable our people to escape to safety, a servant of mine arrived with a horse for me. So much mud had been dragged onto the causeway, however, by those who had escaped from the water, that it was difficult for anyone to stand upright, especially as all were being pushed and shoved by men striving to save themselves. I mounted, but found it impossible to fight from horseback. If it had been possible, the eight horsemen I had left on a small island up the street would have been here, but they could do nothing but retreat.

Even retreat, however, was perilous. Two mares, each carrying a servant of mine, fell from the causeway into the water, and the Indians killed one. The other was rescued by foot-soldiers. Another servant of mine, a young man named Cristóbal de Guzmán, had been given a horse on that island to bring to me for my escape, but the enemy killed both him and the horse before he reached me. His death plunged our camp into deep sorrow, and those who knew him feel that grief to this day. **– Cortés**

Then all the Aztecs sprang up and charged into battle. The Spaniards were so astonished that they blundered here and there like drunkards; they ran through the streets with the warriors in pursuit. This was when the taking of captives began. A great many of the allies from Tlaxcala, Acolhuacán, Chalco and Xochimilco were overpowered by the Aztecs, and there was a great harvesting of prisoners, a great reaping of victims to be sacrificed.

The Spaniards and their allies waded into the lake because the road had become too slippery for them. The mud was so slick that they sprawled and floundered and could not stand up to fight. The Aztecs seized them as captives and dragged them across the mud.

The Spanish standard was taken and carried off during this encounter. The warriors from Tlatelolco captured it in the place known today as San Martín, but they were scornful of their prize and considered it of little importance.

Some of the Spaniards were able to escape with their lives. They retreated in the direction of Culhuacán, on the edge of the canal, and gathered there to recover their strength. **– Aztec account**

In this rout, several dozen Spaniards and an unknown number of their Indian allies were captured. All knew what their fate would be.

The Aztecs took their prisoners to Yacacolco, hurrying them along the road under the strictest guard. Some of the captives were weeping, some were keening, and others were beating their palms against their mouths.

When they arrived in Yacacolco, they were lined up in long rows. One by one they were forced to climb to the temple platform, where they were sacrificed by the priests. **– Aztec account**

Falling back toward our quarters, we passed around a large cove, arriving at a place where their arrows and darts and stones could no longer reach us. Sandoval and Francisco de

Lugo and Andrés de Tapia were standing with Pedro de Alvarado, discussing the day's events and Cortés's latest orders, when the dismal sound of Huichilobos's drum was again heard, accompanied by many conchs, horns, and something like trumpets, a terrifying sound.

We looked toward the high cue where the sound was coming from and we saw that they were dragging our comrades up the steps. They had been captured in our recent rout, and were about to be sacrificed. The men were soon forced up into the small square atop the cue before the shrine where they keep their accursed idols. Plumes were placed on the heads of some of our men, and they were forced to dance before Huichilobos with a sort of fan. After this the papas laid them on their backs on some narrow stones they use for the sacrifice. Then with stone knives they cut open their chests and ripped out their hearts, still beating, offering them to their idols. The bodies they kicked down the steps where their butchers were waiting. These cut off their arms and legs, and flayed their faces, which they later tanned like glove leather with the beards on. They kept these for their drunken orgies, and the flesh they ate with peppers and tomatoes. They sacrificed them all in this manner, eating the legs and arms, and offering the hearts and blood to their idols. The remainder of the bodies, namely, the torsos and entrails, they threw to the tigers and lions and serpents they keep in their bestiaries.

– Díaz

The young king Cuauhtémoc sent the hands and feet of the Spanish soldiers, the skin of their faces, and the heads of four horses, also sacrificed, around to area villages, as a message to any who might be wavering in their loyalty to the Aztec king.

The siege continued, day after day in the bright summer air.

The Spanish blockade caused great anguish in the city. The people were tormented by hunger, and many starved to death. There was no fresh water to drink, only stagnant water and the brine of the lake, and many people died of dysentery.

The only food was lizards, swallows, corncobs and the salt grasses of the lake. The people also ate water lilies and the seeds of the *colorín*,[1] and chewed on deerhides and pieces of

---

[1] *Erythrina americana*, a tree native to Mexico, with gaudy red flowers.

leather. They roasted and seared and scorched whatever they could find and then ate it. They ate the bitterest weeds and even dirt.

Nothing can compare with the horrors of that siege and the agonies of the starving. We were so weakened by hunger that, little by little, the enemy forced us to retreat. Little by little they forced us to the wall. – **Aztec account**

The Spaniards had by now been battling for control of the city for nearly two months, into late June and early July. They were currently licking their wounds in Culhuacán, on the mainland south of the lake. Because of their recent setback, many of their Indian allies had left them. But during this respite it was learned that a ship had arrived at Villa Rica, a ship belonging to Juan Ponce de León, who had recently been defeated (and mortally wounded) in La Florida. From this ship Cortés received new crossbows and powder, and likely new recruits. With this turn of events, even more of the enemy came over to his side.

Some of the Indian lords who had been inside, seeing the danger they were in, and how they were running out of food and water, determined to escape by night. One of these was Ixtlilxochitl, captain-general of Texcoco and the brother of Cuaunacuxtli, lord of Texcoco. He presented himself to our captain and offered his and his men's services to us, promising to help in the war against his people. His renown as a warrior was a dagger driven into the Mexican heart. On another night the lord who ruled Xochimilco and others around the lake came over to us. The defection of these men was a serious blow to their people, because they later waged very cruel war from their canoes and were a large part of the reason we conquered the Mexicans. Then, as these leaders were coming over to our side, with the Christians exhausted from fighting and the Indians packed inside the city with nothing to eat, God saw fit to send them smallpox.[1] Women especially succumbed. It proved nearly impossible for us to pass through the streets, packed as they were with people dying of disease, hunger, and smallpox. – **Alonso de Aguilar**

Yet withal, Cortés was stymied. Why do these people continue to resist us? Can't they see they are doomed? Yet they fight on. He

---

[1] This appears to be a second wave of the disease, which had first struck the previous September.

resolved upon the complete and utter destruction of the city and its people.

> When I saw how rebellious the people of this city were, and how determined they were to die—more determined than any race ever born—I didn't know how we could relieve ourselves of the dangers and hardships they caused us without destroying their city, which was indeed the most beautiful thing in the world. I tried explaining to them that we had no intention of removing our camps, nor of ceasing to attack them from the brigantines. I pointed out that we had already destroyed the people of Matalcingo and Marinalco, and that there was no one anywhere who could help them. No one would bring them maize, or meat, or fruit, or water, or any other provision. But the more I tried to reason with them, the less sign they showed of weakening. They in fact fought with greater spirit and trickery. Seeing the affair continuing in this manner, and reflecting on the fact that we'd spent more than forty-five days in this siege already, I decided to take measures that would increase our safety and squeeze them harder.

> The idea was that, as we advanced along the city streets, we would tear down every house on both sides of the street. We would in fact not advance one step until all of them were in ruins. We would also fill in any waterway we encountered, no matter how long it took. I called together all the chiefs of our Indian allies and told them what I had decided. I asked them to bring as many of their farm laborers as possible, with their *coas*, which are a sort of stick with which they dig, much as spades are used in Spain. They replied that they would gladly do this, that it was a fine idea, and it seemed to them a good way to bring the city to ruin, which they desired more than anything in the world. **– Cortés**

The Spaniards and their allies reentered the city. A fierce battle ensued near temple square, and the Spaniards were again being driven back. Cortés this time laid a trap for their pursuers, creating a turning point in Spanish fortunes.

> When the time came, I passed the word that we were to retreat in good order. I also commanded the horsemen to begin a charge when they reached the square, but then to back off, as if they had lost their nerve. They were to do this, I said, when they saw that the square was full.

The men lying in ambush—keen to do well and tired of the suspense—were anxiously waiting for it all to begin. I joined them, and before long our foot-soldiers and horsemen, along with our Indian allies—who also knew about the ambush—began falling back across the square. The enemy pursued them with such wild shrieks that one might have thought they'd conquered the world. The nine horseman launched their charge across the square, but suddenly pulled up, and by the time they had done this twice, the enemy had reached such a state of fury that they struck at the horses' flanks until they had driven the horsemen to the end of the street, where we were waiting.

Once the Spaniards had passed by us and we heard the signal—an harquebus shot—we knew the time had come. With "Señor Santiago" on our lips,[1] we threw ourselves upon them, charging through the square, lancing them, slashing, cutting them down, leaving them to be finished off by our allies. We killed more than five hundred in this ambush, all of them leaders, zealous and valiant men. Our allies were certain to eat well that night, because every person they killed they took away and cut into pieces for dinner.

The enemy was so shocked and stupefied at being so suddenly routed that they neither spoke nor shouted that evening, nor did they dare appear in the street or on the rooftops, unless certain of being safe. Since it was nearly night when we pulled back, it seems they sent out a few slaves to see if we were retreating, or what else we might be doing. When these slaves showed themselves in the street, ten or twelve horsemen charged them, running them down to ensure that none might escape alive. **– Cortés**

The Spaniards' and their Indian allies fought now with renewed energy, although misfortune was never more than a step away.

The victory that our Lord God gave us that day was the principal cause of the city's being conquered as soon as it was, because the inhabitants were thoroughly shocked by it, and the spirit of our allies was strongly rekindled. We now returned to

---

[1] An invocation of St. James the Greater—apostle, and patron saint of Spain.

our camp intending not to let a day pass without entering the city, so as to bring this war to a speedy conclusion.

We sustained no casualties that day, except for when we broke out of our ambush and a few of our horsemen collided, throwing one rider from his mare. She made directly for the enemy, who quickly shot her full of arrows. Badly wounded, and apparently realizing the grave injury she had received, she fled back to us, dying later that night. Although this distressed us greatly — because horses meant life for us — it was better that she died in our hands than in the enemy's hands, which we feared would happen. If she had died among them, their joy at this would have exceeded their sorrow over the losses of their comrades.

On that day the brigantines and canoes of our allies wrought great havoc upon the city, incurring no damage themselves. **– Cortés**

Although the results of such unbridled warfare, in all its ugliness, were evident on every hand, the Indians would not yield, nor would Cortés.

We already knew that the Indians of the city were quite frightened, but we then learned from two wretched creatures who had escaped from there by night and come to our camp that they were dying of hunger, that they were going out at night to fish among the city's houses, and that they wandered out into the parts of the city that we had already taken in search of firewood, as well as of grasses and roots to eat. Because we had already filled in many of the waterways and leveled many bad stretches of ground, I resolved to enter the city before dawn and do all the damage we could.

The brigantines set out while it was still dark, and I then left with twelve or fifteen horsemen, some foot-soldiers, and a few of our allies. We slipped into the city quickly and sent out a few spies. Remaining hidden as day broke, we awaited their news. When we received the signal we burst out upon what proved to be a large number of people. But they were miserable wretches who had simply come out in search of food, the men for the most part unarmed, and most of the group being women and children. We spread such destruction among them through all the streets we could reach that those we took prisoner or killed totaled more than eight hundred.

The brigantines were also at work, wreaking havoc among them, taking large numbers of people who were out fishing in canoes. When the captains and principal men of the city saw us in the city at this unaccustomed hour, their astonishment was as profound as it had been at the recent ambush, and not a soul dared come out to oppose us. We therefore returned to our camp with plenty of booty and food for our allies' feasting.
– Cortés

Starving, wounded, dispirited refugees now poured into the Spanish camps, pleading for mercy. The filling in of canals was proceeding rapidly; houses—including that of Cuauhtémoc—were being burnt, bridges being captured, and shoreline roads secured. By late July, three-quarters of the ruined city was in Spanish hands.

The next day, which was the feast of St. James the Apostle,[1] we entered the city in the same manner as before, following the broad street that leads to the great marketplace. . . . That day we did nothing but burn and flatten houses on both sides of this street, a pitiful sight to see, but we had no choice if we were to succeed in our aim. As the city's inhabitants looked upon this devastation, they shouted to our Indian allies, encouraging them to get on with the burning and destruction, for if they, the inhabitants, were victorious, our allies—as they well knew—would be the ones forced to rebuild the city. If the Spaniards, on the other hand, were victorious, they shouted, they would still be the ones made to rebuild it.

Thanks be to God, it was we who were victorious, but it was they, not our allies, who were forced to rebuild it. **– Cortés**

The Spaniards were by now running low on powder, and Cortés was being pressured by some of his men who were experienced in European siege warfare to build a catapult, presumably to throw iron or flaming balls into the section of the city that had not yet been captured.[2] Cortés, dubious, told them to proceed, but after several days spent in constructing the machine and setting it up, with most of the fighting men idle during this time, it proved to be a failure, bringing the Mexican forces no closer to surrender.

The day after we had erected the catapult, we returned to the city, and since we had now been three or four days without

---

[1] July 25.

[2] Tlatelolco, the northern part of the island.

fighting, we found the streets filled with women, children, and others—all starving and wretched, skeletal and broken, a truly pitiful sight. I ordered our allies to leave them alone. But none of the enemy's warriors ventured out into a place where we could get at them, although we did notice some on their rooftops, wrapped in the blankets they use, but weaponless. I invited them to talk peace with me, but their responses were evasive. Having spent most of the day in this effort, I finally sent to tell them I intended to attack, and that they should get all their people off the streets or I would loose our allies upon them. They replied that they wished to have peace, but I responded that I saw no lord with whom I could discuss peace terms. He should come out, I said. I would give him all the security he wished, and we would talk peace. We now realized that this was all a joke to them and that they were completely ready to do battle with us.

After having given them so many plain warnings, I felt it was time to put pressure on them, to drive them to even greater extremity. I therefore ordered Pedro de Alvarado to take all his men into that quarter of the city which the enemy still held, and which contained more than a thousand houses. I planned to enter from another direction with our foot-soldiers, since horses would be of no advantage in this place.

Following a brutal combat there, we took the entire quarter, with the toll of dead and captured among the enemy exceeding twelve thousand. Our allies then treated the prisoners most cruelly, leaving not a single person alive, despite our reprimands and threats of punishment. **– Cortés**

The Aztec leaders, their world no longer recognizable, seemed incapable of a saving response.

We returned to the city next day, and I ordered that no one was to fight with or do harm to any of our enemies. They saw our overwhelming numbers and understood that their former subjects, men over whom they had once ruled, had come to kill them. Realizing the dire straits in which they found themselves, having no place even to stand except on the bodies of their dead, and desiring to be delivered from this great misery, they asked our men why we did not just finish them off. They then asked that I be summoned, for they wished to speak with me.

Because all my men wanted to see this war come to an end, and regarded it as a great pity that it had lasted so long, they rejoiced that the Indians at last appeared to want peace. They came to me very eagerly with this message, begging me to go to a barricade where a few chiefs and lords were awaiting me. I knew it would come to nothing. I well knew that, while the people themselves wanted only to be out of this war, dead or alive, it was their prince and three or four of their principal men who wanted to see it prolonged. Nonetheless, I made up my mind to go.

When I reached the barricade I was told by their envoys that they regarded me as a child of the sun. If the sun, they said, in the short span of a day and a night, can circle the entire earth, I should be able, in an equally short time, to kill them all and put an end to their suffering, because they wanted nothing more than to die and go to heaven to rest with the god whom they venerated most—Huichilobos, who awaited them there.

In my reply I did my best to persuade them to surrender, but they would have none of it, even though we had given them more signs of desiring peace than any vanquished people had ever been given by the victors—which, by the grace of Our Lord, we were. **– Cortés**

Cortés's final attempt to end the bloodshed through receiving the defenders' surrender was also thrown in his face.

Having now driven the enemy to the last extremity, as may be gathered from what I've already said, to dissuade them from their evil proposal, namely, for every one of them to die, I spoke with a man we held prisoner, a person of great standing among them, captured two or three days before. . . . Although he was badly wounded, I asked him if he might be willing to return to the city for me. He said he would. When on the next day we again entered the city, I sent him with a few of my men to be handed over to his people. Prior to letting him go, I had spoken to him at length about my desire that he speak to his ruler and the other principal men about peace, and he had promised me to do everything in his power to carry out my wishes.

He was received in the city with great honor, as befitted one of their highest-ranking men. But I later heard that when he was brought before Cuauhtémoc, their prince, and began to speak of peace, he was sent away to be murdered and sacrificed. The reply that we were awaiting came in the form of an attack. Amidst loud war cries, they shouted that they wanted nothing else but to die. Showering us, then, with javelins, arrows, and stones, they closed with us in fierce combat. They in fact fought so strenuously that they succeeded in killing a horse with a blade they had fashioned from one of our swords. This attack cost them dearly, however, for we killed many of them before returning to our camps that day.

– Cortés

Little more could be done by land forces alone. The captain-general decided to counter this stubborn resistance by ordering greater pressure from the brigantines.

On leaving the camp, I had ordered Gonzalo de Sandoval to sail the brigantines in from the other side of the houses where the Indians had taken refuge. We would then have them surrounded. He was ordered not to attack until he had seen that we were engaged. Pressed on all sides, the Indians would have no escape except across the bodies of their dead, or across whatever rooftops were left. By this time they neither had nor could find arrows or javelins or stones with which to attack us.

– Cortés

His hold over his Tlaxcalan allies, however—flush with victory over their former oppressors—had vanished. They engaged in an orgy of slaughter.

Our allies accompanied us with swords and shields, slaughtering right and left, whether on land or water. On that day they slew or took prisoner more than forty thousand souls. Not a man among us remained unmoved by the wailing and shrieking of the women and children, a sound to break the heart of anyone. We expended greater effort in dissuading our allies from their murderous and cruel behavior than we did in battling the enemy. No nation has ever witnessed the level of unnatural cruelty practiced by these people. And our allies took much plunder that day, which we could by no means stop. After all, we were only some nine hundred men and they were 150,000. Nothing we could do or say was sufficient to halt their robberies, although we made a great effort to do so.

– Cortés

In the midst of all the death and the stench and universal weariness, Cortés's eyes nonetheless remained fixed on the true prize: the great wealth he believed to be still residing in the Aztec capital.

> One of the reasons why I had not wanted to enter the city in force over the past few days was that if we did try to take it by storm, the inhabitants would have thrown all they possessed into the water. Even if they did not do this, our allies would have taken it. Either way, I feared that Your Majesty would receive only a small part of the great wealth that this city once held, such as what I had once set aside for Your Highness. Because it was late now, and we could no longer tolerate the stench from the dead bodies that had been lying in the streets for several days—the most loathsome thing imaginable—we returned to our camps. **– Cortés**

The horror of the scene is almost inconceivable.

> The people of the city had to walk upon the bodies of their dead. Others jumped into the water, some swimming, many drowning in that large lake. Their suffering was so great as to surpass understanding.

> The survivors—men, women, and children—now poured out of the city toward us in vast numbers. In their eagerness to escape, some threw themselves into the water, only to drown amidst a multitude of floating corpses. It seemed to us that starvation, imbibing of salt water, or exposure to the stench had killed more than fifty thousand of them. In order that we might not see their plight, they had not thrown the bodies of their dead into the water, out of fear that our brigantines would find them, . . . They had left them in the streets, where we encountered mountains of corpses. We could not avoid walking on them since there was no other place to put one's feet.

> Because people were now streaming out of the city, I stationed Spaniards in all these streets to ensure that our allies would not kill these poor wretches, who were numberless. I also told all the captains of our allies that they must not allow these people to be harmed. Despite this, since our Indian friends far outnumbered us, they succeeded in killing and sacrificing more than fifteen thousand of them that day. The chiefs and warriors of the city were still hiding in corners or on rooftops or in houses or in canoes on the water, where no

artifice nor any other strategy could help them, since their weakness and ruin was clearly visible.

Seeing that it was getting late, and still they refused to surrender, I had the two guns fired at them. This did them some damage, but firing guns at them, I reasoned, would damage them far less than giving our allies permission to attack. When this effort proved futile, I had the harquebus fired, and that bastion was finally overrun, with many of its defenders driven into the water. The rest surrendered without a fight. **– Cortés**

12

AFTERMATH

By August 13, 1521, following three months of butchery and
death, it was over. The city's last bastion—Tlatelolco—had been
definitively taken. On that date the young king Cuauhtémoc
and his family attempted to escape across the lake in a flotilla of small
craft, but they were captured. Cuauhtémoc begged mercy for his
family and insisted on being brought before Cortés himself, who was
at Tlatelolco. News of the leader's capture was greeted with joy
throughout the army. Cortés ordered a guest chamber to be prepared
for the young man and directed that it be well supplied with food. He
then reclined on a rooftop to await delivery of his captive, whose
eventual arrival touched off enthusiastic celebration in the Spanish
camp.

> The Spaniards came out to meet [Cuauhtémoc]. They took
> him by the hand, led him up to the rooftop and brought him
> into the presence of Cortés. The captain stared at him for a
> moment and then patted him on the head. Then he gestured
> toward a chair and the two leaders sat down side by side.
>
> The Spaniards began to shoot off their cannons, but they
> were not trying to hit anyone. They merely loaded and fired,
> and the cannonballs flew over the Indians' heads. **– Aztec
> account**

Díaz stood by as the now-legendary young Indian joined Cortés.

> Cuauhtémoc was an agreeable person in body and
> features. His somewhat long face was cheerful, but his
> unwavering gaze, when it fell on you, was more grave than
> pleasing. He was about twenty-six years old, a little lighter in
> complexion than the brown of other Indians. **– Díaz**

It was evening now, and rain was beginning to fall. Cortés ordered
the men back to their camps, and directed that the young ruler and his
family be sent to his own camp at Coyoacán, near the lake's
southwestern shore. Whether in mourning or in celebration for the
close of this day, the heavens opened with heavy rain, thunder, and
lightning.

Once Cuauhtémoc had been captured, once the celebrations had
subsided and the storm had passed, an eerie silence settled over this

land that had been enveloped in endless din, day and night, for months. The silence was especially deep over the city itself, which remained a charnel house.

> I'd like to speak now of the dead bodies and heads that were in those houses where Cuauhtémoc had taken refuge. I solemnly swear that all the dwellings and storage houses around the lake were full of heads and corpses. I don't know how to write it. In the streets and courtyards of Tlatelolco it was the only thing we saw. Here we had to thread our way among the bodies and heads of dead Indians — we couldn't do otherwise. I've read about the destruction of Jerusalem. But I'm not sure there was more death in Jerusalem than here. So many people perished here, warriors from all the provinces and towns subject to Mexico who had gathered here, and all of them died, leaving the ground and the lake and the storage houses all full of dead bodies. The stench was so great that none of us could stand it, and for this reason, once Cuauhtémoc was in custody, all our captains returned to their camps. Even Cortés was sick from the odor. He also suffered from headaches during his days at Tlatelolco. **– Díaz**

Those Indians who survived did not know what they would be allowed to do. The city was untenable, but to attempt to leave it might have been to risk death. In his conversations with Cortés — now carried on through Marina only, since Aguilar was dead and she now spoke Spanish — Cuauhtémoc brought this matter up.

> Because the stench in the city was so great, Cuauhtémoc begged Cortés's permission to evacuate the survivors to the shoreline towns, and Cortés told him to go ahead. For three days and nights, therefore, all three causeways were crowded with men, women, and children flowing out of the city, all of them skin and bones, sallow, filthy, and stinking. It was heart-wrenching to see them. **– Díaz**

As the living dead fled the city, the Spaniards nonetheless remained pitiless.

> With this [flight from the city] the war came to an end. The people cried: "We have suffered enough! Let us leave the city! Let us go live on weeds!" Some fled across the lake, others along the causeways, and even then there were many killings.[1]

---

[1] Many of them by the Spaniards' dogs.

The Spaniards were angry because our warriors still carried their shields and *macanas*.[1]

Those who lived in the center of the city went straight toward Amaxac, to the fork in the road. From there they fled in various directions, some toward Tepeyacac, others toward Xoxohuiltitlán and Nonohualco; but no one went toward Xoloco or Mazatzintamalco. Those who lived in boats or on the wooden rafts anchored in the lake fled by water, as did the inhabitants of Tolmayecán. Some of them waded in water up to their chests and even up to their necks. Others drowned when they reached water above their heads.

The grownups carried their young children on their shoulders. Many of the children were weeping with terror, but a few of them laughed and smiled, thinking it was great sport to be carried like that along the road.

Some of the people who owned canoes departed in the daytime, but the others, the majority, left by night. They almost crashed into each other in their haste as they paddled away from the city.

The Spanish soldiers were stationed along the roads to search the fleeing inhabitants. They were looking only for gold and paid no attention to jade, turquoise or quetzal feathers. The women carried their gold under their skirts and the men carried it in their mouths or under their loincloths. Some of the women, knowing they would be searched if they looked prosperous, covered their faces with mud and dressed themselves in rags. They put on rags for skirts and rags for blouses; everything they wore was in tatters. But the Spaniards searched all the women without exception: those with light skins, those with dark skins, those with dark bodies.

A few of the men were separated from the others. These men were the bravest and strongest warriors, the warriors with manly hearts. The youths who served them were also told to stand apart. The Spaniards immediately branded them with hot irons, either on the cheek or the lips. . . .

---

[1] The flattened clubs or swords seen by the Spaniards among the island Indians, the word applied here to the more deadly *macuahuitl*, edged with razor-sharp obsidian chips.

Thirty thousand men from the kingdom of Tezcoco were killed during this [siege], of the more than two hundred thousand who fought on the side of the Spaniards. Of the Aztecs, more than 240,000 were killed. Almost all of the nobility perished: there remained alive only a few lords and knights and the little children. **– Aztec account**

Once this flow had ceased, we went with Cortés to inspect the city. We found the houses overflowing with corpses, and among them some living Mexicans who had been unable to move. Their excretions resembled the filth passed by thin swine who have been feeding on grass alone. The city looked as though it had been plowed up as they had dug for roots of edible plants, which they ate boiled. They had even consumed tree bark. We could find no potable water, only brackish.

I must say that they did not eat the flesh of Indians but only of our men and the Tlaxcalans whom they captured. Due to the hunger, thirst, and continual fighting suffered by this people, there had been no live births here for a long time. **– Díaz**

The first order Cortés gave to Cuauhtémoc was to repair and restore the water conduits from Chapultepec so that fresh water could again be brought into the city. To clean up the streets and eliminate the source of the stench, he had him organize the removal and burial of all corpses and heads. He also ordered him to put the causeways back into their former condition, and to make the city's houses and palaces habitable within two months. He marked out what quarter of the city would be assigned to the Indian population, and what part should be left clear for us.

Cuauhtémoc and his captains now complained to Cortés that many of our soldiers and captains had carried off the wives and daughters of the city's principal men, and begged Cortés as a favor to have these women returned. Cortés told them it would be difficult to take them from their present owners, but that they could search through the camps if they liked, bring the women before him, and he would determine if they had become Christians, or if they wished to return to their families, in which case he would order that they be released. He then gave the chiefs permission to search through all three camps, and announced that any woman who wished to return to her family must be given up.

A number of chiefs now started going through our camps from house to house, very thoroughly, looking for their wives and daughters. Many whom they found did not wish to return to their parents or husbands, but rather to stay with the soldiers with whom they were living. Some hid themselves from the searchers, others said they did not wish to return to idolatry. Some were already pregnant.

The searchers found only three women who wished to return, and Cortés expressly commanded that they be handed over. – **Díaz**

Cuauhtémoc doubtless had few illusions about his future. Cortés had no further need of him. He was in fact soon taken away by Spanish captains and his feet burned with hot oil—crippling him—until he should tell where he had hidden his gold. Very little was ever found. This last king of the Aztec empire was then imprisoned to await his ultimate fate.

Cortés remained in camp at Coyoacán. Now that common cause had been made by his cobbled-together army, and the great end achieved, hostility toward him among Spanish troops began to resurface. He was widely perceived as having looted Mexico for himself.

While Cortés was at Coyoacán, he stayed in some palaces with whitewashed walls, surfaces on which one could very easily write with charcoal or ink. Every morning malicious messages—like lampoons—would appear on one of these walls, some in prose, others in verse. One of the writers said that the sun, moon, heavens, stars, sea, and earth had their appointed movements, and if at some time they were knocked out of the planes which they were intended to occupy, they would soon return to their natural state. And so it would be, he said, with Cortés's ambition to command: he would soon revert to his natural condition.

Others said he had dealt us, his men, a more serious blow than he had dealt to Mexico, and that we should think of ourselves not as the conquerors of New Spain, but rather as the victims of Hernán Cortés.

Still others said that he wasn't satisfied with taking a general's share, but that he also took a portion of the king's, not counting the other ways in which he had profited.

Another wrote, "Oh how sad my soul will be until the day I see again the gold that Cortés has stolen and hidden away." It was also written that Diego Velázquez had spent his whole fortune and discovered the northern coast as far as Pánuco, but that Cortés had then come along to reap the benefits, stealing not only the land, but its treasure. There were other messages like this, some using words unfit to reprint here.

Cortés would come out of his quarters every morning and read these messages. He found the style quite good and the verses well-rhymed, with each couplet making its meaning perfectly clear—and not quite as naïvely as I may have suggested.

Now since Cortés was a bit of a poet himself, he prided himself on his witty replies, which played up his own deeds to the denigration of those of Diego Velázquez, Grijalva, and Francisco Hernández de Córdoba. He in fact made some well-written, pointed remarks of his own, with the result that every day the poetry and riddles became more scurrilous, until Cortés finally scrawled, "A blank wall is a fool's writing-paper." This was answered during the night by, "It's also the paper of wise men who know the truth, as His Majesty will soon be told." Cortés understood very well who had written this—one Tirado, a friend of Diego Velázquez, and one allied with others who wished to make their defiance clear.

Cortés eventually got angry enough that he ordered an end to these libelous messages, promising publicly to punish anyone who kept it up. **– Díaz**

Cortés, who was never bothered for long by criticism or hostility, turned his attention now to the rebuilding of this country in the image and likeness of Spain. Possessing far greater organizational ability than Columbus, he had devoted much thought to the proper administration of a Spanish colony. The city of Tenochtitlan, leveled and stinking of death, would be cleared and rebuilt in the Spanish style; Spaniards would be encouraged to immigrate and settle throughout this new land, from coast to coast; laws would be drafted to ensure the development of a peaceful and productive society; exploration and pacification of this new possession and of the lands beyond would proceed apace.

He soon freed the most intelligent and tractable of the Indian leaders to put them in charge of the native artisans and laborers who would rebuild the city under Spanish direction — a task that would get under way in early 1522 and occupy many thousands of Indian laborers. The enlargement of the island by filling of the lake began. Canals disappeared, and causeways became city streets. The island capital would be extended farther every year, reaching out for eventual contact with the surrounding shore.

To the shiploads of settlers beginning to arrive on the coast, and trekking in with their belongings over the now well-beaten mountain paths, he made generous land grants, at the same time promulgating laws designed to keep settlers on the land — an unbroken eight-year residency, for example, was required to gain title to property. He founded a hospital that is still in operation today. He soon established the new city of Medellín — named after his birthplace — just south of today's city of Veracruz. He encouraged the immigration of women, and championed marriage, urging married men to bring their wives to New Spain, and bachelors to marry.[1] He did not believe in the systems of *encomienda* or *repartimiento* — [2]both of which amounted to the

---

[1] If a married man did not bring his wife to New Spain within eighteen months of taking title to his land, the title became forfeit. Somewhat to his chagrin, Cortés's own wife, Catalina Suárez, arrived in New Spain in the summer of 1522. During her brief time there — she died within three months of her arrival — the captain-general made a show of great pleasure, but his discomfiture with her presence became daily more visible. Her death on November 1 was officially attributed to an asthma attack, but it was widely suspected that Cortés had had her poisoned. In 1530 his enemies would see that he was charged with her murder, but neither he nor most others took the charge seriously, and the case was quietly dropped.

[2] The *repartimiento* system was an adjustment to the older system of *encomienda*. Under encomienda, an allotment of Indians came with a particular parcel of Indian lands, and the *encomendero*, the settler upon these lands — if he promised to give his Indians food, shelter, and instruction in the Catholic faith — could work these Indians as a virtual slave force. Under the subsequent repartimiento system, a limited number of Indians was allotted to the landowner by a Crown official as low-paid

distribution of Indians to the colonists as virtual slaves — but he saw no alternative to their continued implementation, especially the older encomienda system. His veterans, he knew, expected to receive Indians along with their new lands, and besides, Spaniards could in no way hope to perform by themselves the immense amount of work needed to settle this land. The system continued unabated,[1] with only his former allies the Tlaxcalans being exempt from a requirement to serve. He dispatched his men and new settlers throughout the country, even to the Southern Sea (Pacific) coast, where he began to build ships, many components of which had to be hauled overland from ports on Mexico's northern coast. Having learned from the conquered Indians the sources of their precious metals, he sent Spaniards all over Mexico to take over and expand these mining operations for the Crown. He sent for seeds, plants, and livestock from Spain and elsewhere,[2] and begged also that priests be sent.[3] He began to collect tithes so that churches might be constructed and the clergy provided for. He dispatched ships from both coasts to search for a strait connecting the Northern with the Southern Sea. He sent a force northward to pacify and put his stamp upon the region around the Pánuco River, the coastal area whose settlement had been licensed to Garay. By early 1524 his men would take over this region in Cortés's name.

One of his earliest acts was to build a quayside fortress, along with a dockyard to preserve the brigantines that had proven so valuable in the reduction of the city. He was, moreover, careful to arm himself against further hostility, whether from the Indian population or from his own men. With shipments of arms and ammunition being held up by his enemies in Spain, notably Bishop Fonseca, he asked his experts

---

or unpaid "day laborers," free to return to their homes at stated intervals. From the viewpoint of the overworked and underpaid Indian, there was little difference in the two systems.

[1] In June 1523 Charles forbade making grants of encomienda, and revoked those already made. Cortés disregarded this order.

[2] The Spaniards introduced wheat at this time. Cattle, horses, and pigs had already been proven to thrive.

[3] Three Franciscans arrived in August 1523, and twelve more the following May. They immediately began to open schools and to stamp out all vestiges of Indian religious practices. Applying themselves assiduously to the study of Nahuatl, they saw to it that the Aztec version of the conquest was set down in writing as early as 1528.

how munitions, especially cannon, might be fabricated and gunpowder mixed here in New Spain. His armorers were soon casting their own copper alloy and cast-iron cannon, fashioning cannonballs out of rock, and filling their need for gunpowder-sulfur by digging it out of fissures — at great risk — around the crater of Popocatépetl. Other cannon he gathered from ships calling at the coast. He mounted them all in defensive positions.

He was in his element. His daily problems were of a different nature than they had been during the conquest, but they were equally challenging. And his word was still law, with potentially fatal consequences for the disobedient. Like a dog shaking off water, he shrugged off all attempts at control from Cuba or Spain.

Back in Spain, from the summer of 1520 to the spring of 1521 — during his advance upon the Aztec capital — the Castilian court had been distracted by an anti-government uprising in a number of Castilian cities. The so-called *comuneros* were in revolt over the coming of Charles to their country, his perceived preference for foreigners, the dispossession of his mother Juana, and the crushing tax burden they had been asked to bear since the young man's accession to the throne. The disturbances had begun shortly after Charles had left for his German states in May 1520,[1] but by the following April, they had been crushed by the Dutch cardinal Adrian of Utrecht, the king's regent.[2] The end of the comunero revolt now permitted greater Crown attention to events across the sea, and heads began to turn in Cortés's direction.

Charles, however, had still granted Cortés no particular status — indeed had not deigned to mention him — nor had his regent in Spain. Waiting in the wings to bring this matter to a head were the partisans

---

[1] During this trip, in October, he would receive the German crown of Holy Roman Emperor at Aachen.

[2] Adrian ruled as regent during Charles's absence from May 1520 to July 1522. He is first encountered in 1507 as the tutor of the seven-year-old Charles. In 1515, with young Charles's influence, he set his foot upon the hierarchical ladder of the Church in Spain, serving as Bishop of Tortosa before being named first a cardinal, then Inquisitor-General of Castile and Aragon. In 1522 he was elected pope as Adrian VI, the last non-Italian pope until John Paul II. He departed Spain for Rome shortly after Charles's return, but his papacy was to be unremarkable and brief. He died in September 1523.

of both Cortés and Velázquez, the latter supported by the powerful Fonseca, Bishop of Burgos. The court now granted the contending parties its attention in their respective suits for the right to govern New Spain. But, despite Cortés's undeniable guilt as a usurper of power in the new colony, Adrian was not unmindful that substantial wealth had begun to flow into Castile as a result of his actions. This boded ill for the Velázquez-Fonseca faction. Likely in consideration of the golden stream turned on by Cortés's outlaw action, Adrian acted against Velázquez to the extent of excluding his agent Fonseca from further participation in the governor's suit.

Charles returned to Castile in July 1522. After confirming Adrian's decision to exclude Fonseca, he referred the matter of the government of New Spain to a tribunal, which, to the horror of Fonseca and Velázquez, decided in favor of the renegade Cortés. The emperor upheld the decision, in October officially proclaiming Cortés governor, captain-general, and chief justice of New Spain. This was Cortés's first-ever recognition by the Crown, the prize he had coveted throughout a long, difficult, and highly dangerous game. Charles's proclamation also sounded the death knell for the Velázquez faction, whose legitimate claim to rule New Spain had finally been erased by the usurper.

Prior to receiving the emperor's blessing, however, Cortés had had to shake off two attacks on his authority that had been set in motion beforehand. The first was a bald attempt by Fonseca (still chafing from the failure of the Narváez gambit) to remove him from command, and the second, a Fonseca-sanctioned attempt to put limits on the lands under his influence. He handled these plots with smiling diplomacy, chicanery, and veiled threats as needed.

In early December 1521, four months after the fall of the Aztec capital, the first challenge to his authority appeared in the form of one Cristóbal de Tapia, a colorless functionary sent from Cuba with a commission from Fonseca giving himself authority to take over the government of New Spain from Cortés. To Fonseca this was probably a cut-and-dried matter, with a predictably favorable outcome. On hearing of Tapia's arrival at Villa Rica, however, and of his announced mission, Cortés commanded his representatives there to detain Tapia for as long as possible on the coast, and under no circumstance to allow him to carry out a formal reading of his orders. He then began to send Tapia a series of flattering messages, meant to be dilatory, pledging his utmost cooperation and begging pardon for not being able to attend to the business of examining Tapia's orders just yet.[1] Tapia was left cooling his heels on the coast till Christmas. Eventually the totally flummoxed and impotent official was told straight out by Cortés's men on the coast that compliance with his warrant, which they knew had come from Fonseca, not the emperor, would not be in the royal interest, and that he should return to Cuba at once — his remonstrances likely abated by a generous sweetening of his purse. In any case, in January, after the meekest of protests, Tapia returned to his masters, never having formally read out his orders and never even having met with Cortés, who remained in sole charge of the land that he had conquered.[2]

Velázquez had sent Narváez, Fonseca had sent Tapia. Cortés had dealt with them both. Yet in the back of his mind he knew that one day he would have to deal with the governor of Jamaica, Francisco de Garay, and his settlement at Pánuco, some two hundred miles north of Villa Rica near today's Tampico. Garay's expeditionaries had made frequent attempts to settle the area, but with spectacular lack of success. Strenuously opposed by local Indians, they had proven unable to gain a foothold. Cortés, made uncomfortable by these incursions into what he regarded as his own land, spent much of 1522 thinking about Pánuco.

In the summer of 1522, just prior to the arrival of his wife, he was engaged in planning a large-scale expedition to settle the Pánuco question. Shortly after his wife's death in November, he led this expedition northward himself, subduing the local Indians with very great effort, and eventually founding his own town of Santisteban del Puerto on the Pánuco River, some miles inland from the coast. Putting this success behind him, he turned his attention southward now to Guatemala — to which he planned to dispatch a force overland under Pedro de Alvarado — and the Gulf of Honduras — to which he planned to send a shipborne force under Cristóbal de Olid for establishment of

[1] During this period Cortés arranged for "spontaneous" votes of support from already established town councils, and even caused the new port town of Medellín to be founded under Tapia's nose, so that its town council might add its vote for Cortés's continuance in the governorship.
[2] Tapia's departure from New Spain was understandably slow and reluctant, so slow and reluctant in fact that young Sandoval, in charge of watching him for Cortés, told the official in January that if he didn't take ship immediately he would be sent home in a canoe.

a presence there. He may not have known that another expedition under Gil González de Ávila was already in the area.

In July 1523, however, as Alvarado and Olid were about to depart, Cortés received word that Garay himself had landed in Pánuco in force, with several ships and over five hundred men — including infantry, horse, and artillery — and was proclaiming to the Indians that he was now governor of the Pánuco region.[1] Cortés, stunned, held his two captains and their armies back for assistance in handling this new threat, quickly dispatching a force under Alvarado to treat with Garay and his men.[2] They found Garay's forces in disarray, loyalties divided, food running short, men deserting in droves. Moreover, the recently pacified Indians, detecting a new lack of unity among the Spaniards and angered by the actions of Garay's undisciplined men, were returning to their marauding ways. Cortés, meanwhile, having just received a spectacularly welcome decree from the emperor affirming his own right to govern the Pánuco region — superseding Garay's mandate — was licking his lips in anticipation of a meeting with the governor. At length Garay, his forces hopelessly dispersed and depleted, was shown the decree and declared his submission to Cortés, who amicably sent him an invitation to the capital, all bygones being bygones.

Garay, on his arrival in Mexico City in December 1523, repeated to Cortés what he had previously told him via messenger — namely, that his forces were so depleted he was unsure how he could even accomplish a return trip to Cuba. The ebullient Cortés promised him complete cooperation, including food, supplies, manpower, or any other assistance he might require for a timely departure. The governor stayed with Cortés for the remainder of the month, discussing with him possible joint projects in other parts of Mexico. They even discussed uniting their families in marriage. On Christmas Eve they attended Mass together and breakfasted afterwards. The governor, who had been complaining of feeling poorly, fell ill immediately following the meal and began to vomit. A physician was summoned, but the patient ultimately could not be saved. Garay died a few days after Christmas, and nearly the last vestige of Cortés's Pánuco problem vanished with him. The question of whether Cortés had had him

---

[1] Garay possessed a patent from the Crown to settle here.
[2] Cortés himself was bedridden at the time, having broken his arm in a fall from a horse.

poisoned naturally arose, but modern scholars think it entirely possible that the governor's death was due to food poisoning or to some other non-sinister cause.

The way was now clear to mop up the Pánuco-area Indians once again and to establish order among the Spanish factions there. Upon Garay's death, Cortés sent Sandoval north with a punishing force to relieve the beleaguered Spaniards and to put a final end to the Indian problem. In the bloody action that followed, the region was at last brought under Cortés's control. Sandoval's orders were to round up all Indian leaders and burn them alive. The condemned Indians remonstrated with Sandoval, telling him that the order to attack Garay's Spaniards had come ultimately from Cortés himself, a claim that—given Cortés's duplicity and his absolute intention to be rid of Garay—may well have been true. Sandoval, following his own orders—also from Cortés—burned the Indians anyway.[1]

Cortés's appointment as governor had not come without attached strings. In early 1524, four officials arrived to "assist" him in the government of New Spain. As the months went by, this "assistance" began to weigh on the nominal governor. Something that weighed on him even more heavily, however, was the news that Olid, after meeting with Velázquez in Cuba en route to his assignment in Honduras, had repudiated Cortés's authority in favor of founding a colony on his own. The enormity of this betrayal caused Cortés to write, very imprudently, to the emperor that he was considering arresting the governor of Cuba. Perhaps fortunately for Cortés, Velázquez passed away in June. Unfortunately for him, however, his ill-advised threat would cause the Crown to have second thoughts about their man in New Spain.

With the arrival of the four men sent from Spain, Cortés's sphere of authority had been seriously restricted, and the colony now began to dissolve into factions. The thought of Olid's betrayal gnawed at him and he first tried to assuage the hurt by sending a cousin, Francisco de las Casas, to Honduras by ship to deal with him. But the growing intolerability of his present situation soon made him decide to lead an overland expedition to Honduras himself. It would be an escape to the old times, setting his own agenda, with no more palace intrigues, no more administration, no more concessions. And he could deal personally with his former captain Olid.

---

[1] Several hundred were burned at the stake.

In October 1524 he departed upon what would turn into a grueling two-year odyssey to present-day eastern Guatemala and northwestern Honduras. He took with him 130 horse, 120 foot, and three thousand Tlaxcalan warriors. Marina went with him as translator and mistress.[1] He also took with him a number of Aztec captives, among them the last king of Tenochtitlan, young Cuauhtémoc, who, crippled from torture, had been languishing in prison for three years. Cuauhtémoc would never see the Gulf of Honduras; in February 1525, in northeast Guatemala, Cortés would have him and several other Indian nobles hanged.[2]

The expedition had to pass through endless miles of coastal swampland, horses struggling through sucking mud up to their bellies. The men were forced to negotiate deep rivers, penetrate thick forests, endure clouds of mosquitoes and torrential rains. They crossed a short but difficult stretch of mountain where sixty-eight horses either fell to their deaths or became hamstrung. Then, on the army's arrival at Nito it was discovered that Olid was dead.[3] He had taken Cortés's kinsman Las Casas prisoner, along with Gil González de Ávila. The two men, however, had succeeded in freeing themselves, and, after an unsuccessful attempt to knife Olid, had captured him. Olid had then been beheaded in the public square at Naco.[4]

In April 1526, having succeeded in little but ensuring his own exhaustion, Cortés took ship and returned, via Cuba, to Mexico. He staggered ashore a virtually unrecognizable shadow of what he had once been. Given up for dead by many in the land he supposedly ruled — a land that, in his absence, had fallen nearly into anarchy — he soon made it clear that he was alive, and once again in charge. His own partisans, on the strength of his return, began to reassert their authority and to restore order.

The Crown, in Cortés's absence, had been searching for ways to control its increasingly unmanageable colony. As a first step, and in an attempt to curb Cortés's power, Pánuco — the northern region that

---

[1] Marina by this time had borne Cortés a son, Martín (now two years old), who was left in the care of another.

[2] The reason given for their execution was a suspected conspiracy among them to murder Cortés and his men, then to raise a rebellion against Spaniards from Honduras to Tenochtitlan.

[3] Nito lay near the mouth of the Dulce River in Guatemala.

[4] Fifty miles southeast of Nito, near the Chamelecón River, Honduras.

Cortés had been awarded shortly before—was administratively separated from New Spain, and Nuño Beltrán de Guzmán, a lawyer, was named its governor. As a second step, a magistrate named Luis Ponce de León was sent with a Crown mandate to suspend Cortés from his governorship,[1] to conduct an investigation into his conduct as governor, and, at the end of such investigation, either to reinstate him or to take his place. This official arrived on the coast in early July 1526, shortly after Cortés's return from Honduras.

Ponce was feted by Cortés, and was promised the fullest cooperation with his inquiry. Because the judge had been ill since his arrival on the coast, however, little of the investigation took place beyond a presentation of credentials. As the magistrate's health appeared to improve, Cortés invited him to a banquet at Iztapalapa. In a now-familiar pattern, Cortés's guest was taken seriously ill following the meal, and a few days later, on July 20, he died (having appointed a new investigator and a new governor prior to his death). Some thirty of Ponce's retinue also died.[2]

When the newly appointed Crown investigator, an aged man, also passed away not long after assuming office, zeal for looking into Cortés's conduct in office waned.

Cortés yielded to the new governor—and to a subsequent series of claimants to that post—retiring to his estates near Cuernavaca to plan further ventures. The Crown, however, still bent on establishing effective and responsible government in its new colony, at the end of 1527 appointed a four-man Royal Audience to rule it. This governing body would be presided over by Guzmán, a man hostile to Cortés.[3]

---

[1] This is not the explorer Ponce de León, who by this time was dead.

[2] Despite the familiarity of the pattern, modern scholars think it entirely likely that the men died of a tropical disease.

[3] Since May 1527, Guzmán had been serving as governor of Pánuco. Exceedingly cruel in his treatment of Indians, he had also been repressive of Cortés's partisans. He and two members of the four-man Audience— the other two having died before reaching the capital—would rule Mexico for about a year, after which time Guzmán was removed, with the remaining two members ruling for about one more year, to January 1531. At this time—amid charges of maladministration and corruption—they were replaced by a second Audience. Still serving as governor of Pánuco, and in search of the rumored Seven Cities of Gold, Guzmán now pushed north and west from the Spanish capital into what soon became known as

During the anarchical period following his return from Honduras, the emarginated Cortés occupied himself not only with his estates, but with exploration, even to sending a three-vessel squadron from a Pacific coast harbor to the Maluku Islands (part of today's Indonesia).[1] By 1528, however, he not only could bear no more of New Spain, but he had developed an overriding desire to clear his name at court. In March, therefore, he took ship for the homeland that he had left twenty-four eventful years before. With him went Sandoval and Andrés de Tapia, as well as Indian acrobats and jugglers, collections of plants and animals, and chests of gold and silver.[2] At Toledo he was treated by the 28-year-old monarch, who had never before met him, with great deference, and shown every sign of royal favor—every sign but one. It was made clear to him that, although he had thorough royal support for his continuance as captain-general, he would never again serve as governor of New Spain.[3] Cortés's rash threat to arrest a sitting governor—Velázquez—had perhaps helped Charles to decide that issue. Distracting him somewhat from this disappointment was a royal grant of title to millions of acres of Mexican land, with all the towns and Indian populations these lands encompassed, as well as complete rights of further exploration. A year later his cup would be filled to

---

Nueva Galicia, where he continued his savage suppression and enslavement of Indians. In 1531 he was named governor of this new kingdom. In 1536 he was arrested for excessive cruelty to Indians and a year later sent to Spain, where he remained in prison until 1538. He never returned to New Spain.

[1] This expedition was sent in support of a Spanish effort to prove Spain's claim that the Maluku, or Spice, Islands, lay in the half of the world allotted to Spain by the 1494 Treaty of Tordesillas (via extension of the agreed-upon meridian into the Pacific), or, in the absence of such proof, to help establish a Spanish beachhead there. Given the inability of mariners of the time to measure longitude with accuracy, the Spanish claim could not be proven, and, in any case, the only one of Cortés's ships to arrive there never returned. The matter was amicably settled by the 1529 Treaty of Zaragoza, in which Spain—in return for a fat payment from the Portuguese—relinquished its claim to the Malukus.

[2] Shortly after arrival at Palos, the 31-year old Sandoval, one of Cortés's right-hand men throughout the conquest, was taken ill and died. Also, while at Palos, Cortés happened to encounter his kinsman Francisco Pizarro, on the threshold of his destiny in Peru.

[3] Charles had recently appointed the first Royal Audience.

overflowing by the emperor's bestowal on him of the title Marquis of the Valley of Oaxaca, a royal action that, at a stroke, elevated the bold usurper to the ranks of the hereditary nobility.

In late summer 1529 Charles left Spain for Italy, and early the following year Cortés reembarked for Mexico, taking with him his now-widowed mother and the highborn Juana Ramírez de Arellano y Zúñiga, his new wife. On arrival at Hispaniola he found himself formally charged by the Royal Audience of New Spain with several counts of criminal misconduct, including the murder of his first wife. This corrupt and unpopular government, however, was about to be replaced by a second Audience, as Cortés soon learned. The new group of administrators, to be chaired by the Bishop of Santo Domingo, promised to be more sympathetic to the captain-general, and the threat of prosecution diminished to the point where he felt it safe, in July 1530, to return to New Spain. Having been instructed by the queen regent,[1] however, to keep his distance from the present rulers — still the first Audience — he and his wife and mother established themselves across the lake in Texcoco. Following a falling out with the new Audience, he retired to his estates at Cuernavaca, where he attended to agricultural and domestic pursuits. He continued, however, to send out expeditions, himself leading a disastrous expedition of four hundred Spaniards and three hundred black African slaves to plant a colony in Baja California.[2] The Gulf of California today is in fact also known as the Sea of Cortés.

---

[1] Isabella of Portugal, whom Charles had wed in 1526. The queen consort served competently as his regent during this and a later absence of the emperor from Spain.

[2] Black African slaves had been imported to the Indies — although from Lisbon — since the first decade of the 1500s. The practice originally had the support of Las Casas, who, to his later shame, suggested that the enslavement of Africans was morally preferable to the enslavement of Indians. From 1518, slaves were brought directly from West Africa in a business managed by Portuguese slave-hunters and traders. Regarded as a necessity to run sugar mills, mines, and farms, this trade in human beings caused outrage among many Spaniards — chiefly ecclesiastics — but it continued to grow in volume, to the point where blacks very soon outnumbered whites throughout all Spanish colonies. In addition to providing labor in field, factory, and mine, blacks served as skilled workers in many occupations, and West African warriors came to provide

By April 1535 the second Audience had been superseded by a viceroy in the person of Antonio de Mendoza, one of the ablest administrators ever sent out by Spain. The new viceroy, however, eventually curtailed Cortés's explorations, especially toward the north, whence rumors of the Seven Cities of Gold had continued to filter into New Spain.[1] Mendoza, interested in exploration, likely wished to place leadership of probes in this direction in the hands of men whom he could control, and he wasted little time in getting such men appointed.[2] Cortés took this as an encroachment on rights of exploration granted expressly to him.

In January 1540 Cortés and his 8-year-old son Martín (born to his second wife, Juana),[3] accompanied by Bernal Díaz and others, left for Spain, where Cortés hoped to present his lengthening list of grievances to the emperor directly. On his arrival in Spain, he learned that the emperor, widowed during the past year, was in Ghent. In the following year, perhaps on the chance that he would meet the now-returned emperor, he joined an enormous naval force led by Charles

---

a significant contribution to Spanish exploratory and military missions. In a very real sense, the New World was settled and civilized more by black Africans than by white Europeans.

[1] Such fantastic rumors of great wealth to the north had been accreting around the reports of four survivors of a 1527 Spanish expedition to Florida, men who had arrived in Mexico in 1536 at the end of an eight-year odyssey that had taken them from the Florida peninsula west and southward through today's Texas and beyond. Their remarkable journey, treated in Volume II, was chronicled by one of their number, Álvar Núñez Cabeza de Vaca.

[2] In 1539, at Mendoza's instigation, the Franciscan friar Marcos de Niza pushed northward into today's Arizona and New Mexico, and in 1540 — on the strength of that friar's highly imaginative report of what he had seen — Francisco Vázquez de Coronado advanced north and eastward as far as today's Kansas. Neither expedition found a city of gold.

[3] By now Cortés had fathered eleven children. In addition to a son Martín, born to Marina in 1522 (and legitimized by the pope in 1529), he had fathered a daughter with one Spanish woman and a son with another, as well as a daughter with each of two women of the Aztec royal line. His first wife, Catalina, had borne him no children, but he had had six with Juana, his second wife — four daughters and two sons, one of whom was the Martín who accompanied him to Spain. His eldest son and daughter with Juana had died shortly after birth.

himself against the Ottoman Turks at Algiers. With the fleet scattered and many vessels sunk by a powerful storm, the mission was a failure. On his return to Castile, he began to haunt the court, sending petition after petition to the emperor, but without response. Charles, more absorbed now with his ongoing wars against France, and the tangled affairs of Peru, apparently had little time for old news.[1] In 1547, having spent more than seven years in fruitless effort, Cortés and his now 15-year-old son made their way to Seville, whence they planned to embark again for New Spain. The captain-general, however, fell ill on arrival there. As his condition worsened, he refined his last will and testament, and on December 2, 1547, his life's work completed and his remaining wealth distributed, he died.[2] He was sixty-two years old.

He had rested little during his hectic life, and his remains have rested less. They have been moved from place to place under threat of vandalism, theft, and destruction. What is left of them reposes in Mexico City's Church of Jesús Nazareno, adjacent to the older Hospital de Jesús, an institution founded by the conqueror himself shortly after the fall of Tenochtitlan.

It is said that no memorials exist in Mexico to either Cortés or Marina, and it is uncommon to find a respectful representation of either of them anywhere in that nation. The founding father and mother of today's Mexico, both indispensable to the success of the Spanish conquest, have been soundly repudiated by their descendants.

> Now that they are Christians, and as though in punishment for our sins, they come to Mass because they must, and with very little reverence or fear. They gossip and talk amongst themselves and, during the most solemn parts of the Mass or during the sermon, get up and walk out. Whereas in previous times they observed the rites of their gods very strictly, now they show neither fear nor shame. – **Alonso de Aguilar**

---

[1] It is said that Cortés once tried to reach the emperor by pushing through a crowd around the royal carriage and attempting to mount the carriage step. When Charles inquired who that man was—presumably as the carriage accelerated away—Cortés reportedly shouted, "One who has given you more kingdoms than you had cities before!"

[2] He died at Castilleja de la Cuesta, today a municipality in the province of Seville.

FOR FURTHER READING

The following brief list is intended to guide the reader to a few rich sources of information on the events and conditions of life in Europe, Spain, and the Americas in the fifteenth and sixteenth centuries, as well as to a few works related particularly to the persons and events treated in the present volume.

General

Bethell, Leslie, ed. *The Cambridge History of Latin America*. Vols. 1 and 2, *Colonial Latin America*. Cambridge: Cambridge University Press, 1984.

Collard, Andrée M., ed. and trans. *Bartolomé de las Casas: History of the Indies*. New York: Harper & Row, 1971.

Kamen, Henry. *A Concise History of Spain*. New York: Charles Scribner's Sons, 1973.

_____. *Empire: How Spain Became a World Power 1492-1763*. New York: HarperCollins, 2003.

Knight, Franklin W., ed. *Bartolomé de las Casas: An Account Much Abbreviated of the Destruction of the Indies*. Trans. Andrew Hurley. Indianapolis: Hackett, 2003.

Mann, Charles C. *1491*. New York: Vintage Books, 2006.

_____. *1493*. New York: Vintage Books, 2012.

Marks, Robert B. *The Origins of the Modern World*. Lanham, MD: Rowman & Littlefield, 2007.

Columbus

Cohen, J.M., ed. and trans. *Christopher Columbus: The Four Voyages.* London: Penguin, 1969.

Jane, Cecil, ed. and trans. *The Four Voyages of Columbus.* New York, NY: Dover, 1988.

Keen, Benjamin, trans. and annot. *The Life of the Admiral Christopher Columbus by his Son Ferdinand.* New Brunswick, NJ: Rutgers University Press, 1992.

Morison, Samuel Eliot. *Admiral of the Ocean Sea.* Boston: Little, Brown and Company, 1942.

_____, ed. and trans. *Journals and Other Documents on the Life and Voyages of Christopher Columbus.* New York: The Heritage Press, 1963.

Cortés

Cohen, J.M., ed. and trans. *Bernal Díaz: The Conquest of New Spain.* London: Penguin, 1963.

Fuentes, Patricia de, ed. and trans. *The Conquistadors.* Norman: University of Oklahoma Press, 1993.

León-Portilla, Miguel, ed. *The Broken Spears.* Trans. from Nahuatl to Spanish by Angel María Garibay K., and from Spanish to English by Lysander Kemp. Boston: Beacon Press, 2006.

Pagden, Anthony, ed. and trans. *Hernan Cortes: Letters from Mexico.* New Haven: Yale University Press, 1986.

Prescott, W.H. *History of the Conquest of Mexico.* London: Phoenix Press, 2002.

INDEX

Columbus

Afonso V, 12

Bobadilla, Francisco de, 74, 75, 77, 78, 83

Casas, Bartolomé de, 46

Chanca, Diego Álvarez, 47, 48, 50, 51, 52, 53, 54, 55, 56

Columbus, Bartholomew, 15, 46, 47, 61, 62, 63, 67, 72, 73, 75, 82, 88, 89, 102, 120, 123

Columbus, Diego (Admiral's brother), 46, 59, 62, 75

Columbus, Diego (Admiral's son), 9, 10, 15

Columbus, Ferdinand, 14, 20, 70, 82, 84, 85, 86, 87, 88, 90, 91, 92, 94, 95, 96, 97, 98, 99, 100, 101, 102, 104, 105, 106, 108, 109, 111, 112, 113, 114, 115, 117, 118, 119, 120, 122, 123, 124

Cuneo, Michele da, 47, 49, 50, 59, 60, 61

Enríquez de Arana, Beatriz, 14

Ferdinand, King, 12, 13, 14, 26, 43, 124

Fieschi, Bartolomeo, 106, 107, 108, 109, 110, 111, 113, 116, 117, 122, 124

Fonseca, Juan Rodríguez de, 45, 66, 74, 82, 111

Garay, Francisco de, 46

Hispaniola
discovery of, 31

Isabela, settlement of

abandonment of, 67

foundation of, 56

Isabella, Queen, 10, 12, 13, 16, 45

death of, 124

João II, 10, 41, 45

Juana, Queen, 66

La Navidad, 37, 38, 51, 53
discovery of destruction of, 51
founding of, 36

Las Casas, Bartolomé de, 20, 21, 22, 28, 43, 65, 66, 79

Méndez, Diego, 92, 93, 102, 103, 106, 107, 108, 109, 110, 111, 113, 116, 117, 118, 119, 120, 122, 123, 124

Ojeda, Alonso de, 46, 75, 76

Ovando, Nicolás de, 78, 81, 82, 109, 111, 117, 118, 123

Perestrelo, Filipa Moniz, 9, 10

Pérez, Fray Juan, 15

Pinzón, Martín Alonso, 21, 30, 38, 43

Ponce de León, Juan, 46

Porras, Francisco de, 111, 112, 113, 119, 121, 122, 123

Roldán, Francisco, 46, 63, 73, 74, 83, 111, 120

Santa María
destruction of, 34

Santángel, Luis de, 15, 16, 40, 41

Santo Domingo
foundation of, 67

Spain, background of, 11–15

Tordesillas, Treaty of, 45

Torres, Antonio de, 56, 57, 58, 59, 60, 61, 62, 65, 75, 78, 82, 83
Torres, Juana de, 65, 75, 78
Velázquez de Cuéllar, Diego, 46
Vespucci, Amerigo, 75
Yáñez, Vicente, 21
Zaragoza, Treaty of, 45

Cortés
Adrian of Utrecht (Pope Adrian VI), 309, 310
Aguilar, Alonso de, 189, 207, 240, 241, 255, 258, 259, 260, 291, 319
Aguilar, Jerónimo de, 147, 148, 150, 151, 153, 156, 164, 166, 183, 209, 302
Alvarado, Pedro de, 139, 140, 141, 146, 157, 187, 228, 229, 231, 232, 240, 242, 243, 245, 258, 261, 278, 283, 287, 290, 296, 311, 312
Balboa, Vasco Nuñez de, 134, 136, 140
Cabeza de Vaca, Álvar Núñez, 318
Charles, King and Emperor, 135, 136, 149, 151, 156, 164, 165, 169, 223, 232, 235, 267, 308, 309, 310, 316, 317, 318, 319
Columbus, Diego, 133, 135, 137, 140
Columbus, Ferdinand, 133
Coronado, Francisco Vázquez de, 318

Cuauhtémoc, 131, 275, 290, 295, 297, 301, 302, 304, 305, 314
Cuitláhuac, 254, 256, 265, 268, 275
Dávila, Pedrarias, 134
Díaz del Castillo, Bernal, 138, 139, 144, 145, 146, 147, 148, 149, 150, 151, 156, 157, 158, 164, 165, 166, 167, 168, 170, 171, 172, 173, 174, 176, 180, 182, 183, 186, 188, 190, 191, 192, 193, 194, 196, 197, 198, 199, 201, 203, 204, 205, 208, 209, 210, 211, 213, 214, 217, 218, 219,220, 221, 225, 226, 227, 228, 229, 230, 232, 236, 239, 246, 247, 248, 249, 250, 253, 254, 256, 257, 259, 260, 262, 264, 270, 275, 276, 278, 279, 280, 281, 290, 301, 302, 304, 305, 306, 318
Ferdinand, King, 132, 133, 135, 136
Fonseca, Juan Rodríguez de, 132, 175, 276, 308, 310, 311
Garay, Francisco de, 140, 141, 177, 267, 308, 311, 312, 313
Grijalva, Juan de, 137, 138, 139, 140, 143, 144, 146, 148, 152, 210, 306
Guzmán, Nuño Beltrán de, 315
Hernández de Córdoba, Francisco, 136, 137, 138, 143, 146, 148, 210, 306
Isabella, Queen, 132, 133
Jiménez de Cisneros, Francisco, 133, 135
Juana, Queen, 132, 135, 309

Las Casas, Bartolomé de, 133, 134, 135, 138, 143, 155, 194, 195, 196, 317

Marina (La Malinche), 153, 156, 164, 166, 172, 174, 183, 191, 192, 193, 204, 205, 209, 226, 250, 258, 262, 302, 314, 318, 319

Mendoza, Antonio de, 318

Montezuma, 137, 153, 154, 155, 156, 157, 159, 160, 161, 163, 164, 165, 166, 167, 168, 169, 170, 172, 173, 176, 180, 183, 184, 186, 187, 189, 190, 191, 193, 197, 198, 199, 200, 201, 202, 203, 204, 205, 206, 207, 208, 209, 210, 211, 212, 213, 215, 216, 217, 218, 220, 221, 223, 224, 225, 226, 227, 228, 229, 230, 231, 232, 234, 235, 236, 237, 239, 242, 244, 251, 252, 254, 255, 257, 262, 265, 273, 275, 286

Narváez, Pánfilo de, 237, 238, 239, 240, 241, 242, 245, 253, 258, 259, 261, 262, 265, 267, 268, 277, 281, 310, 311

Olea, Cristóbal de, 274, 275

Olid, Cristóbal de, 140, 146, 231, 254, 258, 275, 278, 283, 311, 312, 313, 314

Olmedo, Bartolomé de (Mercedarian friar), 173, 187, 230, 254

Ordaz, Diego de, 199, 228, 258

Ovando, Nicolás de, 131, 132, 133

Pineda, Alonso Álvarez de, 140, 177

Ponce de León, Juan, 134, 136, 291, 315

Ponce de León, Luis, 315

Puertocarrero, Alonso Hernández, 151, 153, 170, 174

Quiahuiztlán, 163, 164, 168

Ramírez de Arellano y Zúñiga, Juana, 317, 318

Sahagún, Bernadino de, 153

Sandoval, Gonzalo de, 145, 238, 258, 271, 272, 278, 283, 289, 298, 311, 313, 316

Smallpox outbreak, 268

Súarez Marcaida, Catalina, 143, 307, 318

Tapia, Andrés de, 145, 147, 214, 239, 240, 241, 275, 278, 290, 316

Tapia, Cristóbal de, 310, 311

Tordesillas, Treaty of, 316

Velázquez de Cuéllar, Diego, 133, 136, 137, 140, 143, 144, 145, 149, 162, 163, 167, 169, 174, 175, 176, 199, 212, 237, 238, 253, 277, 278, 306, 310, 311, 313, 316

Velázquez de León, Juan, 225, 226, 228, 231, 232, 258, 261

Villa Rica de la Vera Cruz, 163, 169, 174, 176, 177, 179, 183, 186, 223, 224, 233, 238, 242, 267, 269, 274, 291, 310, 311

Villafaña, Antonio de plot, 277

Zaragoza, Treaty of, 316

Excerpt from *Conquistador Voices* Vol. II

After the helmsman took charge of the raft, I lay down for a short time without being able to rest at all, nor was there anything farther from me at that moment than sleep. Later, near dawn, it seemed to me that I was hearing the rise and fall of the sea because, since the coast was a shoal, the waves broke loudly. And with this startlement, I called the helmsman, who replied that he thought we were near land. And we took a sounding and found ourselves in seven fathoms of water. And it seemed to him that we should stay at sea until daybreak. And thus I took an oar and rowed on the land side as we were a league away from it, and we turned the stern toward the sea. And near land a wave took us that pitched the raft out of the water the distance of a horseshoe's throw, and with the great blow that its fall occasioned, almost all the people who were nearly dead upon it regained consciousness. And since they saw themselves near land, they began to leave the raft half walking, half crawling. And as they came on land to some bluffs, we made a fire and toasted some of the maize that we carried. And we found rainwater, and with the heat of the fire the men revived and began to regain strength. . . . Half an hour later, . . . one hundred Indian archers arrived, and now, whether or not they were of great stature, our fear made them seem like giants. **– Álvar Núñez Cabeza de Vaca**

Spruce Tree Press

Quick Order Form

Please send me _____ copies of *Conquistador Voices*, vol. I
Price: 23.95

Please send me _____ copies of *Conquistador Voices*, vol. II
Price: 28.95

Name: _____

Address: _____

_____

City: _____ State: _____ ZIP: _____

Phone: _____

E-mail address: _____

Add shipping cost: one book, 4.00; two books, 5.00; three books, 6.00, four books, 7.00.

For shipping details on more than four books call 716-601-4850 or e-mail sales@spruce-tree-press.com.

For products to be shipped to a **New York State** address, **add sales tax** paid in that jurisdiction. Compute tax on order total, including shipping costs. Enclose check made out for full amount to **Spruce Tree Press**.

Mail this form, with check, to:
Spruce Tree Press, PO Box 211, Angola, NY 14006

You may also call 716-601-4850 or order through our website at: www.spruce-tree-press.com.

Made in the USA
Columbia, SC
15 October 2024

44423127R00187